The Tribes of Northern and Central Kordofan

H. A. MacMichael

Cambridge University Press

CAMBRIDGE UNIVERSITY PRESS

Cambridge, New York, Melbourne, Madrid, Cape Town, Singapore,
São Paolo, Delhi, Dubai, Tokyo, Mexico City

Published in the United States of America by Cambridge University Press, New York

www.cambridge.org
Information on this title: www.cambridge.org/9781108010771

This edition first published 1912
This digitally printed version 2010

ISBN 978-1-108-01077-1 Paperback

CAMBRIDGE LIBRARY COLLECTION

Books of enduring scholarly value

Travel and Exploration

The history of travel writing dates back to the Bible, Caesar, the Vikings and the Crusaders, and its many themes include war, trade, science and recreation. Explorers from Columbus to Cook charted lands not previously visited by Western travellers, and were followed by merchants, missionaries, and colonists, who wrote accounts of their experiences. The development of steam power in the nineteenth century provided opportunities for increasing numbers of 'ordinary' people to travel further, more economically, and more safely, and resulted in great enthusiasm for travel writing among the reading public. Works included in this series range from first-hand descriptions of previously unrecorded places, to literary accounts of the strange habits of foreigners, to examples of the burgeoning numbers of guidebooks produced to satisfy the needs of a new kind of traveller - the tourist.

The Tribes of Northern and Central Kordofan

H.A MacMichael (1882–1969) was a member of the Anglo-Egyptian Sudan government between 1905 and 1933 and was the deputy Inspector of Kordofan province in Sudan between 1906 and 1912. After combining his administrative duties with ethnographic research, he published this volume as part of the Cambridge Archaeological and Ethnographic Series in 1912; it was the first major ethnographic work on the Sudan. The book combines the history of the province with genealogical information based on interviews MacMichael conducted with local people during his long tenure in Kordofan. The ethnography's focus on local history and the history of different ethnic groups in Kordofan remains the primary source for the local history of the province and the genealogies of the indigenous population. This volume contains opinions on ethnicity which were acceptable at the time it was first published.

Cambridge University Press has long been a pioneer in the reissuing of out-of-print titles from its own backlist, producing digital reprints of books that are still sought after by scholars and students but could not be reprinted economically using traditional technology. The Cambridge Library Collection extends this activity to a wider range of books which are still of importance to researchers and professionals, either for the source material they contain, or as landmarks in the history of their academic discipline.

Drawing from the world-renowned collections in the Cambridge University Library, and guided by the advice of experts in each subject area, Cambridge University Press is using state-of-the-art scanning machines in its own Printing House to capture the content of each book selected for inclusion. The files are processed to give a consistently clear, crisp image, and the books finished to the high quality standard for which the Press is recognised around the world. The latest print-on-demand technology ensures that the books will remain available indefinitely, and that orders for single or multiple copies can quickly be supplied.

The Cambridge Library Collection will bring back to life books of enduring scholarly value (including out-of-copyright works originally issued by other publishers) across a wide range of disciplines in the humanities and social sciences and in science and technology.

Cambridge Archaeological and Ethnological Series

THE TRIBES OF NORTHERN AND CENTRAL KORDOFÁN

THE TRIBES OF NORTHERN AND CENTRAL KORDOFÁN

BY

H. A. MacMICHAEL
SUDAN CIVIL SERVICE
LATE SCHOLAR OF MAGDALENE COLLEGE, CAMBRIDGE

Cambridge :
at the University Press
1912

CAMBRIDGE UNIVERSITY PRESS
London: FETTER LANE, E.C.
C. F. CLAY, Manager

Edinburgh: 100, PRINCES STREET
Berlin: A. ASHER AND CO.
Leipzig: F. A. BROCKHAUS
New York: G. P. PUTNAM'S SONS
Bombay and Calcutta: MACMILLAN AND CO., Ltd.

PREFACE

THIS book makes no pretence of giving a complete account of Kordofán, nor can the materials from which it has been composed be said to shew the solidarity which is an essential qualification of a scientifically historical work.

My aim has been to describe, however imperfect may be the result, the antecedents of the tribes at present inhabiting the province in so far as any information upon the subject can be gleaned from extraneous sources or from current native tradition.

At the same time, while as a general rule planning to omit minute descriptions of people and places, and avoiding discussion of current questions, whether political or commercial, I have found it advisable to make occasional exceptions where understanding of the conditions of the past and the links connecting it with the present would have been impaired by such unnecessary limitation in the scope of the work. In so far as the work purports to deal with some aspects of ethnology, I must plead in excuse for its manifold shortcomings that I am a mere tyro with no expert knowledge of the science whatever.

One ethnological fact, however, is certain, and as the truth of it applies with varying force to every tribe in the country, it is of primary importance to bear it in mind:—breeding from slave-women captured from the numerous black tribes of the south and west has for centuries affected the racial characteristics and status of the so-called Arabs to a very marked degree. Many of the sedentary population and of the Baḳḳára could almost be called negroid in appearance; but the camel-owning nomads have preserved a greater purity of type.

Southern Kordofán ("Dár el Nūba"), though now reckoned a part of the province for administrative reasons, is to all intents and purposes entirely distinct from it, and to the native is not included in the term Kordofán. My acquaintance with it and its inhabitants, except at second hand, is very slight, and I have only mentioned the Nūba incidentally and in so far as their affairs have influenced the course of events in Kordofán proper.

For similar reasons I have said little of the riverain people now under the White Nile Province.

No separate chapter is devoted to the Danagla, of whom there are numbers settled in Kordofán, though allusions to them are frequent. Their history would more properly be described in a work upon the ancient peoples of the Nile valley; and indeed no inconsiderable amount of information concerning them is easily accessible in the literature of the last hundred years.

Of the present condition of affairs it is sufficient to say that the greatest need of Kordofán is an increased agricultural and industrial population. Its revenue is consistently and considerably in excess of its expenditure, thanks to the wealth, still largely undeveloped, of its extensive gum forests. At present the less productive or more expensive provinces of the Anglo-Egyptian Sudan swallow the surplus provided by Kordofán; but when they become self-supporting Kordofán will be able amply to justify a more generous expenditure upon its own necessities of the funds that it supplies.

Though irrigated by no river, its natural resources are not inconsiderable. Cattle and sheep in immense numbers can be reared, and the wells can be greatly increased in number and improved: huge areas can be placed under cultivation by corn, sesame, ground nuts, "senát," and similar products: the trade in ostrich-feathers, which is already considerable, would offer no mean prospects if adequately organised and controlled under expert management; and the gum forests are capable of almost indefinite development. Hitherto the expense of transport to the river has been a serious drawback but in January 1912 the railway reached El Obeid, and the effect of the changed conditions is already apparent.

The reader may perhaps complain that undue prominence has been given in this book to native "nisbas" or genealogical tables, for they are admittedly inaccurate, vague, and inconsistent—and, as Escayrac de Lauture remarks, "la généalogie des chefs arabes n'est pas du reste toujours tenue avec cet ordre merveilleux et cette rare exactitude qui caractérisent les généalogies allemandes." On the other hand, great store is set on them by the tribes concerned, and the belief in them, however misplaced, undoubtedly exercises considerable influence in inter-tribal affairs. Moreover, however inaccurate their details, certain glimmerings of truth appear here and there and cannot be neglected by one trying to find some dim light in the general darkness.

One point may be noticed in this connection: the Kabábísh, Dár Ḥámid, Ḥamar, and several other tribes of Northern and Central Kordofán, claim ultimate descent from a certain 'Abdulla el Guhani of the tribe of Guhayna. No particulars of his life or times are forthcoming, and in fact the "fekis" ignorant of the Ḳaḥṭánite origin of the tribe of Guhayna universally attribute to it a descent from 'Adnán the Ismá'ílitic ancestor of the Prophet. It is in one respect particularly curious that the Ḳaḥṭánite origin of Guhayna has thus come to be considered of insufficient nobility, and a connection with the Prophet invented to enhance it; for, on similar grounds, but on precisely contrary lines, Arab historians, realizing the superior purity of the Ḳaḥṭánite blood, and unwilling to admit any inferiority in the ancestry of Muḥammad, credited Ismá'íl with a fictitious wife of noble Ḳaḥṭánite blood, and ignored the Jewish version, followed in other respects, that Ismá'íl took a wife from the land of Egypt.

A word is perhaps necessary as to the scheme of transliteration adopted. I have endeavoured to pursue a uniform and coherent system, but no doubt inaccuracies will be found, more especially in the spelling of the names of tribal subsections, which seldom appear in writing, and which when written are as often mis-spelt as not. In such cases one has to trust mainly to the ear and to the probable derivation of the word. In the case of certain stereotyped words such as "Omdurman" (Um Durmán), "El Obeid" (El Obayyiḍ), "El Gleit" (El Ḳilayt), and "Khartoum" (Kharṭūm) I have left the more usual spelling unchanged in order to avoid an appearance of undue pedantry.

It only remains for me to express my great indebtedness to the books of the present Sirdar and Governor-General of the Sudan, Lieut.-General Sir F. R. Wingate, and the Inspector-General, Major-General Sir Rudolf Baron von Slatin, for information regarding the period of the Dervish revolt. So vague, disconnected, and often contradictory, are native accounts that the two historical works mentioned were of inestimable value to me. My thanks are also due to Professor William Ridgeway, Dr A. C. Haddon, and Dr C. G. Seligmann for their invaluable advice and help; to Mr S. A. Tippetts for information kindly given me by him about the Habbánía, and certain sections of the Gawáma'a; to Captain W. Lloyd of the Scottish Rifles, late Governor of Kordofán, for various notes upon the tribes of Western Kordofán; to Mr H. R. Palmer, Commissioner for Revenue, Northern Nigeria, for several valuable notes on the tribes of the Western Sudan; to Dr F. A. Bather of the British Museum and Mr G. W. Grabham of the Education Department of the Sudan Government for kindly assisting me in the identification of the objects found in the Northern Hills and at Faragáb and depicted in the two plates; and to Captain H. R. Headlam for permission to use photographs taken by him of the "náẓirs" of the Kabábísh and the Kawáhla.

H. A. M.

September, 1912.

CONTENTS

*This map is available as a download from www.cambridge.org/9781108010771

LIST OF ILLUSTRATIONS

BIBLIOGRAPHY

ABU EL FIDÁ. "Historia anteislamica." Ed. Fleischer (Arabic and Latin). 1831.

ALDRETE. "Varias Antiguedades de España Africa y otras provincias." El Doctor Bernardo Aldrete canonigo en la sancta Iglesia de Cordoua. 1614.

EL BAKRI. "Kitáb el Mesálek wa el Memálek" (cited by Leo Africanus, Cooley, Ibn Khaldūn, Barth and Carette; q.v.).

BARTH (H.). "Travels and Discoveries in North and Central Africa." 1849–55. 5 vols. Dr Heinrich Barth. 1857–8.

BROWN (R.). Edition of "The History and Description of Africa...etc." by Leo Africanus (q.v.) in the Hakluyt Society's publications, edited by Dr Robert Brown. 1896.

BROWNE (W. G.). "Travels in Africa, Egypt and Syria from 1792 to 1798." London, 1806.

BRUCE (J.). "Travels to discover the Source of the Nile, in the years 1768–1773." 6 vols. Edinburgh, 1790.

BUDGE (E. A. W.). "The Egyptian Sudan, its History and Monuments." 1907.

BURCKHARDT (J. L.). "Travels in Nubia." London, 1819.

BURTON (R. F.). "Narrative of a Pilgrimage to Meccah and Medinah." London, 1879 (1st ed. 1855–6).

BURTON (R. F.) and DRAKE (C. F. T.). "Unexplored Syria." London, 1872.

CAILLIAUD. "Voyage à Méroé, au Fleuve Blanc, au delà de Fâzoql...fait dans les années 1819, 1820, 1821 et 1822." Paris, 1826–7.

CAMERON (D. A.). "On the Tribes of the Eastern Sudan." *Journal of the Anthropological Institute.* February, 1887.

CARETTE (A. E. H.). "Recherches sur l'origine et les migrations des principales tribus de l'Afrique septentrionale et particulièrement de l'Algérie." (Exploration scientifique de l'Algérie. Sciences historiques et géographiques. 3.) Paris, 1853.

CLAUDIUS PTOLEMAEUS. "Geographia." Ed. Carolus Müller. Paris, 1883.

COOLEY (W. D.). "The Negroland of the Arabs examined and explained." London, 1841.

CROWFOOT. "The Anthropological Field in the Anglo-Egyptian Sudan." *Report of the British Association.* 1907.

CUST (R. N.). "A sketch of the modern languages of Africa." (Trübner's Oriental Series.) London, 1883.

DAVIS (N.). "Evenings in my tent; or, wanderings in Balad Ejjareed." London, 1854.

DENHAM, CLAPPERTON...etc. "Narrative of travels and discoveries in Northern and Central Africa in the years 1822, 1823 and 1824." London, 1826.

DIODORUS SICULUS. "Bibliothecae historicae libri qui supersunt. Interprete Laurentio Rhodomano, recensuit Petrus Wesselingius." Amsterdam, 1746.

DONGOLA "NISBA." An Arab MS. in possession of El feki el Dardíri of Khorsi in Kordofán. It is described as follows, "This work is the compilation of the works of three different persons: from the beginning as far as the story of the Khalífas (Caliphs) and that of the Prophet of God Ísa (Jesus) is by El Sayyid Ghulámulla: from the first 'tanbíh' (full-stop), at which point begins the history of Khuzám and the Beni Khuzíma, is by El Sayyid Muḥammad walad Dólíb the elder: the latter's work continues as far as the second 'tanbíh,' where the origin of the Sudanese is begun. From here to the end is by El Sayyid Muḥammad walad Dólíb the younger, who was buried at Khorsi. Now this history was copied by my father (i.e. the present owner's father, Muḥammad el Khalífa) in his own hand in A.H. 1252 (A.D. 1836) from the history whose date was A.H. 1151 (A.D. 1738); and I made this copy in Ramadan A.H. 1302."

For the genealogy and approximate dates of the above-mentioned persons see Chapter VI, on the Northern Hills.

DOUGHTY (C. M.). "Wanderings in Arabia." London, 1908.

ENSOR (F. S.). "Incidents on a journey through Nubia to Darfoor." London, 1881.

ESCAYRAC DE LAUTURE (Le Comte de). (*a*) "Le Désert et le Soudan." Paris, 1853; (*b*) "Mémoire sur le Sudan." *Bulletin de la Soc. de Geogr.* Paris, 1855.

FOURNEL (H.). "Les Berbers. Étude sur la conquête de l'Afrique par les Arabes." Paris, 1875–81.

GELÁL EL DÍN AL SIŪTI. "Ḥusn el Maḥáḍira fí akhbár Miṣr wa el Ḳáhira." 2 vols. litho. Cairo.

GLEICHEN (see sub "Handbook").

HAMAKER. "Specimen Catalogi codicum MSS. orientalium...." Paris, 1820.

HAMILTON (W. R.). "Remarks on several parts of Turkey. Part I.

Aegyptiaca, or some account of the antient and modern state of Egypt.' London, 1809.

HAMY (E. T.). "Les Pays des Troglodytes." *L'Anthropologie*, Vol. II, 1891.

HANDBOOK. "Handbook of the Sudan." Compiled by Captain Count Gleichen. London, 1898.

HARTMANN (R.). (*a*) "Skizze der Nillander." Berlin, 1866; (*b*) "Die Nigritier." Berlin, 1876.

HELMOLT. "The World's History." Ed. by H. F. Helmolt. Vol. III.

HERODOTUS. Trans. from Baehr's text by H. Cary. London, 1891.

HOLROYD. "Notes on a Journey to Kordofán in 1836–7." *R. G. S.* Vol. IX, Part 2. February, 1839.

HUART (C.). "A History of Arabic Literature." London, 1903.

IBN BAṬŪṬA. "Voyages d'Ibn Batoutah." Arabic text, trans. by C. Defrémery and Dr B. R. Sanguinetti. Paris, 1853–9.

IBN DUḲMÁḲ. "Description de l'Égypte." Publ. by Dr Vollers. Cairo, 1893.

IBN KHALDŪN. "Histoire des Berbères et des dynasties musulmanes de l'Afrique septentrionale." Trans. by M. le Baron de Slane. Algiers, 1852–6.

IBN SA'ÍD (quoted by Maḳrízi, q.v.).

IDRÍSÍ. "Géographie d'Édrisi." Trans. in French by P. A. Jaubert. Paris, 1836, 1840.

JOHNSTON (Sir H. H.). "The Nile Quest." London, 1903.

JUNKER (Dr W.). "Travels in Africa during the years 1875–1878." Trans A. H. Keane. 1890.

KEANE (A. H.). (*a*) Article "Sudan." *Encyclopaedia Britannica*; (*b*) "Man Past and Present." Cambridge, 1899.

KLIPPEL (ERNST). "Études sur le Folklore Bédouin de l'Égypte." [From *Bull. Soc. Khédiviale de Géographie*, Série VII, Num. 10.] Cairo, 1911.

KLUNZINGER (C. B.). "Upper Egypt: its people and its products." London, 1878.

LANE (E. W.). "An account of the Manners and Customs of the Modern Egyptians written in Egypt during the years 1833–5." London, 1836.

LANE-POOLE (S.). "A History of Egypt in the Middle Ages." London, 1901.

LEO AFRICANUS. "The History and Description of Africa. Done into English, 1600, by John Pory." Ed. by R. Brown (Hakluyt Soc. Publ.). London, 1896.

LEPSIUS (R.). "Nubische Grammatik." Berlin, 1880.

LINANT (A.). "Journal of a voyage on the White Nile...." *Journal of the R. G. S.* Vol. II, 1832.

MACMICHAEL (H. A.). (*a*) "Rock Pictures in Kordofan." *Journal of the Royal Anthropological Inst.* Vol. XXXIX, 1909; (*b*) "The Kabábísh. Some remarks on the Ethnology of a Sudan Arab tribe." *Journ. R. A. Inst.* Vol. XL, 1910; (*c*) "The Zagháwa and people of Gebel Mídób." *Journ. R. A. Inst.* Vol. XLII, 1912.

MAḲRÍZI (quoted by Quatremère, q.v.).

MARMOL. "L'Afrique de Marmol." Trans. by N. Perrot. 1667.

MAS'ŪDI. "Les Prairies d'Or." Text and trans. by C. B. de Meynard and P. de Courteille. Paris, 1861.

MÜLLER (C.) (see sub Claudius Ptolemaeus).

VON MÜLLER. "Extract from notes during Travels in Africa in 1847–8–9." *Journ. of R. G. S.* Vol. XX, 1851.

NACHTIGAL (G.). "Sahărâ und Sûdân." Berlin, 1879.

NA'ŪM BEY SHŪḲAYR. "History of the Sudan" (Arabic text). Cairo, 1904.

EL NUAYRI. (MS. Arab 683, fol. 17; quoted by Quatremère, q.v.)

OHRWALDER (see Wingate).

PALGRAVE (W. G.). "Narrative of a Year's Journey through Central and Eastern Arabia." London and Cambridge, 1865.

PALLME (J.). "Travels in Kordofan." London, 1844 (translation).

PARKYNS. "The Kubbabish Arabs between Dongola and Kordofan." *Journal of R. G. S.* Vol. XX, 1851.

DE PERCEVAL (A. P. CAUSSIN). "Essai sur l'histoire des Arabes avant l'Islamisme...." Paris, 1847.

PETHERICK (J.). (*a*) "The Soudan and Central Africa...." Edinburgh, 1861; (*b*) "Travels in Central Africa, and Explorations of the Western Nile." 2 vols. London. 1869.

PLINY. "Naturalis Historiae, Libri XXXVII." Ex edit. G. Brotier (Delphin Classics).

POMPONIUS MELA. "De Situ Orbis." Ed. Bâsle. 1543.

PONCET. "A voyage to Æthiopia made in the years 1698, 1699, and 1700." Trans. London, 1709.

PORY (see sub Leo Africanus).

PROUT. "General Report on the Province of Kordofan 1876." Cairo, 1877.

PRUDHOE (Lord). "Extracts from Private Memoranda kept by Lord Prudhoe on a Journey from Cairo to Sennar in 1829." *Journal of R. G. S.* Vol. V, 1835.

QUATREMÈRE. "Mémoires géographiques et historiques sur l'Égypte, et sur quelques contrées voisines." 2 vols. Paris, 1811.

RINN (L.). "Les Origines berbères. Études linguistiques et ethnologiques." Algiers, 1889.

RÜPPELL. "Reisen in Nubien, Kordofan und dem peträischen Arabien." Frankfurt, 1829.

SCHURTZ. (Chapter by Schurtz in *The World's History*, Vol. III [see sub Helmolt].)

SCHWEINFURTH (G.). "The heart of Africa." Trans. by Frewer. London, 1868.

"SENNÁR HISTORY." An Arabic MS. found in Sennár by Maj.-Gen. Sir Rudolf Baron von Slatin. It purports to have been finished on "the 19th of Sha'abán 1322 A.H." and to give a history of Sennár from the time of 'Amára Dunkas (c. 1509 A.D.) onwards.

SLATIN (Sir R. C.). "Fire and Sword in the Sudan, 1879–1895." Trans. by Sir F. R. Wingate. London, 1896–7.

SPRENGER (A.). "Historical Encyclopaedia, entitled 'Meadows of Gold...'" [Mas'ūdi]. Trans. by A. Sprenger. Vol. I. (Orient. Trans. Fund Publ.) London, 1841.

STEWART (C. E.). "Extracts from a Report on the Sudan by Lt.-Col. Stewart. Khartoum, Feb. 1883." (Appendix to "Mahdiism and the Egyptian Sudan" q.v. sub Wingate.)

STRABO. "Rerum Geographicarum Libri XVII." Ed. Casaubon. 1620.

TRÉMAUX (P.). "Voyage en Éthiopie au Soudan oriental et dans la Nigritie." Paris, 1862.

EL TUNÍSÍ. "Voyage au Darfour" by Sheikh Muḥammad Bey 'Omar el Tunísí. Trans. by Perron. Paris, 1845.

WALLIN (G. A.). "Notes taken during a journey through part of Northern Arabia in 1848." *Journ. of R. G. S.* Vol. XX, 1851.

WILKINSON (Sir J. G.). "Modern Egypt and Thebes." 2 vols. London 1843.

WILSON (Sir C. W.). "On the Tribes of the Nile Valley north of Khartoum." *Journal of the Anthropological Institute*, August, 1887.

WILSON (C. T.) and FELKIN (R. W.). "Uganda and the Egyptian Sudan." 2 vols. London, 1882.

WINGATE (Sir F. R.). (*a*) "Mahdiism and the Egyptian Sudan." London, 1891; (*b*) "Ten Year's Captivity in the Mahdi's Camp..." (from the original MSS. of Father Joseph Ohrwalder). 15th ed. London.

CHAPTER I

GENERAL HISTORY OF KORDOFÁN

THE area at present known as Kordofán[1] may very roughly be divided into three parallel latitudinal belts, viz.:—the southern mountains inhabited by sedentary autochthonous Nūba and in part by nomad Baḳḳára; the central and comparatively fertile district peopled by a mixed Arab and black race; and the rough open wastes of the north, the home of the nomad Arab.

In the earliest days and for thousands of subsequent years the ancestors of the Nūba probably held the greater part of this country, excepting the northernmost deserts. Beaten back by other races that ruled the Nile banks in successive generations, or by tribes from the interior, and finally by the nomad Arabs, the Nūba have now retired to the mountains of Southern Kordofán.

Of the circumstances prevailing in Kordofán in the time of the Pharaohs we know nothing and can guess but little. The data available for determining the state of the Sudan as a whole in those dim days is very scanty, but such as we have is often applicable to Kordofán as much as to any other part of the country[2]. In the fourth millennium B.C. the Pharaohs of the fourth, fifth, and sixth dynasties at intervals raided or traded with the Sudan. The power of Egypt in the Sudan then waned until about 2500 B.C. when the twelfth dynasty to some extent reasserted its power.

[1] For the origin of the word Kordofán see Appendix I.

[2] The following remarks on the Pharaonic period are mainly abridged from Budge's *History of the Sudan*.

Of what happened in the Sudan in the days of the thirteenth, fourteenth, fifteenth, sixteenth, and seventeenth dynasties next to nothing is known. Amasis I, first king of the eighteenth dynasty, invaded Nubia and probably penetrated Kordofán.

His son Amenhetep I, his grandson Thothmes I, and the latter's two successors all had to cope with raids and rebellions by the wild nomad tribes of the Sudan. The nineteenth dynasty were chiefly concerned with Syria and their south-eastern border, and in the time of the twentieth dynasty the power of Egypt over her vassals was fast waning.

When Shashanq I (the Shishak of the Bible) founder of the twenty-second dynasty drove the priests of Amen from Egypt they fled to Napata, and the native Nubian princes ruling there were encouraged to form an independent kingdom. So great did the power of these princes become that Piankhi king of Napata about 750 B.C. invaded and conquered Egypt, and his successor Shabaka some 40 years later completed the work of conquest.

About 693 B.C. Tirháḳáh, who was acting as vassal king of Nubia, seized the throne of Egypt, but the power of the Nubians in Egypt lasted only about 88 years (c. 750–662 B.C.) and then declined.

Psammetichus I of the twenty-sixth dynasty established garrisons at Assuwán and concerned himself with the strengthening of his power to the north.

It was in his reign that the "Automoloi" or "Sembritae" of the classical authors deserted their posts on the frontier and settled in the Sudan to the south of the junction of the White and Blue rivers, and there mixed with the native population.

About 580 B.C. Ḥeru-sa-atef, king of Napata, in nine expeditions conquered the Nile valley from near Ḥalfa to about the latitude of Sennár.

Nastasenen (died 517 B.C.) ruled a great part of the Sudan from Napata and it was in his time that Cambyses made his mad attempt to invade the country. From 517 B.C. there is a gap of over 200 years in our knowledge of affairs; and then in the reign of Ptolemy II (283–247 B.C.) we hear of a king of Nubia "bred up in Grecian discipline and philosophy," who abolished the barbarous customs of his predecessors and put to death the priests by whom the country was ridden[1]. About 30 B.C. the Nubians first came into contact with the Romans, who in that year had established a prefecture in Egypt, and we hear that the nomad Blemmyes of the East in alliance with these heathen "Nobatae" were a continual source of trouble. So strong did they become that eventually Diocletian (284–305 A.D.) was reduced to the expedient of subsidizing them and entrusting the guardianship of his frontier at Assuwán to the Nobatae, who at that time extended as far north as the oasis of Kharga. About 540 A.D. these Nobatae (Nūba) were converted to Christianity and little more is heard of them until the Arab conquest of Egypt.

From the conquest of Egypt onwards the Nubians were continuously engaged in wars, raids, counter raids, and rebellions against the Arabs with a decreasing measure of success, and Kordofán and the rest of the Sudan became gradually permeated by a constant influx of Semitic blood.

It is true that in 1275 A.D. the Arabs annexed the Sudan, but until about the middle of the fourteenth century the Christian kingdom of Dongola formed a partial dam to the tide of Arab immigration along the river. It is not however to be supposed that it could impose any serious check on the southern movement of the nomads in the interior, nor on the unknown migrations of the non-Arab tribes to the south and west of its territories.

In 1365 A.D. and again 20 years later the rebellious Awlád Kanz conquered Assuwán, and though defeated in 1412 by the Howára Berbers who had been forced southwards from Northern Africa by the Arabs, held the chief power in the Northern Sudan till 1517. During these years the power of the Nubians disappeared and the blacks to the south were practically left face to face with the Arabs: the result of the facts summarized was a general commingling of stocks and the conversion, often from political motives, of all but the Southern Sudan to Islam.

From 1517, when Selím conquered Egypt, little is known of

[1] This king was called Ergamenes. He is alluded to as *μετασχηκὼς Ἑλληνικῆς ἀγωγῆς καὶ φιλοσοφήσας*. See Diodorus Siculus, Bk III, pp. 174 et seq.

the affairs of the Sudan for 300 years. There were mercenary garrisons of "Ghuzz" scattered all over the country and the mixed tribes of Arabs Hamites and blacks were to some extent held in check.

What part in the events described was played by Kordofán can only be determined by guesswork. That part of the country north of Gebel el Ḥaráza we may be sure was from first to last no more than refuge for the untameable nomads, whatever their race, whose hand was against that of each successive ruler of the Nile banks.

Central Kordofán, being fertile, was probably inhabited by various Nubian races and by the black races of the western kingdoms, until both were displaced or absorbed by the Arab immigrants.

The mountains of Southern Kordofán may have been inhabited by Nūba or by negro races that gave place to the Nūba as the latter lost their power to the north and were forced southwards.

Kordofán has never, like Sennár, Dárfūr, Wadái, Bagirmi, Bornu, etc. itself been an independent kingdom, and consequently its records have not been kept continuously, as happened to some extent in the case of the above-mentioned states, whose rulers, for their own glorification and according to the common usage of all independent states, have preserved a more or less true, though highly coloured, account of their past history.

Nor has Kordofán, which has formed the only break in a chain of dynastic kingdoms stretching across Central Africa from east to west, obtained an equal share of attention from those who have been interested in unravelling the tangled skein of the early history of Africa.

Consequently the history of Kordofán, from the time when it ceases to be guesswork until the Egyptian invasion in 1821, has to be collected from (1) the records of Sennár which formed a kingdom separated from Kordofán by the Nile, (2) the records of Dárfūr which bounds Kordofán on the west, and (3) from oral native traditions in Kordofán and elsewhere. Of antiquarian remains that would assist the enquirer practically nothing has been discovered. The history of Kordofán, in brief, is the history of a buffer territory, now the prey of its eastern, now of its western neighbours.

It is not impossible that Northern Kordofán may have been the early home of those mysterious Anag to whom any signs of human occupation previous to the coming of the Arabs is always attributed, and whose name is therefore used as practically synonymous with aborigines[1].

Another ancient people, of whom there are traces in Kordofán, are the Dágu[2].

Very little is known about the latter but tradition speaks of them as being heathen and black and with a strain of Arab blood. Barth records a tradition that they came from Fazuglo and were known as "Nas Fara'ón" ("Pharaoh's folk"). Assuming that they came from the east, possibly about the eleventh or twelfth century A.D., it appears that they did not settle in Kordofán to the extent to which they did in Dárfūr, where they seem to have lived side by side with the aboriginal Fūr for some centuries and to have in time become the ruling power.

To understand in the least what subsequently happened in Kordofán we must now follow the general trend of events in Dárfūr.

Probably about the fourteenth century a race of pagan Arabs called the Tungur[3] began immigrating into Dárfūr. They were of a more advanced civilization than the Dágu or the Fūr but they intermarried with the Dágu ruling family, gradually gained in power and influence at their expense, and finally displaced them entirely and seized the reins of government. In time however the Tungur themselves began to lose their racial individuality and to coalesce with the old Fūr inhabitants of the country; until, about the fifteenth century, there succeeded to the throne one Dáli, whose mother was a Kera-Fūr and whose father was only partly Tungur.

At this time the Fūr seem to have been more predominant in the east and the Tungur to have been gradually extending their power westward over Bagirmi, under pressure from the east.

[1] For the Anag see Chapter VI.

[2] See Chapter II.

[3] See Chapter II.

The Dáli mentioned above is the ancestor of the two dynasties whom tradition invariably describes as having subsequently ruled Kordofán, and of whom mention will be made later, viz. the Kungára and the Musaba'át.

In the meantime, about the date of the end of the Tungur dynasty in Dárfūr, events fraught with great importance to Kordofán in the future were taking place on the eastern side of Kordofán. About the close of the fifteenth century[1] 'Amára Dunkas had united under his leadership the assortment of tribes known as Fung[2], and, in alliance with the chief of the Keri district[3] east of the Blue Nile, swept over the country between Fazuglo and Khartoum. The force led by 'Amára Dunkas was largely Arab, nominally at least of Muḥammadan religion, and almost certainly included the forefathers of many sections of the so-called Arab tribes now in Kordofán.

After conquering the Gezíra it appears that the Fung also extended their immigrations to Kordofán and that some of them settled there.

It is known without doubt that of the tribes which at present inhabit Kordofán the earliest comers were the Ghodiát, the Bedayría, the Gawáma'a, the Gima'a, the Gilaydát, and the Shuwayḥát, and traditions say that they, more especially the Ghodiát, are connected with the Fung.

It is therefore probable that their settlement in Kordofán dates approximately from the beginning of the sixteenth century.

These tribes took up their abode for the most part in the neighbourhood of El Rahad, El Birka, and Gebel Kordofán, and, to judge from probability, tradition, and external evidence, largely intermarried with the Nūba tribes. They appear to have been to some extent united under a sort of supreme arbitrator chosen from among themselves, who decided all important disputes.

[1] Bruce gives the date as 1504; Col. Stewart as 1493; Cailliaud as 1484; and the "Sennár History" as 915 A.H. (1509 A.D.). Tremaux shews how Bruce's and Cailliaud's dates came to differ; he prefers 1504. Stewart calls the leader of the movement "Amara Dunkas"; Cailliaud "Amârah Dounaqs"; Bruce "Amru wad Adlan."

[2] See Appendix 2.

[3] "Abdulla Gemáa-el-Kerinani" (Stewart); "'Abdulla Gemá'a" ("Sennár History").

The story that these tribes were the ancestors of the Baḳḳára of Western Kordofán is not supported by the traditions: it is more likely that the Baḳḳára (i.e. Ḥumr, Messiría, Rizayḳát, etc.) arrived in Dárfūr and Kordofán about the same time or rather later from the north and north-west *via* the interior. The confusion may have arisen from the fact that the Ghodiát, Bedayría, etc. were at first "Baḳḳára," i.e. "cattle-owners."

It is quite possible that from 1500 A.D. (or thereabouts) onwards the Fung kings of Sennár regarded Kordofán as a province of their kingdom, but whether they actually had any power there is extremely problematical.

We must now return to Dárfūr[1].

King Dáli was according to one tradition the great-grandfather of Tumsáḥ and Kūru the ancestors of the Musaba'át and the Kungára respectively: the two brothers quarrelled and Tumsáḥ migrated eastwards ("ṣobaḥa" [صبح] hence "Musaba'át") to Kordofán.

Another account says that Sulaymán Solong, a descendant of Dáli, had a brother called Musabbá to whom he gave Kordofán after conquering that country, each engaging to respect the other's sphere of influence.

A third version of the story is that Solong and Selmán were two brothers and that the former was ancestor of the Fūr and the latter of the Musaba'át.

In any case this Sulaymán Solong is practically the first historical personage who appears in Kordofán.

He ruled Dárfūr from 1596 A.D. till 1637, and during that period conquered Kordofán—(presumably from the admixture of Fung and Arab who had immigrated since the time of 'Amára Dunkas)—and temporarily extended his dominion over Sennár which was now in an enfeebled condition owing to a series of civil wars[2].

Sulaymán's mother is said to have been an Arab, and he himself took an Arab wife. He too was the first royal convert

[1] For an amplified account of the following see Chapter II.

[2] According to Bruce, Ounsa was deposed in 1606, 'Abd el Ḳádir in 1610, 'Adlán wad Ounsa in 1615, and Ba'adi wad 'Abd el Ḳádir died in 1621.

in Dárfūr to Muḥammadanism[1]. His people, however, were not converted from heathenism at once, but only gradually adopted the religion of Islam, with which they were more and more closely being brought into contact by intercourse with Arab traders. This tendency was facilitated by the conquests of Sulaymán, whose sway was extended as far as the Atbara[2].

It is probable that Southern Kordofán and the mountains of Dáir and Teḳali from the time of 'Amára Dunkas, and perhaps earlier, had been more closely connected with Sennár than with Dárfūr and that Sennár was until about 1788 considered as the paramount power in those regions. In support of this is the fact that Sennár, at any rate previous to the date mentioned, seems to have been well supplied with slaves caught in Southern Kordofán, principally from Dáir and Teḳali[3], and to have almost entirely recruited its army therefrom.

It so happens however that the only actually recorded incident, happening comparatively early, which illustrates this theory is the attack made about the middle of the seventeenth century[4] upon Teḳali by Ba'adi abu Duḳn (Ibn Rebát). Sulaymán Solong had died in 1637 and the power of Dárfūr had waned: Ba'adi no doubt took advantage of this: he "destroyed Kordofán" and subjected Teḳali and made it tributary to Sennár, and,

[1] So Nachtigal, followed by Ensor and Schurtz (p. 544). Of Sulaymán Solong Escayrac de Lauture says "son père était Toumourki, sa mère seule appartenait à la tribu des Bederieh, et c'est en Égypte qu'il connut l'Islamisme, dont les Bederieh savaient probablement à peine le nom."

[2] See Schurtz, p. 545.

[3] Bruce says of these Nūba whom he met in Sennár "Many of them that I have conversed with seem a much gentler sort of negro than those from Bahr el Aice, i.e., than those of whom the Funge or Government of Sennar are composed" (Vol. IV, p. 420). They were said also by Bruce to adore the moon but not the sun, and also a tree and a stone "though I could never find out what tree or stone it was, only that it did not exist in the country of Sennar but in that where they were born." See also Stewart's *Report*..., p. 3. He thus accounts for the number of villages in Sennár with the same names as places in Kordofán.

Bruce also heard it related in Sennár that the original home of the Fung race was near Dáir and Teḳali, whence they migrated "after having been preserved from a great deluge."

[4] Stewart gives the date as 1635. The "Sennár History" gives the surname "Abu Duḳn" to Ba'adi Ibn Rebát and describes his attack on Teḳali and its results. Bruce gives the dates of Ba'adi Ibn Rebát as 1651–89; the "Sennár History" gives them as 1641–77; and Cailliaud as 1638–75. 1635 is therefore too early.

whatever may have been the case previous to Ba'adi's time, Teḳali and the surrounding country remained subject to Sennár, with interludes, until about 1788[1].

Whatever power they may have had in the south the Fung were not at any time supreme in Central Kordofán before about 1748, and in Northern Kordofán never. It is true that after the decline in the power of Dárfūr following upon the death of Sulaymán Solong, the Fung seem to have had more power in Kordofán than had Dárfūr, but the fortunes of both parties varied so greatly in proportion as their affairs were more or less prosperous at home, and the Musaba'át were by now so firmly established in Kordofán, that neither can be said to have been supreme. Each power seems to have regarded Kordofán as a province of its kingdom, though without adequate justification, and no doubt extorted whatever it could: the Musaba'át appear meanwhile to have considered themselves subject to neither.

From the time of Ba'adi abu Duḳn until the real Fung conquest of Kordofán we have no knowledge of any definite events that may have occurred.

However in 1733[2], while 'Omar Lele was Sultan of Dárfūr, and the Musaba'át predominant, if not independent, in Kordofán, Ba'adi abu Shilluk ibn el Nul came to the throne of Sennár. Soon after his succession he became involved in a prolonged war with Abyssinia, and we hear from Bruce that he was assisted in his councils by "Hamis, Prince of Dar Fowr [who] had been banished from his country in a late revolution occasioned by an unsuccessful war against Selé and Bagirma and had fled to Sennar." "Hamis" [Khamís?] also probably furnished a contingent of men[3]. After long years of fighting the Abyssinians were driven off. Some years later, having recouped his strength, Ba'adi engaged in a war with the Musaba'át[4], possibly at the

[1] The "meks" of several of the southern gebels, e.g. Debatna, are said to be Fung to this day.

[2] 1733 is the date given by Bruce. The "Sennár History" gives it as 1135 A.H. (1723 A.D.), and Cailliaud as 1721.

[3] The "Sennár History" states that Sennár was aided by the Fūr; and gives the date of the defeat of the Abyssinians as 1743. Bruce (Vol. II, p. 635) dates the outbreak of the war about 1736 or 1737.

[4] The "Sennár History" gives the date of the war with the Musaba'át as 1747 (1160 A.H.), i.e., four or five years after the close of the Abyssinian war.

instigation of Hamis, for we are told that "it was by his [Hamis's] assistance the Funge had subdued Kordofán[1]." Ba'adi was twice repulsed, but about 1748[2] the Fung general Muḥammad

[1] Bruce does not describe the war with the Musaba'át, and from his remark when first mentioning "Hamis" as flying to Sennár that "it was by his assistance the Funge had (sic) subdued Kordofan," one might suppose, but for the "Sennár History," that the Musaba'át war preceded the Abyssinian, instead of vice versa.

[2] The date of the defeat of the Musaba'át is not given by Bruce, but is an important one as marking the beginning of the Fung supremacy in Kordofán. The following are my reasons for placing it about 1748:

Bruce gives Ba'adi abu Shilluk's dates as 1733–66; the "Sennár History" as 1723–62; Cailliaud as 1721–61. The "Sennár History" describes the campaign as beginning in 1747; but it is not said how long after the outbreak of the war Abu Lekaylak gained his victory. We will now refer to the popular account regarding the number of years that the several dynasties prior to the coming of the Turks lasted:—The "Dongola nisba" says, "Kordofán was ruled by the Fung for seven years, then by the Ghodiát (who are Hameg by descent) thirteen years, then by the Musaba'át for seventeen years, then by the Kungára for thirty-six years, and it was from them that the Turks took it." Now the Kungára conquered Kordofán about 1784—(Tiráb died in 1785 [vide Schurtz, p. 545] and El Tunísí mentions that his death was in the year following his victorious campaign. Budge however puts his death in 1787.)—the date of the Fung conquest will therefore be 1784 minus 37 Muḥammadan, or about 36 solar, years, i.e. about 1748. Allowing one year for the course of the war after its outbreak, this agrees so well with the date given by the "Sennár History" that it is probably fairly correct.

Even if Bruce's dates for the reign of Ba'adi are correct, the theory that Kordofán was conquered in 1748 is not impaired.

Now Pallme (p. 12) says the cattle-breeding tribes round Gebel Kordofán "became towards the middle of the last century [eighteenth] better acquainted with Sennaar. The king of Sennaar, namely, sent in the year 1779, the Sheikh Nacib, with 2000 cavalry, to take possession of the country, and the tribes surrendered, with a pretty good grace, to their fate, without offering much resistance. Thus they remained for about five years, under the government of Sennaar." Petherick (*Upper Egypt*, p. 263) says, "Towards the middle of the last century the kingdom of Sennaar had been increased by various conquests until it stretched...to the White River....Its King Adlán,...having gleaned a knowledge of the tribes inhabiting the (sic) Kordofan...conceived the idea of subjugating them....About the year 1770, under Sheikh Nasseeb, he invaded the country with 2000 horsemen....Nasseeb acquitted himself so much to the satisfaction of Adlán, that he named him his Melek or viceroy; and under his lenient administration the country prospered." Both Pallme and Petherick speak of the Fũr as reconquering the country later from "Melek el Hashma" (i.e. Háshim the Musaba'áwi), but both are apparently under the impression that Háshim was one of the Fung. As a matter of fact Petherick plagiarizes freely and without acknowledgement from Pallme and adds flowery details of his own:—both are vague and very inaccurate. In spite of this the story of Nacib (Nasseeb) has occasionally been accepted. No one in Kordofán at present has ever heard of him though Abu Lekaylak and Háshim are well known names, nor is any such person mentioned by Bruce, Burckhardt, or Browne. It is almost certain that Pallme's informants, vaguely as usual, spoke of the ruler of Sennár as sending

abu Lekaylak[1] inflicted a crushing defeat on the Musaba'át and was appointed governor of Kordofán.

He ruled justly and well and was long the hero of the people. His career however was most adventurous and chequered. He and his brother 'Adlán in 1764[2] rebelled against Ba'adi, deposed him, and raised Naṣr his son to the throne of Sennár. Again in 1769 Abu Lekaylak deposed and exiled Naṣr, and when the latter tried to recover his throne he was slain. Naṣr was succeeded in 1769[3] by Ismá'íl, but the whole power remained in the hands of Abu Lekaylak and his brother 'Adlán the vizier, the latter residing near Sennár, and the former spending much of his time in his province of Kordofán[4].

Bruce has the following entry in his journal, dated August 1, 1772: "News brought that the people of Darfoor have marched with an army to take Kordofan, which, it is apprehended they soon will do, being about 12,000 horse, with Mahomet Abu Calec; who, it is thought, will fall back on Sennaar, if not surrounded.... The army of Foor was encamped at a place called Reel, south-west of Lebeid, about seven or eight days, where there is plenty of water. It is their place of rendezvous, about the same distance as Foor."

Since Bruce mentions too that at this time Kordofán was being frequently taken and retaken by Dárfūr, and since Abu Lekaylak must evidently have spent much of his time king-making in Sennár, we may suppose that his governorship of Kordofán was intermittent, and more especially so after his first few years there.

"nasíbu" (نسيبه), i.e. his relative, and that Petherick merely copied Pallme. I do not know how they arrived at their dates. 'Adlán is not mentioned by Pallme: Petherick does mention 'Adlán (as king), but in 1770 Ismá'íl was reigning and not 'Adlán at all. There is probably a confusion between the 'Adlán who was the all-powerful vizier and brother ("nasíb"?) of Abu Lekaylak, and the puppet King 'Adlán (1776–88).

1 Bruce calls him "Mohammed Kalec." Browne calls him "Abli calik." Prudhoe (see *Royal Geogr. Soc. Journal*, Vol. v, 1835) calls him "Mohammed Ablee Keylik." The last-mentioned author says Ba'adi's father was put to death by "Ablee Keylik," who later deposed Ba'adi; but that on "Ablee Keylik's death Baadi returned": this is probably not accurate.

2 See Bruce, Vol. II, p. 669.

3 Bruce, the "Sennár History," and Cailliaud are in agreement as to this date.

4 He was in Sennár at the time of Bruce's visit to Sennár in 1772.

According to the traditional estimate the Fung ruled supreme in Kordofán for seven years only, and it would therefore seem that Abu Lekaylak after about 1755 retired frequently to Sennár. That he was, almost if not altogether up to his death in 1776, a power in Kordofán is suggested by Browne's remark that "...a king of the name of Abli Calik is the idol of the people of Kordofan where he reigned about fourteen years ago [i.e. about fourteen years previous to 1793, the date of Browne's arrival in Dárfūr], and is renowned for probity and justice[1]." It is said that from about 1755 till about 1768 the Ghodiát, who, it will be remembered, were themselves a mixture of Fung, Hameg, Nūba, and debased Arab races settled in Southern Kordofán north of the mountainous country, were predominant: they most probably rose to the height of their power under the *régime* of their relatives from Sennár and succeeded them more or less peacefully[2]. It is said that El Obeid was built and became the capital in their day[3].

When Abu Lekaylak died in 1776 he was succeeded as sheikh in Sennár by Ba'adi wad Ragab: this man had almost as much power as had been in the hands of Abu Lekaylak, and when Ismá'íl tried to shake off his yoke Ba'adi exiled him and raised 'Adlán II to the throne (1776).

Now at some period in the second half of the eighteenth century, and probably between 1768 and 1776 (the date of Abu Lekaylak's death), there came into prominence in Kordofán one Háshim el Musaba'áwi: he was Sultan of the Musaba'át in Kordofán and lineal descendant of that Muḥammad Tumsáḥ

[1] 1776 is the date given by the "Sennár History" for the death of Abu Lekaylak: it is probably correct since both Bruce and the "Sennár History" agree in the dates they give for the reigns of Ismá'íl and 'Adlán II. See Browne, p. 352.

[2] The Ghodiát claim that the Fung on evacuating the country left them in charge: the Musaba'át make the same claim for themselves. Browne (p. 352) says, "the Kings of Kordofan had been deputed by the Mecque of Sennaar till after the death of the son of Abli Calik, when it was usurped by the Fur, in consequence of the weakness and dissensions of the Government at Sennaar."

[3] It is said that when the Ghodiát were setting about building a village on the banks of the Khor and could not decide what to call it, a white donkey belonging to a woman called Manfūra died; so the village was named El Obayyid ("El Obeid"—Ar. الابيّض). Others say the Musaba'át built the town, but this is less probable.

who is mentioned above as the alleged founder of the Musaba'át dynasty. Háshim is said to have warred with the Fung (or may be their successors the Ghodiát), and to have been driven by them to Katūl in the north-west. From this point of vantage he raided the country to the south, and before long became the most powerful man in Northern and Central Kordofán. When the Fung retreated Háshim returned to El Obeid and regained his power. The entry from Bruce's Journals, dated August 1, 1772, may very probably refer to Háshim's attack. As Bruce left Sennár on September 5 we do not know the result of the threatened invasion which he reports. At any rate, when once Háshim was established in power he became involved in a war with Dárfūr, now under the rule of Tiráb, who had succeeded in 1752[1]. It is impossible and unimportant to decide whether Háshim or Tiráb was the aggressor: the important fact is that war broke out about 1784–5.

Before dealing with this war we will note that it was between 1780 and 1788, and probably nearer to the latter date, that Sennár made its last effort to assert its disappearing power in Kordofán.

In 1780[2] the sheikhs of Sennár revolted against Ba'adi's power and made Ragab wad Muḥammad sheikh and vizier in his stead. Ragab attacked Southern Kordofán, but, as the king 'Adlán took advantage of his absence to murder most of the vizier's relations, and Sennár was a prey to anarchy, Ragab hurried back from Kordofán only to be defeated and killed in 1788[3].

From now onwards Sennár was in too anarchical a condition to exercise any influence at all in Kordofán. In fact Ragab's expedition was probably little more than an isolated raid for slaves and booty: the real power of the Fung in Kordofán ceased before the death of Abu Lekaylak.

To return now to Háshim and Tiráb:—Háshim collected an army of 10,000 men, chiefly Danagla Sháíḳía Kabábísh and Rizayḳát[4], and began a series of raids over the border (which

[1] So Schurtz (p. 545). Budge gives the date as 1768.

[2] So the "Sennár History."

[3] See note 2, p. 68.

[4] See El Tunísí.

at this time was probably not further west than Um Sumayma, since that place is mentioned by Burckhardt in 1814 as being the western limit of Kordofán and three days west of El Obeid).

According to one story[1] Tiráb on Háshim's approach wrote deprecating the invasion on the grounds that they two were of a common stock. A peace was made but on Tiráb's return his "amírs" were not satisfied and urged that Háshim had no right to Kordofán, which had been conquered by the ancestors of Tiráb and therefore belonged to Dárfūr. Tiráb then collected an army and sent it under one of the "amírs" against El Obeid. Háshim utterly defeated this force between Ḥuoi, El Tína, and Abu Gu'ūd. The Kungára sent another force, which suffered the same fate. Tiráb was now thoroughly enraged and swore that in the dry summer he would march to El Obeid, and that he would take so great a force with him that the very drops of water leaking from the waterskins should make the grass grow high enough to give shelter to the guinea fowl. Tiráb marched as far as El Dóma with this gigantic force, and Háshim, after detaching all the old men women and children from his adherents and sending them on towards the river, himself followed and camped at Gebel Ḥinayk near Omdurman. Thence he retreated across the Nile, destroying all boats behind him. Tiráb after taking El Obeid pursued Háshim to the river, and finding all the boats were gone spent several months choking up the river with trees, hoping by this expedient to cross. Before he had carried out this project he was fortunate enough to capture a few boats, so crossed over in them. He soon returned however and started back for El Fásher.

The narrative of El Tunísí is more circumstantial, and more likely to be true. He gives the following account of the war between Háshim and Tiráb:—

When Háshim began raiding Dárfūr Tiráb protested, but his protests were as a matter of fact insincere, since Dárfūr was in a state of discontent, and he was not sorry to adopt the common expedient of making a foreign expedition in order

[1] I.e. that of the Musaba'át, told by "Sultan" Ḥámid Gabr el Dár, descendant of Háshim.

to relieve pressure at home, excite a common enthusiasm, and distract the popular attention. In addition, Tiráb wished his son Isḥáḳ to succeed him, whereas under the terms of the will of his father, Aḥmad Bukr, he should have been succeeded by his brothers, one after the other. Tiráb hoped that if he left Isḥáḳ behind and sent his brothers to the front they might find the fate of Uriah the Hittite.

There seems to have been some difficulty in collecting an army, as Tiráb had hitherto only some 200 negro slaves and some unpaid levies of villagers; but he gradually raised an army of 2000 slaves (by levying contributions from merchants and accepting slaves in lieu of tribute) and 3000 Bedouin cavalry, and entered Kordofán by Kága el Surrūg. Marching south-east he met Háshim at the head of 1500 cavalry and 2500 foot at "Farsha" in Dár Ḥamar and defeated him[1].

Háshim now fled eastward to Sennár to seek protection from the inveterate foes of Dárfūr and left vast stores of plunder to Tiráb, who posed as the deliverer of Kordofán.

Tiráb led his victorious army across Kordofán as far as Omdurman, where he built those stone walls at the south end of the town, the ruins of which are still to be seen[2]. The people of Kordofán were treated with great leniency, and instead of being plundered were only required to feed the troops quartered on them. The Bedouin troops were granted three years' remission of taxation and returned to Dárfūr, and a happy era commenced: taxation was light, and trade flourished with Arabia, Egypt, India, and Abyssinia.

It was at this time too that Bára, built originally by Danagla, was beautified with trees and gardens[3].

The year following the conquest of Kordofán by the Kungára the troops demanded to return home. Tiráb, however, not yet having got rid of his brothers, and preferring Kordofán to a disturbed Dárfūr, temporized. Before long a plot was hatched against him by his father-in-law, 'Ali wad Bargan, but the plot failed and 'Ali was killed by the guards.

[1] See Petherick, *Upper Egypt...*, p. 267: but "Ibn Fadl" was not the Sultan of Dárfūr as he states. "Farsha" is Firsháḥa near Rihaywa.

[2] See Slatin, Chap. II.

[3] See Petherick.

Tiráb's next move was to pretend illness. Unfortunately the pretence became a reality, and Tiráb seeing his end near sent to Dárfūr for his son Isḥáḳ, and laid upon his "amírs" a last injunction to acknowledge Isḥáḳ as his successor. Meanwhile another plot was in process: Kinána, the chief wife of Tiráb, hoping to secure the succession for her own son Ḥabíb, thought the safest method of doing so was to promise her support to 'Abd el Raḥmán el Rashíd, the youngest brother of Tiráb, on condition that he should marry her, succeed Tiráb, and appoint Ḥabíb his successor.

At this point Tiráb died (1785).

'Abd el Raḥmán, who had fallen in with Kinána's plot, promptly seized the royal insignia and proclaimed himself Sultan. The "amírs" who had tried to conceal the fact of Tiráb's death till Isḥáḳ had been proclaimed Sultan were now in a dilemma, and their hand being forced they agreed to abide by the terms of Aḥmad Bukr's will. There were various objections to the elder brothers, and by a process of elimination 'Abd el Raḥmán was finally chosen Sultan of Dárfūr and Kordofán[1].

'Abd el Raḥmán, after popularizing himself by largess on a regal scale returned to Dárfūr, raiding Gebel Turu on the way. He took with him the Rizayḳát and Messiría Baḳḳára in order to suppress Isḥáḳ. This he successfully did; and Isḥáḳ was utterly defeated and killed[2].

When 'Abd el Raḥmán retired from Kordofán he left a governor there, but Háshim about 1791[3] reappeared and chased him out.

Now Browne was in Dárfūr from 1793 till 1796, and gives some information as to the course of events after Háshim's return to Kordofán. During 1794 five important personages in Dárfūr were executed on the charge of having carried on treasonable correspondence with Háshim: again, towards the end of 1795 "a body of troops was mustered and reviewed,

[1] El Tunísí's story is resumed from here. It was in this reign that Browne visited Dárfūr.

[2] Cf. Nachtigal.

[3] Browne arrived in Dárfūr in 1793 and says the Sultan "for about two years had been engaged in a very serious war with the usurper of Kordofan."

who were to replace those that had died of the small-pox in Kordofán, which it was said amounted to more than half the army." The original levy was reported to have been about 2000 men, and reinforcements had been frequently dispatched. The war had not ended when Browne left in 1796.

For the close of the war we turn to El Tunísí. He visited Dárfūr in 1803 in the reign of Muḥammad Faḍl, and tells us that 'Abd el Raḥmán sent Muḥammad Kourra[1], who with Kinána had been mainly instrumental in gaining him the throne, to eject Háshim.

This Kourra did[2] and remained as governor in Kordofán for seven years, ruling wisely and well, and periodically sending huge stores of riches to Dárfūr. However, intriguers in Dárfūr now poisoned the mind of 'Abd el Raḥmán against Kourra, and the "amír" Muḥammad, son of 'Ali wad Gáma'i, was sent at the head of an army to arrest Kourra and bring him to El Fásher. Kourra made no resistance, but adopted a calm and dignified manner and so appeared before his Sultan. 'Abd el Raḥmán was convinced by his demeanour and reinstated him in Kordofán with even greater power than before, and showered honours upon him.

In 1799 'Abd el Raḥmán died and Kourra returned to Dárfūr, where he assured the succession to Muḥammad Faḍl, son of 'Abd el Raḥmán, and after putting him on the throne, helped him to reorganize the two kingdoms[3]. We have little information

[1] Muḥammad Kourra was known as "Abu Sheikh," the name given to the principal eunuch of the royal household (see Ensor, and Slatin, Chap. II).

[2] So El Tunísí and Ensor. On the other hand Burckhardt (*Nubia*...) speaks of Háshemí "King of Kordofan" as being ejected by "Metsellim" from Kordofán. This is probably incorrect. Musallem was, as Burckhardt says, ruling Kordofán in 1814; but Browne was in Dárfūr from 1793 till 1796 while the war with Háshim was in full swing and met Musallem at El Fásher (see Browne, page 216): he says of him that he had been a palace slave, was castrated for interfering with women, and was an ignorant and uneducated buffoon,—though, a principal minister. He may have succeeded Muḥammad Kourra. He was known as El Meḳdūm Musallem; but Holroyd (*R. G. S. Journal*, Feb. 1839) calls him Towashi Emm Sellam. "Meḳdūm" was a title only given to palace eunuchs—such as Dárfūr usually sent to govern tributary provinces (see Wingate, *Mahdiism*...). For the subsequent history of Háshim see note 3, p. 63.

[3] Muḥammad Faḍl reigned from 1799 till 1839. Muḥammad Kourra eventually rebelled against him and was killed.

about this period in the history of Kordofán, but several interesting facts are mentioned by Burckhardt, who in 1814 visited Shendi, then the largest town in the Sudan with the exception of Sennár and Kobbe, while El Meḳdūm Musallem[1] was with a bodyguard of 500 horsemen ruling Kordofán from El Obeid.

A valuable part of Burckhardt's narrative concerns the trade between Kordofán and Shendi. From Kordofán came red pepper, gum, "allób" nuts (from the "heglig" tree and eaten as a dainty and considered a remedy for flatulency), blue cambric, leather ropes, leather sacks of ox-hide, seamless water-skins, wooden bowls, and ostrich feathers. But the bulk of the trade consisted in slaves: few of these were Kordofánis: the merchants for the most part bought the slaves, who came from Dár Fertít (on the present French Congo border) and elsewhere, in Dárfūr, and thence proceeded to El Obeid, where they rested awhile with their families, after which they proceeded to Shendi, where they generally had a second family ready to receive them. These merchants on arriving at Shendi sold the slaves, and with part of the proceeds bought beads with which to purchase a second batch of slaves in Dárfūr. As 1000 beads would suffice to buy six female slaves in Dárfūr, the profits of these merchants can be imagined. Natron was also imported to Shendi from Dárfūr. The imports to Kordofán from Shendi were antimony, beads, spices, hardware, "dammūr," cotton stuffs, silk, coffee beans, and especially agate beads[2].

The events which led to the Egyptian conquest of Kordofán in 1821 may be very briefly summarized as follows:—

Muḥammad 'Ali had overcome the Mamlūk dynasty in 1811,

[1] See note 2, p. 17.

[2] Bruce mentions three great caravan routes in Kordofán between 1768 and 1773.

(1) The Great Caravan route from the Niger to Cairo which passed about 60 miles N. of G. el Ḥaráza, coming from the S.W.; and which went to Cairo *via* a point some 50 miles west of the Nile and 30 miles south of the Tropic of Cancer; and thence due north.

(2) The Caravan route to Mekka *via* Suákin; which coming from the west passed 30 miles north of El Ḥaráza to a point on the river 10 miles north of Ḥalfaia (i.e. Khartoum North).

(3) Number two is crossed from S.W. to N.E. (at a point 30 miles N. of El Ḥaráza) by the Caravan road from Dárfūr to Mekka *via* Dongola.

(See map appended to Bruce's work.)

and wished to make himself independent of Turkish control. To the furthering of this purpose money and men were required, and the Sudan offered to him an opportunity of procuring both.

His innate love of conquest and great enterprises also urged him forward. Accordingly he invaded and captured Dongola, and sent one army to attack Sennár, and the other to Kordofán under his son-in-law[1], Muḥammad Bey Defterdár.

The Defterdár with 4000 cavalry and infantry, ten pieces of artillery and about 1000 Bedouins invaded Kordofán, now under Meḳdūm Musallem, by way of Kagmár[2]. To the north of Bára he was met by the raw Kordofán levies under Musallem[3].

To these latter firearms were unknown: the cavalry were clad in mail, their horses caparisoned with copper, and were armed with swords: the infantry, that is the bulk of the army of Kordofán, were armed with rude shields, spears, and axes, and were almost naked. However, they made a most gallant fight, and indeed the victory hung in the balance till Musallem

[1] Muḥammad Bey Defterdár had married Názla Hánem, daughter of Muḥammad Ali (see Wilkinson, *Modern Egypt...*, Vol. I, p. 199).

[2] It is said that the "Turks" travelled in the winter months and followed the following route from Dongola:—El Ḥáfir, El Ordi, Khandaḳ, Abu Ḳutsi, Debba (here leaving the river), Um Belíla, El 'Ámri, Ḥóbagi, El Ṣáfia, Um Masárín, G. el Ḥaráza, G. 'Aṭshán, Kagmár, El Ḳernáia ("Um Nála"), Um Daióka el feki, Bára, Um Sóṭ, El Ghabūsh, Keríta, Fūla Kurbág, El Obeid. El Ḥaráza, as Escayrac de Lauture points out in *Le Désert...* (p. 439), would have been the most advantageous position for the ruler of Kordofán to oppose the Defterdár's advance. The author alluded to says, "Le chef indigène auquel appartenait le commandement de ces montagnes demanda en 1821 au Sultan de Darfour les troupes nécessaires à la défense de ces défilés, dans lesquels il s'engageait à arrêter la marche victorieuse de l'armée égyptienne et à anéantir entièrement cette armée. Le Sultan de Darfour ne comprit que trop tard l'importance stratégique du djebel Haraza, qui fut franchi par les Égyptiens, et dont le chef, abandonné à lui-même, fut fait prisonnier et décapité."

[3] Holroyd says "Emm Sellam" was aided by "Ibrahim Idwir, a Sultán of Darfur." Cailliaud calls Musallem "Sâlem."

Budge says that when Ismá'íl passed through Nubia in 1820 the "Kâshef Hasīn Suleiman" after trying to stop him "fled to Kordofan with 300 slaves and slew Makdûm Musallim and took his harim and his treasury to the Sultân of Darfur, whose daughter he married." He also, however, later speaks of the Defterdár as seizing Kordofán, then going to Shendi to avenge Ismá'íl's murder by the Sháíkía, and afterwards returning to capture El Obeid. It was undoubtedly the Defterdár who fought with Meḳdūm Musallem.

was killed by a Gimi'ábi sheikh: then the Kordofánis broke and fled. Bára was pillaged and two days later the same fate befell El Obeid, where great wealth fell into the hands of the Turks. The last resistance from the Kordofánis was encountered in Dár Ḥamar, where a further victory was shortly afterwards gained by the invaders. The whole of Kordofán, with the exception of the southern mountains, was now surrendered; and Kordofán entered upon the blackest period of its history.

Previously, it is true, Kordofán had seen wars and tumults, but taxation had been light and the rulers just according to the standard of the day. Now all was altered: a foreign race seized the country and administered it exclusively for their own benefit, and in defiance of every law of humanity and justice.

The Defterdár was a monster of inhuman cruelty, and gruesome stories are told of the outrages perpetrated by him and his successors[1]. Money and the gratification of lusts were their only objects. Not only did they crush the native under a heel of iron, but they incidentally swindled their own government at the natives' expense at every turn.

A military despotism, with the power of farming out the administrative posts at its disposal to the highest bidders, can hardly tend to the welfare of the natives under the most favourable circumstances: when the despots are utterly unscrupulous and the successful bidders the same, the results are wholly deplorable. This was the case in Kordofán. The existence of a code of laws, regulations whereby matters of importance should be referred to headquarters, and a more or less qualified "Ḳádi" is to give judgement in judicial cases, are of little use where the code is with impunity ignored, when the only test of the merits of an administrative measure is the amount of money it will produce at once, where the "Ḳádi" is a puppet and the governor in supreme power is a wanton tyrant. Yet this was the condition of affairs in Kordofán for the greater part of the nineteenth century.

The province, of which the administrative boundaries were Gebel el Ḥaráza on the north, Gebel Kadero on the south, and

[1] E.g. see Pallme, pp. 17–26 and Petherick, *Upper Egypt*, pp. 276–281.

a line from Kága to Ḥuoi on the west[1], was divided into four districts, viz. Khorsi, Bára, El Taiára, and Abu Ḥaráz[2].

After the recall of the Defterdár in 1822 the governor of the province was generally the colonel in command of the troops in El Obeid[3]. Under him were the "káshefs," officers in charge of the districts. Under the "káshefs" were subordinate officials distributed in the more distant localities. The governor and the "káshefs" were Turks, their clerks usually Copts, the subordinate officials generally lettered persons of influence belonging to the riverain tribes, or sometimes natives of the country. Between the native and this horde of adventurers, all anxious to enrich themselves before outbid by a rival aspirant to the governor's favour, stood only the local sheikhs; and the system of tax collecting, the only affair of any importance, usually involved the fleecing of the native for the

[1] Burckhardt (*Nubia*) speaks of Um Sumayma, three days west of El Obeid, as on the frontier of Kordofán and Dárfūr in 1814. Pallme (p. 1) says, "Kordofan extends in the North from Haraza to Kodero, in the South from the Nuba mountains, and eastwards from Caccia [? Kága] to the Shilluk or Shillook mountains, about four degrees of longitude." Again he says (p. 2), "Kordofan has no townships on the Bahr-Abiad, or White Nile, for the village nearest to this river is situate at a distance of about four hours' march from its banks. The nomadic tribes, inhabiting the western shore, belong to the realms of Sennaar, and are entirely distinct from the natives of Kordofan."

Ḥuoi ("El Khoeï") is mentioned as being on the Dárfūr frontier by Baron von Müller (1847–9): the village of Markab was in Dárfūr. Prout (1876) remarks that the western boundary ran near Kága (to the north) and Abu Ḥaráz (to the south). In all probability the western boundary was never exactly fixed and varied at different times; but the tendency obvious throughout has been for the expansion of Kordofán at the expense of Dárfūr. It appears too that a traditional boundary for some years previous to 1877 was a line drawn north and south through Gebel Ba'ashóm; and in 1902 the Sultan of Dárfūr still claimed this as operative.

The present approximate boundary which runs west of Um Badr, Kága el Surrūg and the districts of Mūmū and Muglad was very roughly fixed in 1877, after the conquest of Dárfūr by Zubayr. It has been readjusted and corrected in minor particulars since the reoccupation. Disputes arose on the subject in 1903 and after the settlement the boundary was defined. At present it runs west of Um Badr through Gebels Darasáni and Sukunja. Thence southwards to Abu Tóg: thence south-westwards to the east of Um Shanga through Gebel el Kebsh, and on southwards, west of Zalata district, to Ḥáfir Ogr. Thence it runs southwards and very slightly eastwards to the Baḥr El 'Arab.

[2] Kagmár was not a district as Pallme says but only a military post for the collection of tribute from the nomads.

[3] This account of the province is mainly gathered from Pallme.

private benefit in different degrees of every person in authority over him, including his own sheikhs.

The taxes and customs duties were on no fixed scale or proper proportion, and were collected by "káshefs" and their subordinates, in money, in slaves, or in kind, and always in excess, at a rate fixed by the governor, or by summary confiscation. If one district was milked dry and yet had not provided the amount at which it was rated, the deficit was extracted from another district.

Justice was but a name: tortures were used to extract confessions: barbarous punishments were inflicted for ill-doing or non-complaisance.

The following passages from Pallme's *Travels in Kordofán* give some idea of the state of affairs:—

1[1]. "The revenue is collected partly in money, partly in kind, i.e., in products, or slaves; there is no systematic arrangement in the mode in which the contribution is levied....In the year 1838, the country was obliged to contribute, in addition to the imposts in money, beside cattle, butter, and slaves, 4000 árdeb (about 118,000 sacks) of doura, or millet; and the Bakkara nomadic tribes, 12,000 oxen, and kine. Cattle is only received from the villagers when they cannot produce cash; a large ox is then taken by the government to the value of 35 piasters, (...about 9 shillings sterling). During several years, 8000 heads of horned cattle were annually sent to Cairo, the greater part of which perished on the road....It is impossible to describe the cruelty with which the taxes and contributions are collected; and it is really wonderful that it should be yet possible to drain a country, where so little trade is carried on, of such large sums annually...the people will, in fact, eventually be obliged to emigrate, as they have already from several parts, or a general insurrection will be the result.... Droughts, or excess of rains, may cause the harvest, in many districts, to fail, or the locusts may totally devour it; the cattle, moreover, may fall a prey to epidemic diseases; but none of these circumstances is ever taken into consideration, and the

[1] pp. 37–39.

contributions are levied without mercy or compassion.... When a village has nothing left wherewith to pay its taxes, it is obliged to find a certain number of slaves, who are drafted as recruits into the various regiments, or publicly sold; in the former case, the government receives these slaves at a value of 150 to 300 piasters (...from 30 shillings to £3. 10*s*.) a head; children at 30 piasters, or more; but always below the market price, in order that Mehemed Ali, the great slave merchant, may gain something by the bargain, at the expense of his oppressed subjects. A great portion of the imposts is even now paid in slaves."

2[1]. "The Viceroy of Egypt institutes annually, once or twice in the course of the year, an actual hunt in the mountains of Nuba, and in the bordering countries, and seizes upon a certain number of the negroes by stratagem or force, in order either to pay the arrears due to his troops in Kordofan with these unfortunate men, instead of with ready money, or to increase his revenue by the sale of his fellow creatures.... The burden of this sanguinary fate falls most heavily upon the miserable inhabitants of the Nuba mountains. In the year 1825, four years, therefore, after the conquest, the number of slaves which had been led away into captivity was estimated at forty thousand; and in the year 1839 the total number amounted at least to two hundred thousand, without reckoning the thousands stolen by the Bakkara and bought by the Djelabi." The force taking part in these slave hunts usually numbered 1000 to 2000 regular troops, 400 to 800 Moghrabín, and 300 to 1000 natives. Grain and meat for the force were of course seized where found without any payment.

Of actual events that took place in Kordofán from 1821 till the expulsion of the Turks little can be said.

In October, 1822, while the Defterdár was engaged in ruining Kordofán for his own amusement, Ismá'íl the son of Muḥammad 'Ali, after conquering Sennár, was murdered at Shendi by Nimr the "mek" of the Sháíḳía. The Defterdár at once marched *en force* to Shendi, put it and Metemma to the sword, pursued

[1] pp. 306 et seq.

the rebels to Tūti Island, again defeated them, and returned to Kordofán[1].

Almost immediately afterwards he was recalled to Egypt by Muḥammad 'Ali, who had been warned by the number of complaints he had received and the news of several small outbreaks that there was a limit beyond which it might not be wise to drive the natives.

The Defterdár died in Egypt in 1883—it is said poisoned by his father-in-law[2].

The removal of the Defterdár did not effect much change in the methods employed by him in administration. Some slight amelioration in the condition of affairs may have temporarily been effected, but rapine and embezzlement remained the watchwords of the rulers of Kordofán. During these years nothing out of the ordinary seems to have happened[3]. Central Kordofán was in a state of abject subjugation, and was gradually being depleted of all its wealth: many of its inhabitants migrated to Dárfūr and the southern mountains. The northern nomads paid as much tribute as could be extorted from them, and were swindled in their transport contracts. In the south a heavy toll was taken yearly from the Baḳḳára and the "gebels" were raided by government and Baḳḳára, together or by turns, for slaves.

Two "gebels" however, of which previous mention has been made, repelled all attempts to subdue them entirely. These were Dáir and Teḳali. The former was never subdued though assaulted time and time again. Its sturdy inhabitants lived by robbery and raided successfully as far north as Melbis: even the "gellába" hesitated to visit it.

[1] See Stewart.

[2] An account of the Defterdár is to be found in Sir G. Wilkinson's *Modern Egypt and Thebes*, Vol. I, p. 199.

[3] It is worth noting that Major Denham and Captain Clapperton when at Socoto in August 1824 received a letter from a sheikh in Bornu saying "the news from the interior is that...the ruler of Foor also sent an army against the Turks who are in Kordafal or Kordofal and it is reported that they had a battle at a place called Kajah which ended in the defeat of the army of the Foor and the death of three of their grandees besides what fell of the troops, but that the said chieftain is gathering a larger army and means to send it against them" (see *Narrative of Travels*..., by Major Denham, &c....).

Teḳali on the other hand paid tribute at the conquest of the country, but when the usual extortion was attempted it reverted to a state of passive revolt, and a series of expeditions against it effected nothing for about twenty years[1].

Its inhabitants were Muḥammadans and had a large admixture of Fung and Fūr elements, and were joined from time to time by turbulent spirits from Central Kordofán. They lived under an absolute Sultan, and were altogether in a more advanced state of civilization than any other of the southern hills. Their refusal to pay tribute never prevented their trading freely with the "gellába," chiefly in slaves, captured from neighbouring hills, and ivory[2].

Some time in the middle of the century while Naṣr was "mek" they are said to have been subjugated and ordered to pay 90 adult slaves and 380 oz. of gold per annum[3], but the result seems to have been much the same as before: they continually evaded payment and defeated all attempts to coerce them.

To revert now to Kordofán proper :—

Matters continued in their evil state, and about 1838–9 Muḥammad 'Ali went to Khartoum and made enquiries into

[1] Khurshid Pasha when Governor General, between 1826 and 1834, himself conducted an expedition against Teḳali.

[2] Baron J. W. von Müller the Austrian Consul General in Central Africa (1847–9) puts the annual importation of ivory from Teḳali at 60 to 100 cwt. and says the usual price of ivory of the best quality per "Ḳantár" was 850 to 900 piastres in ready money; 1050 piastres if paid for half in ready money and half in merchandize; 12,000 piastres if paid for one-third in ready money and two-thirds in merchandize (see *R. G. S. J.* Vol. xx).

[3] Pallme was in Kordofán in 1839 and speaks of Teḳali as still independent. Petherick in 1863 says, "Tekkela has been subjugated, and although not invested with a garrison is tributary to Egypt by a payment of an annual tax of slaves and gold," see *Travels in Central Africa*, Vol. II, p. 7. Escayrac de Lauture writing between the dates of Pallme and Petherick describes (p. 453) how the governor of Kordofán, Muṣṭafa Pasha, captured Naṣr the brother of the ruling "mek" in a raid and imprisoned him. Naṣr promised that if Muṣṭafa would place at his service a company of infantry he would take Teḳali and pay a tribute of 4000 slaves annually. This plan succeeded to the extent that Naṣr actually seized Teḳali and killed his brother: his next move, however, was to settle Muṣṭafa Pasha's black troops at Teḳali in the enjoyment of lands and wives and cut the throats of the officers. He paid, it is unnecessary to say, no tribute at this time; and successive governors attempted without success to dislodge him.

the many abuses of which he had heard from his numerous spies. The governor of Kordofán, Muḥammad Bey—a rascal of the worst order—was deposed[1], and all the staff-officers and nine other officers and Copts were brought to trial: but the outcome was still of no advantage to the people, because conviction of the offenders merely resulted in the confiscation of their plunder by Muḥammad 'Ali.

At the same time the Viceroy summoned several of the sheikhs to Khartoum: among these was the head sheikh of the Kabábísh. This tribe was particularly aggrieved: their complaint was a typical one: much of the transport of gum was in their hands, and they were expected to deliver the same weight at the end of the journey as had been delivered to them, no account being taken of loss of weight due to the heat. Even so, the deficiency which they were compelled to make good was rated according to the prices in Alexandria. Again 45 piastres only was the hire paid by government for a camel carrying goods from El Obeid to Debba, and this sum, subject to various arbitrary deductions, was often paid in cotton goods grossly overestimated in value.

The sheikh of the tribe was held personally responsible for all losses, and in one case when the Kabábísh abandoned 17 camel-loads of gum and hides in the road the authorities at El Obeid compelled the sheikh to pay 30,000 piastres, although the value of the goods was about 1000 piastres, and both gum and hides were subsequently delivered safely at Dongola.

Muḥammad 'Ali conciliated the Kabábísh by raising the rate of freightage from 45 to 80 piastres: the abuses however continued, and the 45 to 60 piastres paid in cash by "gellába" was always preferable to the nominal 80 piastres promised by the government.

Muḥammad 'Ali's reforms on the whole were valueless to

[1] See Pallme, pp. 42, 114, and 264–266. Muḥammad Bey was colonel of the 1st regiment of the line and a Circassian by birth. He was brought to Egypt as a slave, was uneducated, dense in wit, pompous and superstitious. He succeeded Muṣṭafa Bey as governor of Kordofán in 1835 or 1836 (see Holroyd). In 1827 one Rustum Bey was governor (see Linant), but the dates of his appointment and transfer are not known.

everyone except himself. He left the system of slave raiding unaffected, though compelled by European representations periodically to make pretence of forbidding it. In 1838 he demanded and obtained 5000 slaves from Kordofán.

An account of El Obeid as it appeared in 1838–9 is given by Pallme, and repeated by Petherick in part. The following are the chief points of interest:—

After the Turks took the place they rebuilt it in the form of six sections ("Ḥára"): one was inhabited by Danagla and merchants, one ("El Orṭa") included the government buildings and the "sūk," one consisted of blacks from Dárfūr, one of Felláta pilgrims, one of Kungára, one of the irregular troops ("moghrabín"). In the Kungára quarter lived Sultan Tayma, the official castrator of slave boys. These were in great request as eunuchs for harems in Egypt. The fee for castrating a boy was about 150 pt., but about half generally died under the operation.

The total number of inhabitants was about 12,000[1].

The natives lived in straw huts closely packed together, and the whole place was dirty and ill-kempt.

There were four straw mosques and one of brick. The public buildings and officials' houses were of mud.

Opposite the government buildings was the gallows, and near by was the "sūk." In the latter provisions and animals seem to have been very cheap:—a large sheep cost 15 to 18 piastres, and in the villages outside could be bought for 6; the best camels averaged 150 piastres; ordinary ones 40 to 80[2]. Every day the traffic in slaves was conducted by auctioneers, and boys and girls of from 10 to 15 years cost only 100 to 300 piastres: the price of other slaves varied with the demand.

[1] Holroyd (1836–7) estimated the inhabitants at 30,000. Every year the population in the dry season is nearly double that in the rainy season when the people have cultivation and plenty of water in the neighbouring villages. Hence probably the variation in the estimates of Pallme and Holroyd. In 1908 it was calculated that the maximum population of El Obeid was 12,000, i.e. as it was in Pallme's time.

[2] In 1847 Petherick found the following prices usual at El Obeid (see *Upper Egypt*, p. 285): a full grown camel 150, a cow or bullock 45, a heifer 25 to 35, a sheep 5, a bushel of corn 3 piastres. The value of a piastre as used by Petherick was the same as it is now, viz. 5 piastres = 1*s*.

Pallme states that about 15 years before his visit water was found at 20 feet below the surface at El Obeid, but that in his time it was 50 feet down. Petherick, who spent from 1848 to 1853 in the country, says "the wells, and there are many in Lobeid, are sunk to a depth sometimes exceeding one hundred feet....With two or three exceptions, these wells produce hard and brackish water...[1]."

As regards the troops, Pallme says that they consisted of three battalions of 1000 Sudanese, 800 Moghrabín irregulars, about 40 artillerymen, and about 200 Bashi Bazuks (irregular Turkish cavalry):—"Among all Mehemed 'Ali's troops...I never met with a regiment so wretchedly equipped, so badly drilled, and so utterly deficient in discipline[2]." Their arms were in a disgraceful condition, insubordination was rife, and general laxity prevailed. Their pay was 20 paras (*2d.*) a day and a ration of food; "but for their actual pay they have to wait frequently a whole twelvemonth, and their arrears are then liquidated with slaves or camels. It frequently happens on these occasions that a son receives his father or his brother instead of payment." Soldiers' children were paid from the date of their birth, and when old enough enlisted as drummers or pipers. However, Pallme states that a new commandant had lately been appointed and some measure of reform was being effected. The Moghrabín irregulars had to find themselves in clothing, horses, and equipment, without any prospect of compensation in the event of loss. They were armed with a long gun, two pistols, and a sabre. Most of them were quartered in El Obeid, and the rest distributed in the districts. The hospital arrangements for the troops can only be described as vile:—"The Egyptian doctors and apothecaries, scarcely escaped from the elementary schools and placed on their own footing, treat the sick soldiers like cattle, never dream of diagnosis, prescribe whatever enters their heads, and care very little whether they save a man's life or murder him....Every order is

[1] See *Upper Egypt*, p. 306 et seq. In 1911 the average depth of wells in the town was about 18 metres. There were also among them a few poor wells of 13 metres, and, on the higher ground, a few of 28 metres. Most were sweet.

[2] See Pallme, p. 200.

given on the principle of 'Allah Kerím.'" Camels for transport of troops were chiefly supplied by the Ḥamar, who at that time were the largest camel owners of the country: the same tribe was also in charge of the defence of the Dárfūr frontier, and were frequently given a loan of horsemen by the government to assist in raids into Dárfūr to capture animals wherewith to pay their tribute.

The wealthiest and best educated of the tribes were the Danagla, who were *protégés* of the Turks, and largely employed by them in the administration. Practically all the export trade was in their hands, and they also traded for slaves and ivory with the southern mountains. Pallme brands them as utterly dishonest, gross liars, and overfond of brandy. The Baḳḳára, until shortly before Pallme's visit, when the export of cattle to Egypt had been forbidden, suffered greatly at the hands of the Turks. Tribute in kind was always collected from them by the troops, and apart from the 8000 or 9000 head of cattle usually extorted, they had to submit to the depredations of the official tax-collectors.

On the other hand they were allowed an entirely free hand to raid for slaves among the Nūba hills.

The best that Pallme can find to say of the state of affairs is that Yūsef Bey, who succeeded Muḥammad Bey in 1839, attempted to improve the discipline of the troops and ameliorate their lot; that he was rather more lenient and less arbitrary in his methods; and that European travellers were in little danger.

Of the climate Pallme can say nothing sufficiently bad. Of the eight Englishmen who had come to the country to work mines, six died in two months. Fevers, dysenteries, boils, dropsy, small-pox, jiggers, and syphilis (imported by the Egyptian troops) were rife:—"In all my travels I never met with any country where the climate is so unhealthy and where there is such a variety of disease as in Kordofan." Since Kordofán to the north of the southern mountains is now far from being generally unhealthy except perhaps in September, it is to the lack of sanitary methods and the dirty condition of living adopted by a thick population that we must attribute the conditions described by Pallme.

Of commerce he says:—"The monopoly enjoyed by the Egyptian government in this province totally impedes trade in general. The chief articles of commerce are not only bought by the authorities, who are, moreover, protected by a law prohibiting any private person from bringing them into the market; but the immense duties levied on the goods render it impossible to transport them to Egypt; this rule especially applies to ivory. Everyone therefore is compelled to sell to the government." And again:—"The articles of export are: gum, hides, senna leaves, ivory, rhinoceros' horns, cattle, tamarinds, ostrich feathers, ostrich eggs, gold in rings and in grain, water-bags, salt, tobacco, sesame, and slaves. The first three articles named are the most lucrative in a commercial point of view, and monopolized of course by the government. The gum arabic is collected in the forests a few months after the rainy season, and we may say by force; for the government pays the cantaro of 44 oock'ckahs, equivalent to 110 pounds, with 15 piastres (4*s.* 4*d.*) only....Kordofan yields, in average years, from 3500 to 4000 loads of this product, or from 10,000 to 14,000 hundredweight, at 44 oock'ckahs. I have been assured by many persons that an addition of 6000 hundredweight might be made to this quantity, if the labour of the persons employed in the collection were but better remunerated."

Ivory, which formed the tribute paid to Dárfūr by its tributary provinces, was sent thence in considerable quantities to El Obeid and Bára: much was also brought from Shaybūn and the Shilluk country. The price of a "ḳantár" in Kordofán was £10. 18*s.*, including the duty. Practically the whole supply was forwarded to Suákin and little to Egypt, although nominally Muḥammad 'Ali held the monopoly of the trade.

The import trade was carried on by caravan from Cairo, Sennár and Suákin, and was attended with very heavy expense, partly on account of the transport, and chiefly of the exorbitant duties.

A consignment of goods paid duty at Alexandria, Cairo, Dongola, and El Obeid. A camel load of cotton stuffs paid 300 piastres duty at El Obeid, of rice 150 piastres, of wine 100 piastres. Most of the trade goods came from Austria, viz. spikenard, cooking pans, razors, swords[1], camel bells, antimony, arsenic, iron and brass wire, matches, Bohemian products, cloths, mirrors, rings, beads, etc. Calicos were imported from England; coffee from Abyssinia; narghilehs, ablution jugs, syringes, etc. from the Levant. The list of articles imported also included cloves, pepper, sugar, sulphur, rice, soap, chintz, wines, oil, amber, etc. from Prussia.

Less than a decade after Pallme left Kordofán it was visited (in 1847) by John Petherick as a mining engineer to report on the numerous iron ore deposits, and during 1848–53 Petherick was trading in gum in the province. Whether because he was of a more cheerful disposition, or because he was more hardened, he gives a rather less gloomy view of affairs. Many of his facts and anecdotes he borrows unacknowledged from Pallme.

Petherick travelled from Khartoum up the Nile to Tūra el Khaḍra, and thence by camel *via* Abu Garád, where was a large "sūk" and a customs house under charge of an officer in the 1st regiment of the line, Hashába, El Dóm, Zarzūr, and Bára to El Obeid.

The system of overtaxation and unprincipled methods was still in force, and Petherick says[2]: "From the governor and his wakeel, or *chargé d'affaires*, down to the servant of the meanest official, by the whole string of *employés*, including the military officers, whose services are frequently employed in levying the taxes, a system of extortion and pillage is so systematically carried on against the tax-paying community, that the sum paid by the people is more than double the amount of the net income, as shewn in the government books." Although raiding for slaves had by now been discountenanced as a method of gaining recruits, they could be bought for that purpose at £6 to £8, and the El Obeid slave market still throve.

[1] Pallme says, "Two edged swords of Austrian manufacture are 36½ inches in length, and 1¾ inches in breadth, of equal diameter throughout, and rounded off inferiorly. 7¼ inches and marked ŝ with a lion. The scabbards and hilts are made in the country....Those [swords] marked with a death's head from the workshops of Peter Knell in Solingen are preferred" (p. 298). The import of these swords has ceased now. They were used to a great extent by the Dervishes from 1881 to 1899 and have lasted well.

[2] See *Upper Egypt* (p. 245).

The release of the gum trade from the government monopoly had, however, been of great benefit to the natives, and enabled most of them to pay their taxes in cash[1]:—the western and southern tribes still paid in kind. Nor were the same gross cruelties perpetrated by officials as those for which the Defterdár and his successors had become notorious.

The governor of Kordofán in 1847 was Muṣṭafa Pasha, a good natured, comparatively honest, and popular man. He was by birth a Cretan, and had been kidnapped and sold to a Turk. After enlisting he worked his way up to the rank of Colonel. He resided at Bára, and let his *chargé d'affaires* at El Obeid do most of the work.

In 1847 he conducted an expedition with a force of 1500 infantry, 1000 Ḥamar horsemen, 400 Bashi Bazuks, and some Ḥawázma, to collect arrears of tribute from the Selím Baḳḳára on the White Nile. Thousands of cattle were captured, and the troops got 10 months' arrears of pay.

Muṣṭafa Pasha was recalled in 1848.

In 1854 Muḥammad 'Ali died. One of the first acts of his successor, Sa'íd Pasha, was to visit the Sudan in 1855 and effect a number of reforms[2]. The most important of these, as they affected Kordofán, were the prohibition of the custom of collecting taxes by means of soldiery; the order that the taxes were only to be collected after the harvest, when the people were in a position to pay; and the abolition of slavery (in 1857). This last reform was the result of the storm of indignation

[1] At first when Muḥammad 'Ali abandoned the monopoly of trade in general he retained that of gum, senna, and ivory, arguing that they were natural products which belonged to whoever collected them, and as such his perquisite. During this period the official price of gum sold to Muḥammad 'Ali or accepted by him in payment was 50 pt. a "ḳantár" of 120 rotls: the seller, however, would usually prefer a more certain 40 pt. or 45 pt. from the merchants. When the trade was finally freed from the monopoly the output increased enormously and prices dropped. In March and April 1850 gum was down to 27 pt. a "ḳantár."

The cost of transporting a load of five "ḳantárs" (600 rotls) from El Obeid to Cairo *via* Dongola was about 150 pt., and if the cost price at El Obeid be added it generally could be reckoned that the "ḳantár" could be delivered in Cairo at a cost of 80 pt. As 220 pt. a "ḳantár" was obtainable in Cairo it is obvious that profits were considerable: the buyer paid the import duty (see Escayrac de Lauture, *Le Désert*...).

[2] See Stewart.

roused in Europe by the reports of missionaries and explorers. Egypt was compelled to yield to the pressure, but the prohibition of the trade and of official slave raids into the country of the blacks deprived the officials of much of their income, and a consequence was that the trade "if more dangerous was also more lucrative, and...the officials covered their loss of income with bribes and hush money[1]." A brief account may here be given of the system of local administration in vogue under the superintendence of governor and "káshefs" during the period from 1821 to 1881, and the modifications through which it passed[2].

The Turks found in force the usual Arab tribal system: each tribe of nomads was under a head sheikh, under whom were the sheikhs of the various sections. The sedentary people had likewise their head sheikhs, and under them were both sheikhs of sections and sheikhs of villages. In the tribe the authority of the sheikhs of sections and the sheikhs of villages overlapped, as is unavoidable where a people is in process of transition from the nomad to the settled state, and as is still the case. Upon this system the Turks at first superimposed another by appointing a "sheikh masháikh" with authority over all other sheikhs. Head sheikhs of sedentary tribes were henceforward called "masháikh akhṭáṭ" (singular "sheikh khaṭṭ") and the village sheikhs were left under them. The heads of the great nomad tribes were of course practically free from the control of the "sheikh el masháikh."

In addition there were "muowins," i.e. native officials residing at headquarters, and liable to be dispatched in any direction to assist in collecting taxes.

This system was followed for about 40 years. The last to hold the position of "sheikh el masháikh" was Muḥammad Yasín a Dolábi of Khorsi, of a powerful Dongola family. His father, Yasín Muḥammad Dólíb, held the same position before him for many years[3].

Mūsa Pasha when governor about 1860, found it more

[1] See Schurtz, p. 558.
[2] The following has been gleaned from native sources.
[3] See the genealogical tree of the Doálíb given in Chapter VI.

convenient to abolish the post of "sheikh el masháikh," and distribute the duties among four local "náẓirs," with similar duties and powers, one "náẓir" being appointed to each district.

Muḥammad Yasín was therefore made a "muowin" at headquarters, Maḥmūd Dólíb Nesi appointed "náẓir" of Khorsi, one Ṣaláḥ, of the Gawábra Danagla at As'ḥáf, "náẓir" of Bára, El Ṭáhir el feki Bedawi "náẓir" of Abu Ḥaráz, and a fourth "náẓir" of El Taiára[1].

Each of these "náẓirs" had under him two "'uhdas" ("'uhad"—singular "'uhda") as assistant tax collectors.

All these persons were as a rule Danagla or members of riverain tribes. To each "'uhda" a certain group of tribes was apportioned: these tribes were generally the settled ones: other tribes had as "'uhdas" their own sheikhs, who paid taxes direct to headquarters, and whose status was practically that of the "náẓirs" of the present day. This system continued until Ḥasan Pasha Ḥelmi el Guwaizer (subsequently governor of Dárfūr) came as governor to Kordofán. He abolished the four "náẓirs" and reverting to the older system appointed 'Abd el Hádi Ṣubr as "náẓir" of Bára, Khorsi, El Taiára, and the country near the White Nile: Abu Ḥaráz however was left under its own "náẓir." Just before the Mahdía Giegler Pasha again reinstituted the system of a "náẓir" for each district[2].

To revert now to the course of events:—1865 was a year of terrible famine, and is still remembered as "Sannat el

[1] Muḥammad Yasín subsequently succeeded 'Abd el Hádi Ṣubr (successor of Maḥmūd Dólíb Nesi) as "náẓir" of Khorsi.

[2] As the result of insistent complaints against 'Abd el Hádi he was removed by Giegler Pasha shortly before the outbreak of the Mahdía (see Slatin, Chap. IV). The "náẓirs" then appointed were:—Bára, Muḥammad Ágha Sheddád; Khorsi, Muḥammad Yasín; El Taiára, Sulaymán Ágha; Abu Ḥaráz, (remained in office) 'Abd el Raḥím el feki abu Ṣofi'a. The following were the various "náẓirs" of Bára district:—(1) Ṣaláh, (2) El Taib, (3) 'Othmán Aḥmad, (4) 'Othmán Ḥámid, (5) Aḥmad Yasín,—all these were Gawábra of As'ḥáf—(6) 'Abd el Hádi Ṣubr (general "náẓir"), (7) Muḥammad Sheddád. The last named was objected to by the As'ḥáf people and Gábir wad Taib a Gabri acted in his place until the Mahdía. Gábir and Sheikh el Dardíri a Dólábi of Khorsi had previously been "'uhdas" to Muḥammad Sheddád; the former with charge over the nomads' portion of the tribute of the tribes apportioned to him, and the latter over the tribute of the settled population of these tribes. The tribes that paid through the "'uhdas" of Bára were the Merámra, the Habábín, the Gilaydát, some of the Nawáhía and of the 'Arífia—(all sections of Dar Ḥámid)—and various other scattered sections.

Fatásha." In 1874 Dárfūr was annexed by Egypt, and Colonels Purdy and Colston were sent into Dárfūr and Kordofán respectively to make reconnaissances. In the following year too a survey was made by F. S. Ensor, C.E., for a proposed line of railway from Dongola to El Fásher along the Wádi el Melik.

In 1877 Gordon was appointed Governor-General of the Sudan, and on August 4 a convention was concluded between Great Britain and Egypt by which all public traffic in slaves was prohibited. In 1879 Gordon resigned his post, and the slave trade was at once covertly renewed with the connivance of the Egyptian officials—in fact it cannot be said that the slave trade had ever been completely stamped out.

The country was now ripe for rebellion. The limit of endurance had been reached: what reforms had been effected were insufficient, and the greatest of them all, viz. the prohibition in more than name of the slave trade was by the irony of fate intensely unpopular.

The officials were for the most part corrupt and unprincipled as ever; the country had been robbed of all its wealth; and justice was a farce. It was the Baḳḳára in particular who were furious at the spasmodic attempts of the government to put a stop to their immemorial custom of raiding for slaves.

The following extract from the work of Messrs Wilson and Felkin gives some idea of the efficacy of so-called reforms. The incident occurred at Um Shanga in 1881:—

"The camels could go no farther. Mr Wilson rode off in search of fresh ones, and found a certain Woad Ali Effendi Bimbashi, who promised that he would try to secure some for us. After we had gone to bed his cavass, a Circassian, came to see us, and said he had been ordered by his master to get the camels, and asked if we had any slaves to sell, for he was in great want of some. He said he had bought a girl and a woman the week before for $43. The bimbashi had been dismissed from the government service at Obeid, and, as the officials there had no money with which to pay his salary, he was sent to levy a small tax on his own account. The sum due to him was between $200 and $300, and the cavass told us that he feared he would not be able to get more than $1000, as the people in that district were very poor. The next morning we saw one way in which he collected his dues. Twenty camels were requisitioned, and first one owner and then another redeemed his beast by from $1 to $5, which went into the pocket of the bimbashi."

In 1881 Muḥammad Aḥmad ("the Mahdi") quarrelled with the head of the Sammánía "ṭaríḳa" and established himself as a religious teacher on Abba Island. He adopted the *rôle* of an ardent revivalist, and preached against the gross corruption of the times much as Muḥammad ibn 'Abd el Wahháb a century before had done with such overwhelming success in Arabia. The all-important difference between the two men lay in the fact that the Wahhábi was an honest single-minded zealot, while Muḥammad Aḥmad after tasting of success shewed himself no more than a licentious, brutal, and ambitious fanatic.

His first act was to make a short tour through Kordofán and gauge his chances of success there. Some months later at Mesallamía he was joined by 'Abdulláhi Muḥammad of the Guberát Ta'áísha, known later as the "Khalífa."

This man was a most valuable adherent, for he was thoroughly acquainted with the restless Baḳḳára tribes, and had great influence with them. It was at his suggestion that Muḥammad Aḥmad again made a tour through Kordofán,—this time with the definite design of fomenting the discontent that was rife. Passing through the Gima'a country he visited El Obeid and secured the support of El Sayyid el Mekki, the head of the Ismá'ílía "ṭaríḳa," and many others. Thence he went to Teḳali and sounded Mek Ádam Deballu. The latter had lately refused to pay his tribute to Eliás Pasha wad Um Berayr, a Ga'ali whom Gordon had appointed governor of Kordofán in defiance of local prejudice; but he was too astute to commit himself as yet.

From Teḳali Muḥammad went back *via* Sherkayla to Abba Island.

By this time the government at Khartoum had realized the danger of allowing him to remain unmolested and sent Muḥammad Bey abu el Sa'ūd to bring him to Khartoum. Muḥammad Aḥmad flatly refused, and seeing that the time was ripe openly proclaimed a "jehad," and declared himself the Mahdi expected of all true believers.

Ra'ūf Pasha, the governor-general, now sent an expedition to capture him, but the attempt ended in the discomfiture of the government troops and a corresponding impetus being given to the Mahdi's cause. As the true Mahdi of Islam is to come from Gebel Mása, it now seemed politic to the pretender to give that name to his next destination, and from there to start his campaign in earnest. The place he decided upon was Gebel Gedír in Southern Kordofán, and thither he moved by way of Teḳali with a band of Kenána and Deghaym through the Gima'a country, collecting adherents as he went. At Teḳali he was disappointed in his hopes of support, though nothing was done to hinder his progress to Gedír.

On December 9, 1881, near Gedír, the Mahdi was attacked by Rashíd Bey, the governor of Fashóda, but he dispersed the over-confident government troops and killed their leader. An expedition of some 4000 men was now organized at Khartoum, and placed under command of Yūsef Pasha el Shelláli: a battalion of infantry and some volunteers under 'Abdulla wad Dafa'alla was also to cooperate from Kordofán.

The Khartoum expedition started on March 15, 1882, and waited at Kawa for the Kordofán contingent. The latter had to cope with considerable difficulties, as 'Abdulla Dafa'alla was hampered at every turn by the intrigues of his enemy, Eliás Pasha, the ex-governor, who had now been succeeded by Muḥammad Pasha Sa'íd. However, 2000 odd troops from Kordofán eventually got to Kawa, and the joint force under Yūsef Pasha proceeded in May to Fashóda, and thence marched inland to Mesát near Gebel Gedír. Here on June 7 they were attacked and practically annihilated.

This success of the Mahdi placed all Southern Kordofán in his hands, and also provided him with munitions of war. At the same time his lieutenants farther north had not been idle. In May, 1882, Muḥammad Pasha Sa'íd had sent a force of 1200 men from El Obeid to relieve El Birka, then a fortified government post, which was being besieged by 'Abdulla wad el Nūr and a mixed horde of Bedayría, Ḥawázma, Ghodiát and

Ḥumr. On May 13 the Dervishes were defeated near Kashgíl, but on the withdrawal of the government troops the siege was resumed and the town fell soon after: 2000 of the garrison were put to death, and about 1000 escaped to El Obeid. In May, too, the Bedayría attacked and wiped out the people of Abu Ḥaráz and killed the "náẓir." Again on May 19 the Dongoláwi village of As'ḥáf, which had provided the Turks with so many tax-collectors, was attacked by a medley of Ḥamar, Dár Ḥámid and Shuwayhát under El Summáni, and most of the inhabitants were put to the sword. The troops dispatched from Bára for the relief of As'ḥáf were defeated.

The Gawáma'a under Raḥma Manófal now began to close in on Bára and cut off its supplies. Early in June Raḥma suffered a check, but the cordon of Dervishes was continually reinforced, and the success of the garrison was only temporary. Bára at this time had a garrison of 2000 men, with eight guns: on June 23 it was attacked by the Dervishes in force. The attack was repulsed, and Raḥma retired to collect reinforcements. About July 7, 1882, a mass of rebels under El Nūr assembled at Shattūra to the south-west of Bára, and a force was detached from Bára to cope with them. The government troops repelled the Dervish attack, but found their return to Bára cut off: however, reinforcements from El Obeid arrived, and the combined forces dispersed the enemy, and were shortly afterwards recalled to El Obeid.

On July 17 Raḥma appeared with a fresh force in front of Bára, and for the rest of the year the town was closely invested. Late in August there arrived there reinforcements from the river under Muḥammad Pasha Imám: these had been urgently summoned, for the Mahdi had now moved northwards in person against El Obeid, and at the same time had detailed a force to assist in the investment of Bára. Part of the reinforcements were therefore kept at Bára, and the rest sent on to El Obeid[1].

After the defeat of Yūsef Pasha near Gedír on June 7 the

[1] It is said that a favourite gibe directed at such Dervishes as were caught and made to work on the trenches was "you call yourselves Anṣár el Dín ['Helpers of Religion'—the Prophet's name for his early converts of El Medína], I call you Anṣár el Ṭín ['Ground Helpers']; yella yá Keláb ['get along with you, dogs']."

Mahdi had entered into negotiations with the religious leaders and the chief merchants of El Obeid, and especially with the traitorous ex-governor, Eliás Pasha, who headed the faction opposed to Muḥammad Bey Sa'īd and Aḥmad Bey Dafa'alla (the brother of the ill-fated 'Abdulla).

On September 3 the Mahdi, at Eliás's invitation, left his uncle Maḥmūd Sheríf at Gedír and marched to El Obeid and demanded its surrender. The government buildings at this time were strongly fortified by a quadruple ring of trenches, and eight forts had been built on the walls. The troops consisted of about 8000 regulars and Bashi Bazuks, and a crowd of newly enlisted irregulars under Aḥmad Bey Dafa'alla. Muḥammad Pasha therefore declined to surrender, and hung the Mahdi's messengers.

Notwithstanding this Muḥammad Pasha Imám, a part of the garrison, and the bulk of the townspeople deserted the same night to the Mahdi. On September 8 the Dervishes attacked El Obeid in the morning, but were repulsed with the loss of about 10,000 men, including the Mahdi's brother Muḥammad and the Khalífa's brother Yūsef, and 63 banners. Only 300 odd of the garrison were killed. The Mahdi now retired for a mile to await more arms and ammunition that were expected from Gedír: on their arrival he closely besieged the town. Two battalions of regulars and 750 Bashi Bazuks as reinforcements for El Obeid and Bára were now (September 24) sent off from Khartoum under 'Ali Bey Luṭfi.

The Gawáma'a under Raḥma fell on these at Kawa and killed over 1100 of them. About 200 escaped, and their entry into Bára was effected by means of a sortie under El Nūr 'Angara.

About the same time El Taiára, defended by two companies of Bashi Bazuks, was besieged by El feki Minna Ismá'íl of the Gawáma'a at the head of a host of Gawáma'a, Gima'a, Bedayría and Ḥawázma, and after a short resistance capitulated. The reinforcements sent from El Obeid to relieve it were annihilated.

To the south again Father Bonomi's missionary establishment at Dilling was besieged from April to September, and was then captured by Mek 'Omar.

In November a treacherous attempt was made by Aḥmad wad Málik, one of the notables of Bára, to set fire to the town during an attack by the enemy: the attempt did not succeed entirely, but most of the grain was burnt and the garrison reduced to great straits for food. El Nūr 'Angara now deserted, and on January 5, 1883, the garrison of 2000 men surrendered to 'Abd el Raḥmán el Negūmi with their arms and ammunition, and joined the rebels.

El Obeid was still holding out, but under the greatest difficulties. Thirty or forty men a day were dying of starvation: not only all the corn (of which an insufficient supply had been laid in) but the very dogs had been eaten, and no better food could now be found than palm fibre, gum, and skins. Finally, on January 16, 1883, it was decided to surrender on condition of the lives of the garrison being spared. The Mahdi accepted these terms, and took possession of the town on January 17.

Of the officers of the garrison Muḥammad Pasha was subsequently sent to 'Allóba, where he was killed with axes by El Minna Ismá'íl; 'Ali Bey Sheríf was sent to El Birka, and there beheaded by Nawái of the Ḥawázma; and Aḥmad Bey Dafa'alla and Muḥammad Yasín deported to Shakka, and put to death by the Rizayḳi sheikh Madibbo on their arrival. Others were exiled to the Nūba mountains or Dár Ḥumr. The garrison of about 3500 men were compelled to join the Dervishes; about £100,000 in specie was captured, and about 6000 rifles with their ammunition. The town was given over to pillage, and all government records were destroyed.

About now El Minna Ismá'íl, who had got into trouble for looting too freely at El Obeid, quarrelled with 'Abdulláhi the Khalífa, and attempted to make himself independent. Abu 'Anga, 'Abdulla el Nūr, and Wad el Negūmi were sent against him, and he was seized suddenly and executed.

The Mahdi now set about securing his position and extending his power by sending out emissaries in every direction. The fame of his exploits, crowned by his capture of El Obeid, rallied practically the whole native population of the Sudan to his cause, but his attempts in one direction were unavailing: the Sennussi sent a delegate to El Obeid, but disgusted at the accounts of rapine and violence that he heard, he warned his people in the west to have no truck with the canting impostor at El Obeid, who, apparently so zealous and high-minded, was living in luxurious vice. The Egyptian Government meanwhile were not entirely idle. 'Abd el Ḳádir Pasha, the governor-general, had wisely advocated a policy of segregating the Mahdist revolt in Kordofán and Dárfūr by a line of strong garrisons along the White Nile. The authorities at Cairo were more ambitious, or less sensible, and 'Abd el Ḳádir was recalled, and preparations made for the reconquest of Kordofán.

General Hicks was appointed for the task. It was from the outset a hopeless one: the troops provided were an utterly incapable rabble, undisciplined and cowardly; Hicks had not sufficient European officers, and he was hampered at every step by intrigues and jealousies.

By March, 1883, Hicks was at Khartoum, and after a month of drilling his unwilling recruits, and effecting a clearance of the country between Khartoum and Sennár, he prepared for the expedition to Kordofán.

Intrigues delayed him till September, and he then started with about 7000 infantry, 400 Bashi Bazuks, 10 mountain guns, 500 cavalry, 100 cuirassiers, and 2000 camp followers, and reached El Dueim. From here Hicks had intended to go *via* Bára to El Obeid, but he was persuaded to take a more southernly route by 'Alá el Dín Pasha, his second in command, who had succeeded 'Abd el Ḳádir Pasha, and who feared that there was not sufficient water for the troops on the northern road.

Hicks therefore advanced slowly with his whole force and guides to Sherkayla, which he reached on October 14, marching *via* Shatt, Zerayḳa, Derayfísa, Serakna, Nurábi, Geleben Ḥar, and 'Aḳayla. He was unable, as he wished, to keep up a line of communications with Dueim by a series of military posts, because in the first place there was not enough water, in the second he could neither spare nor trust the men, in the third the Arabs would have been able with ease to annihilate post after post of the miserable Egyptian recruits. It was also highly improbable that the garrisons of these posts would so much as venture to attempt the forwarding of any supplies that might reach them. As a matter of fact a force of some 3000 Baḳḳára under 'Abd el Ḥalím Musayyid, Muḥammad abu Girga, and 'Omar the son of Eliás Pasha, and a medley of Gima'a and Gawáma'a under 'Asákir wad abu Kalám were dogging Hicks's footsteps the whole way, cutting off his retreat by closing all wells, and sweeping the country clear of food.

On October 20 Hicks reached El Rahad: 'Abd el Ḥalím now went and met the Mahdi at El Obeid, and the latter sent off all the fighting men he could muster to join the "amír's" forces. The two bands, about 40,000 strong, met at 'Allóba, and then lay in waiting for Hicks at Shekán. Relations between Hicks and 'Alá el Dín, meanwhile, were becoming very strained, and the prospects of the expedition were proportionately endangered. The army moved on to 'Allóba and there halted, and Hicks sent a letter to the Mahdi. The latter replied with threats and demanding the surrender of the troops, and on November 1 left El Obeid to join his adherents at Shekán.

On November 3 Hicks advanced with a two days' water supply. The following day Abu 'Anga attacked his rear, and a number of his men were killed and waterskins destroyed. The enemy now completely encircled Hicks's army, and on November 5 at Shekán they fell upon it with fanatical fury. Wad el Negūmi led the attack supported by 'Abdulláhi the Khalífa, the latter's brother Yaḳūb, 'Ali wad Ḥelu and other "amírs"; while Abu Girga and 'Abd el Ḥalím fell upon the rear.

Hicks's troops, who were marching in a formation of three squares at the time of the attack, immediately broke in utter confusion, and began firing at random in every direction. They were massacred like sheep, with a loss to the Dervishes of not more than 500 men. Hicks himself made a most gallant stand, but was speared by Muḥammad Sheríf. Only 300 of the luckless army escaped. The Dervishes captured all the stores and arms and, with the exception of some 12,000 who remained with the Mahdi to enter El Obeid in savage triumph, dispersed to their homes. As soon as the news spread abroad the Mahdi became all powerful from Dongola to the Equator and from the Red Sea to Wadái, and it only remained for him to take possession. He sent his cousin Muḥammad Khálid (Zógal) to take over Dárfūr, where Slatin Bey had been compelled to surrender after a strenuous resistance; Karamalla was supreme in the Baḥr el Ghazál; and Egyptian troops had been annihilated in the Eastern Sudan.

Gordon in the meantime had been sent out by consent of the British Government, and had arrived in Khartoum on February 18, 1884, on his last fateful mission. He at once entered into negotiations with the Mahdi and acknowledged him as Sultan of Kordofán: but the latter was in a position to ignore his advances and merely replied, as he had done to Hicks, with a demand for surrender.

The Mahdi now turned his attention for a time to the unquiet Nūba hills. Mek Ádam of Teḳali had submitted and come to El Obeid, but Gebel Dáir was, as ever, stubborn, and Abu 'Anga was sent against it.

As the water at El Obeid was insufficient for the vast horde of Dervishes, the Mahdi in April moved *en force* to El Rahad, leaving his relative, El Sayyid Maḥmūd, at El Obeid.

The campaign against Khartoum was now begun in earnest, and Abu Girga was sent to besiege it. Wad el Negūmi followed him shortly afterwards. At the end of Ramaḍán Abu 'Anga was recalled from G. Dáir, and the Mahdi proclaimed that he was going to Khartoum. Every "amír" was made to collect his people, and the most dire penalties threatened to the laggard. The greater part of the population of Kordofán marched north-east on August 22, leaving a small garrison under El Sayyid Maḥmūd at El Obeid.

The camel-owning tribes took the northern road by Khorsi Ḥelba and Tūra el Khaḍra; the bulk of the settled population, of whom the Gawáma'a were the most numerous, marched with the Mahdi, the chief "amírs," and El Sayyid el Mekki, by El Taiára, Sherkayla, Shatt and Dueim; and the Baḳḳára, with a large proportion of their cattle, took the better-watered southern road.

This great migration was popular enough at first, but before long it became the chief cause of discontent. The natives had supposed that with the destruction of the government troops and the capture of the country their labours were ended, and they could settle down and enjoy the spoils. They soon found they were grievously mistaken, and now and time and time again they were compelled to leave their beloved herds and cultivation, and live for an indefinite period in the barren country round Omdurman, where diseases broke out among them, food was dear or even unprocurable, and the way of life strange to them,—the only alternative being sudden death or at least complete spoliation if they lagged. To the nomads, camel-owners and Baḳḳára, this was particularly irksome.

We may leave the Mahdi and his "amírs" before Omdurman and Khartoum, and only say that Omdurman fell on January 15, 1885, and Khartoum eleven days later. From the time the Mahdi left Kordofán till January, 1885, all had been quiet in the central and northern districts, for the country was practically desolate.

When Khartoum had fallen Abu 'Anga was again sent by the Mahdi with a large force to Southern Kordofán to quell the Nūba, send slaves to Omdurman, and collect any laggards he could find, and send them to swell the Mahdi's army. Shortly afterwards the Mahdi died and was succeeded by 'Abdulláhi Muḥammad of the Ta'áísha as "Khalífa."

In Southern Kordofán Abu 'Anga met with only partial success in his efforts to storm the mountain fastnesses, and the Khalífa soon after his accession sent 'Othmán Ádam, his cousin, to join him. At the same time he sent Yūnis wad el Dekaym against the Gima'a, many of whom had not left their country for Omdurman as ordered. Their head sheikh 'Asákir wad abu Kalám had already been imprisoned at Omdurman. Yūnis collected about 7000 Gima'a and transported them to Wad el 'Abbás opposite Sennár: others he sent to Omdurman.

Meanwhile El Sayyid Maḥmūd had left 'Abd el Háshimi as his "wakíl" at El Obeid and gone to Omdurman. Almost at once there broke out in El Obeid a mutiny of the black troops, who were chiefly conscripts from the Nūba hills, and 'Abd el Háshimi was killed. Fights ensued between the blacks and the Dervishes in the town and neighbourhood and the former were victorious and decamped joyfully to their hills.

El Sayyid Maḥmūd at once returned to El Obeid and disregarding the Khalífa's instructions followed up the rebels to Gebels Gulfán and Nyima. He was there defeated and lost his life (November 1885) in an attempt to storm Gulfán. Abu 'Anga was at this time in the vicinity: he had been employing himself for most of 1885 in trying to compel "mek" Kumbo of Dáir to surrender, in capturing slaves, and raiding the country-side. In the first of these ventures he was unsuccessful owing to the natural strength of the mountain. In the other two he succeeded to excess.

The Ḥumr, Messiría and Ḥawázma, who had not gone in full strength to Omdurman, broke into revolt in September and annihilated one of Abu 'Anga's raiding parties between Gedír and Talódi: however, when they ventured to attack Abu 'Anga himself they were utterly broken and lost some 10,000 men.

Abu 'Anga would now have liked to avenge El Sayyid Maḥmūd, but the Khalífa wanted him for another work:—

Muḥammad Khálid (Zógal) in Dárfūr was under the Khalífa's suspicion—as were all the close adherents of the late Mahdi—and had been summoned to Omdurman. Abu 'Anga was ordered with all speed to Bára in March 1886 to intercept Zógal and arrest him. He did so, threw him into chains, and sent him to El Obeid, where he lay in chains for a year before being sent to Omdurman. The whole of Zógal's force comprising about 1000 cavalry and a great host of Dervish footmen was enrolled in Abu 'Anga's army. Various of the western "amírs" were allowed to proceed to Omdurman and were there received with great honour by the Khalífa;—an omen not unnoticed by the rest of the tribes who found themselves gradually being subjected more and more to the domination of the western Baḳḳára of the Khalífa's own race.

Abu 'Anga with a greatly strengthened force was now allowed to proceed against the Gulfán rebels. Some of them surrendered, others had already dispersed, and the remainder were killed. During these events 'Othmán Ádam was residing at El Obeid and acting as governor of Kordofán. In this capacity and by his subsequent exploits he earned the fame of being a bold and manly youth—for he was not yet 20 years of age—honourable and considerate and a type of Arab chivalry. He had some trouble with the Ḥumr and Messiría, but the greater part of the province was cowed and quiet: up in the far north however Ṣáliḥ Bey Faḍlulla with a handful of loyal Kabábísh of his own section, the Nūráb, who had never like the bulk of the tribe broken away and joined the Mahdi, had entered upon a chequered career of alternate victory and defeat. After the battle of Ginis in 1885 he had been in correspondence with Sir F. Grenfell and had done good work in cutting off small parties of Dervishes. By June 1885 he had collected a moderate force of Kabábísh and was installed at Gebel el 'Ain. In the following month he suffered a defeat that kept him quiet at Gebel Audūn for the rest of the year.

During 1886 too he achieved nothing, but early in 1887 he renewed his activities and captured 500 camels that were on their way north to join Wad el Negūmi. In March he actually inflicted a reverse upon Wad el Negūmi and was sent the Khedive's thanks and a supply of arms and ammunition from Sir F. Grenfell: unfortunately, few of them ever reached him. In May 'Othmán Ádam by the Khalífa's orders sent a force under Faḍlulla 'Aglán, some Beni Gerár under Wad Nubáwi[1], and some Ma'ália and Meganín under Simáwi Um Beda[2] (whose father and uncle had both been killed by Ṣaliḥ's father Faḍlulla) to capture or kill Ṣáliḥ. An engagement took place at Um Badr, and on the first day Ṣáliḥ was successful. On the next day his brother Gáma'i was killed and a number of Kabábísh deserted. Ṣáliḥ then fled to the north-east but was cut off and killed.

In June 1887 Abu 'Anga returned to Omdurman *via* Tūra el Khaḍra with a force of about 20,000 men and a great store of booty. He was shortly afterwards dispatched to the Abyssinian campaign, never to return. In El Obeid he left 'Othman Ádam as before.

In the same year a revolt had broken out in Dárfūr under the Sultan Yūsef whom Zógal had left as "amír" in El Fásher,

[1] The Kabábísh later revenged themselves on the Beni Gerár by killing Muḥammad wad Nubáwi near Gebel el Ḥaráza.

[2] Nicknamed "Giraygír": (Slatin's "Grieger").

so the Khalífa dispatched 'Othmán Ádam with a large army, composed chiefly of Kordofán tribes, to take over the supreme command and re-establish his authority. No garrison was left in Kordofán, for the Gima'a country was deserted, the Kabábísh had been reduced to impotency, the Gawáma'a were all in Omdurman, the strength of the Nūba had been broken by Abu 'Anga, and the rest of the tribes either marched with 'Othmán Ádam or had been sent to Omdurman.

Although the bulk of every tribe had been collected at Omdurman, in some cases there was left a section of them in Kordofán under 'Othmán: for instance, of the Dár Ḥámid tribes a large proportion remained under their "amír" Simáwi Um Beda in Kordofán and Dárfūr with 'Othmán, while others under their respective sheikhs were at Omdurman with the Khalífa[1].

'Othmán Ádam and his army at once joined the "amír" Karamalla in Dárfūr, defeated the adherents of Sultan Yūsef, and captured Shakka. In December of the same year they also defeated Yūsef's ally Zayd near Dára.

On January 8, 1888, Zayd's troops were again dispersed and El Fásher, the capital, taken.

'Othmán Ádam was now master of Dárfūr and for a short time peace reigned there and in Kordofán. Not so on the river, for at this juncture the Khalífa, determined to have about him an invincible bodyguard whom he could trust implicitly and who would raise no objections to his gradual supplanting of the Mahdi's old adherents in favour of his own, decided to bring to Omdurman the whole of his own tribe, the Ta'áísha. Tempted by the prospect held out to them some 24,000 of these fierce Baḳḳára marched across Kordofán to Omdurman laying waste the country as they went, and others, Ta'áísha and Habbánía for the most part, followed in their train. 'Othmán Ádam ruled Dárfūr with a rod of iron, and the latter half of 1888 was marked by the revolt of the fanatic Abu Gemmayza of the Masálít tribe. He proclaimed himself the Khalífa 'Othmán and obtained immediate and whole-hearted support from a host of Fūr, Bedayát, Zagháwa, and other Dárfūr tribes.

[1] The names of the "amírs" of the Dár Ḥámid tribes and some particulars will be found in Chapter IX on Dár Ḥámid.

On October 16 he cut to pieces the army of 'Abd el Ḳádir Delíl and a week later won a second victory over Muḥammad Bishára. It was not till February 1889 that 'Othmán succeeded in completely defeating the rebels near El Fásher.

From now until his death later in the same year 'Othmán was supreme in Dárfūr and Kordofán; while on the river the Ta'áísha insolently robbed and pillaged either bank and terrorized the other tribes to an extent that even the Khalífa, when willing, could do little to check.

The immense concourse of Dervishes at Omdurman and the abandonment of all peaceful pursuits in the desolated provinces now caused a shortage of corn, and a terrible famine ensued over the whole country: its full force was of course felt at Omdurman, where the population perished of hunger and disease by the thousand.

The troops in Dárfūr also felt the force of the famine, for no cultivation had been prepared, and the tribes to the west prevented all importation of grain to El Fásher. 'Othmán Ádam finally decided in 1889 to attack these western tribes, but he met with a stout resistance and before reinforcements arrived he was carried off by typhoid fever at the early age of twenty.

His successor, Maḥmūd Aḥmad, was a very different type of man; debauched, sensual, grasping and incapable, though daring and ambitious withal. Until the end of 1892 Maḥmūd remained as master in the west: he was then summoned to Omdurman with some 5000 troops; but soon afterwards returned to Dárfūr.

All trade west of the Nile during these years was, needless to say, at a standstill and the greater part of the land lay uncultivated while its inhabitants led a freebooting existence with Maḥmūd. That "amír" was for some years entirely engaged, with varying success, in wars with the Dár Gimr, Masálít, Dár Táma and other western tribes; but at last, late in 1896, when the final British advance had begun and Dongola fallen, Maḥmūd and all the other "amírs" were summoned to the great gathering of the hosts at Omdurman.

It was Maḥmūd's march to the river with his army that finally ruined Kordofán. With some 10,000 men he commenced his terrible march of devastation: every town and village and every paltry patch of corn in his course was utterly destroyed to prevent the possibility of desertion, and every man, woman and child that could be caught and that could not obtain exemption by bribery was reft away to join the host;—and this too at the hands of the very tribes that had owned the country.

In May 1897 Maḥmūd arrived at his destination and in the following month he was sent to Metemma to overawe the wavering Ga'aliín and prevent the further advance of the British troops. On July 1st Maḥmūd attacked Metemma where the Ga'aliín had defied him and almost exterminated its defenders. There he now lay for some time, for the Khalífa would not allow him to advance further. In July Abu Ḥammad fell before the British troops and in September Berber was occupied.

In October, and again in November, a flotilla came up the river and reconnoitred Maḥmūd's position at Metemma, shelled the town and withdrew. At the end of the year the Khalífa ordered a general advance from Omdurman, but dissensions arose and the project failed. It was not till February 1898 that Maḥmūd was allowed to advance towards Berber.

On April 8th was fought the battle of the Atbara. Maḥmūd was captured, his troops were almost wiped off the face of the earth, and the last hopes of the Khalífa were dashed to the ground.

Omdurman now fell and the Khalífa fled *via* Ḥomra to Sherkayla: the Ḥumr and Rizayḳát and other Baḳḳára decamped through Dár Ḥámid. Those who were not waylaid by the Dár Ḥámid tribes and the Nūba of Katūl were seriously harassed by a remnant of Messiría and Ḥamar who had evaded all attempts to inveigle or force them to Omdurman, and only reached their own country in a state of discomfiture and destitution. In one case however the fugitives were successful: Mūsa Madibbo the Rizayḳi inflicted a heavy defeat upon the Ḥamar near Mafūra and killed their leader Muḥammad el Sheikh.

For the winter of 1898–9 the Khalífa remained at Sherkayla, a stronghold of the Habbánía, who with the exception of the Ta'áísha had been his chief favourites. Early in 1899 he went *via* Gedír to Fungor. In September the Sirdar, Sir H. Kitchener, moved up the river, and the Dervishes retired again to Sherkayla, hard pressed all the way by the Nūba who were eager for plunder and had scores to settle for the dealings of Abu 'Anga with them in the past. On November 24th Colonel Wingate, after defeating the Khalífa at Abu 'Adel and destroying his army, inflicted the *coup de grâce* at Um Dibaykerát.

The whole country was now reoccupied, except Dárfūr, and in December Colonel B. Mahon was appointed governor over the desolated wastes of Kordofán. Gradually the broken remnants of the Dervishes, and with them a few of their old foes the Danagla who still survived, came unobtrusively back, settled in their own haunts, and began again the peaceful life from which they had been so rudely swept by the blind fury of fanaticism.

Few incidents have occurred in the last ten years to disturb Kordofán: the province, thanks to a just administration and its own great natural resources in the form of gum forests, has gradually attained to a comparatively large measure of prosperity, and the population, so grievously depleted by war and famine, has steadily increased.

In none but the outlying quarters of Kordofán have any disturbances occurred, though several expeditions against the savage and unruly Nūba of the south have been rendered necessary at different times.

In October 1904 Gebel Dáir was subdued: in May 1906 the half-caste blacks of Gebel Talódi attacked the government garrison there but met with no support from the surrounding tribes and were speedily subdued; and in subsequent years various other refractory hills have brought retribution upon their own heads.

With the Arabs there has been little trouble, though the wild Ḥumr in the south-west have now and then come into conflict with the Dinka to their south or delayed the payment of their tribute: small religious outbreaks have once or twice occurred but proved abortive; and wild nomads from the far north, subject to no man, have occasionally raided the camel-owning Arabs of Northern Kordofán and Dongola. The two riverain districts of Dueim and Gedíd were in 1905 cut away from Kordofán and incorporated in the White Nile Province, and in 1907 a part of the Nūba country was made into a sub-province.

CHAPTER II

THE DÁGU, TUNGUR, KUNGÁRA, AND MUSABA'ÁT

PART I.

THE Dágu (or Tágu) in Kordofán are but a miserable remnant of a great race. They are not Arabs but blacks. The traveller Browne, about 1794, gathered from native tales in Dárfūr that "the Dageou [Dágu] race came originally from the north, having been expelled from that part of Africa...under the dominion of Tunis." Others say they came from the east, and that their first king was one Kosber[1].

So old an authority as Ibn Sa'íd (quoted by Ibn Khaldūn)[2] says:—"Adjoining them [i.e. the Nubians of Dongola] are the Zagháwa, who are Muhammadans, and one of whose tribes is called Tájúah. Next comes al-Kánem...."

Barth's opinion is to the contrary: he says they are of entirely different stock from the Zagháwa, and seem to have originated from Fazuglo. The Zagháwa of the present day disclaim all connection whatever with the Dágu.

Our chief sources of information about the Dágu are short references in the works of Browne, Barth, Nachtigal, and Slatin. From them we hear that at some very early date the Dágu conquered Dárfūr, and ruled the country from the fastnesses of G. Marra. Little more is known of them[3]. Browne relates that

[1] See Schurtz, p. 544.

[2] Ibn Sa'íd lived from 1214 (or 1208) till about 1286. See Ibn Khaldūn's *Histoire des Berbères*... (de Slane), Bk II, pp. 105 et seq. Cp. also Cooley, pp. 116 et seq.

[3] Barth says they dominated Dárfūr in the tenth century of Islam, but they may have been there for ages previously. Schurtz (p. 544) says the number of their kings is variously given as 21, 13, or only 5. Browne erroneously speaks of Sulaymán Solong ("Solyman") as a "Dageou." He also speaks of "Bégo or Dageou" as though they were the same.

they are said to have had a custom whereby at the inauguration of a king they lighted a fire which was never allowed to go out until the king's death. It is said that it was in the reign of a king called Kor that the Dágu were dispossessed in their turn by the invasions of the Tungur[1].

In the eighteenth and nineteenth centuries the Dágu were still to some extent independent in Dárfūr and had Sultans of their own, but they were by no means powerful, and were regarded as tributary vassals[2].

In Kordofán there are a number of Dágu in what are known as the Messiría Gebels near Abu Zubbad, but they are regarded as Nūba and of no account whatever. Another small colony of them lives at G. Dágu, close to the east of El Obeid. All knowledge of their former power in Dárfūr is now utterly forgotten by these latter: they connect themselves with the Fung (and the Ghodiát) and say they came from the east. They have no pedigree, but were thinking of hiring a fiki for 60 pt. to invent one[3]!

PART II.

Like the Dágu the Tungur no doubt were at one time a great tribe, though little is known of their history or whence they came. At present they are almost extinct or merged in other races.

The following is Barth's account of them[4]:—The Tungur are reported to have come originally from Dongola where they had separated from "the Egyptian tribe of the Batálesa," once settled in Bénesé. When they moved westwards in the sixteenth century they found the Dágu in power in Dárfūr, and vanquished them[5]. They then extended their empire from Dárfūr westwards,

[1] See Slatin, *Fire and Sword...*, Bk II, Chap. 2.

[2] See Browne; Ensor; El Tunísí; and Barth, Vol. III, pp. 543 et seq.

[3] The "Dongola nisba" alludes to the Dágu in passing as "Anag," i.e. aboriginals. Slatin says the only small settlements left of the Dágu in Dárfūr are near Dára and in Dár Sula in the west. (See Slatin, Chap. 2.)

[4] See Barth, Chap. 51, p. 429.

[5] This would be soon after Leo Africanus had made his tour as a young man with trading caravans through the negro kingdoms in 1513–1515 A.D. He makes no mention of the Tungur.

thus forming a strong barrier to Islam, and made Kádama their capital. They failed however to maintain their rule in the east at the same time, and Kūro the Fūr, the third predecessor of Slímán[1], defeated them there and founded a pagan kingdom. In Wadái they are said to have held their dominion for 99 years[2]; but they were overthrown in 1020 A.H. (i.e. 1611 A.D.) by 'Abd el Kerím ibn Yamé, the founder of the Muḥammadan empire of Wadái[3].

Dr Schurtz, following Nachtigal in the main and Slatin[4] in part, says the Tungur were a race of superior civilization and came to Dárfūr from the east, supplanted the Dágu in power, and gradually spread over Wadái, and that their first ruler in Dárfūr was Aḥmad el Ma'aḳūr. Their last ruler there was Sháu. The first king of the dynasty of the Kêra, who had fused themselves with and gradually supplanted the Tungur, was Delíl Baḥr, or Dáli, the law-giver, Sháu's own half-brother[5].

[1] I.e. Sulaymán Solong, or "Seling Solong" as he is sometimes called now,—the first Muḥammadan king of Dárfūr. Cp. p. 7. His date is given as 1596–1637 by Dr Helmolt.

[2] 99 is the favourite Arab number to represent any large figure.

[3] Helmolt (p. 584) however gives his date as 1635–55, and the name of the Tungur king (a heathen) at Kádama as Da'ūd:—this "chiefly after G. Nachtigal's *Sahara und Sudan*, Part III."

[4] *Fire and Sword...*, Bk I, Chap. 2.

[5] Dr Helmolt gives the following table:—(see *The World's History*, Vol. III, p. 585):

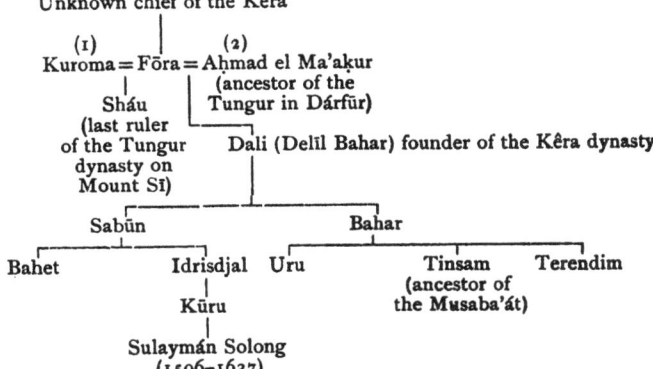

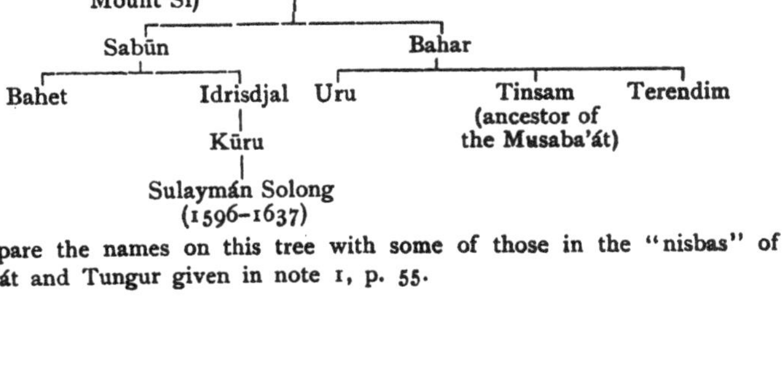
Unknown chief of the Kêra
(1)
(2)
Kuroma = Fōra = Aḥmad el Ma'aḳur
(ancestor of the
Tungur in Dárfūr)
Sháu
(last ruler
of the Tungur
dynasty on
Mount Sī)
Dali (Delīl Bahar) founder of the Kêra dynasty
Sabūn
Bahar
Bahet
Idrisdjal
Uru
Tinsam
(ancestor of
the Musaba'át)
Terendim
Kūru
Sulaymán Solong
(1596–1637)

Compare the names on this tree with some of those in the "nisbas" of the Musaba'át and Tungur given in note 1, p. 55.

Schurtz says :—" This [Dáli's] government may have fallen in the middle of the fifteenth century."

Slatin in his *Fire and Sword*...[1] relates that according to tradition the Tungur came from the north from Tunis under the leadership of 'Ali and Aḥmad, two brothers, about the fourteenth century, and scattered over Bornu and Wadái, eventually reached Dárfūr, and settled near G. Marra. These two brothers quarrelled about a woman, and 'Ali wounded Aḥmad in the tendon Achilles:—hence the latter's surname of " El Ma'aḳūr." 'Ali then moved westwards, leaving two of his slaves to look after Aḥmad : the slaves took Aḥmad to the village of King Kor, the last of the Dágu dynasty and a heathen. Kor was much impressed by Aḥmad's superior civilization, and gradually promoted him in power and married him to his favourite daughter. On Kor's death, Aḥmad succeeded him ; and this event was followed by a large influx of Tungur to Dárfūr. These Tungur mixed freely with the Dágu, but to a large extent displaced them. Aḥmad's great-grandson was Dáli, whose mother was a Kêra-Fúr. The points of resemblance and difference in these accounts are clear, but it is noteworthy that in none of them is there any reference to the Beni Hilál.

At present every Kordofán tradition of the conquest of Dárfūr by the Arabs and the fusing of the Arab and black elements into a single race gives great prominence to the Beni Hilál. For instance, the few Tungur in Kordofán, though vague and haphazard, say Aḥmad el Ma'aḳūr was a Hiláli (and "younger brother of Abu Zayd el Hiláli") and had three children, namely 'Abd el Raḥmán, Kinna (a daughter), and another : of these 'Abd el Raḥmán was ancestor of the Tungur ; Kinna and the other of the Kungára and Musaba'át. I am told too that the present Sultan 'Ali Dínár on similar lines claims descent from the Beni Hilál[2].

The Tungur explain their name by saying that when El Ma'aḳūr was left lamed in Dárfūr, he made a living as a

---

[1] Bk I, Chap. 2.

[2] It is said that the ancestors of the mek's family at Teḳali were Beni Hilál who immigrated from Dárfūr and provided rulers for the blacks.

carpenter (نجار), and the people who wished a job done by him came saying تنجر تنجر [" tungur, tungur "].

A much fuller account is given by the Musaba'át of Dárfūr[1]:

[1] I.e. by Ḥámid Gabr el Dár, himself the lineal descendant of the old Musaba'át Sultans. The following are the traditional pedigrees of the Tungur and Musaba'át respectively as given by them. The former is the less reliable of the two.

Tungur

Ghálib
|
Lūai
|
Ka'ab
|
Háshim
|
'Abd el Muṭṭalib
|
'Abbás
|
'Abdulla
|
.........?
|
Sa'ad
|
El Geráḥ
|
'Ámir
|
Isḥáḳ
|
Mámūn
|
'Agab
|
Baṭnán
|
Ḳuṣayr
|
Germūn
|
Serḥán
|
Sufián el Ma'aḳūr
|
'Abd el Raḥmán el Hiláli
|
Isḥáḳ
|
Nul
|
'Awámil
|
Seríḥ
|

Musaba'át

Khuzaym
|
Kenán
|
Nuḍr
|
'Abd el Salám el Asmar (Imám of Baṣra)
|
Hilál
|
Idrís
|
Mámūn
|
'Ísa
|
Nagíl
|
'Agab
|
Baṭnán
|
Rufá'a
|
Kás
|
Sultan Ga'afir Gurmūn
|
Sufián
|
Riziḳ
|
Aḥmad el Ma'aḳūr
|
Sultan Muḥammad Dáli
|
Sultan Ḥubáya (?)
|
Sultan Muḥammad Ṣábūn Ga'al
|
Muḥammad Tumsáḥ — Aḥmad Kūru (ancestor of Kungára)

(Muḥammad Tumsáḥ)
|
Sultan Idrís Guruwábaḥt
|
Sultan Baḥr
|
Sultan Muḥammad Gunḳul
|

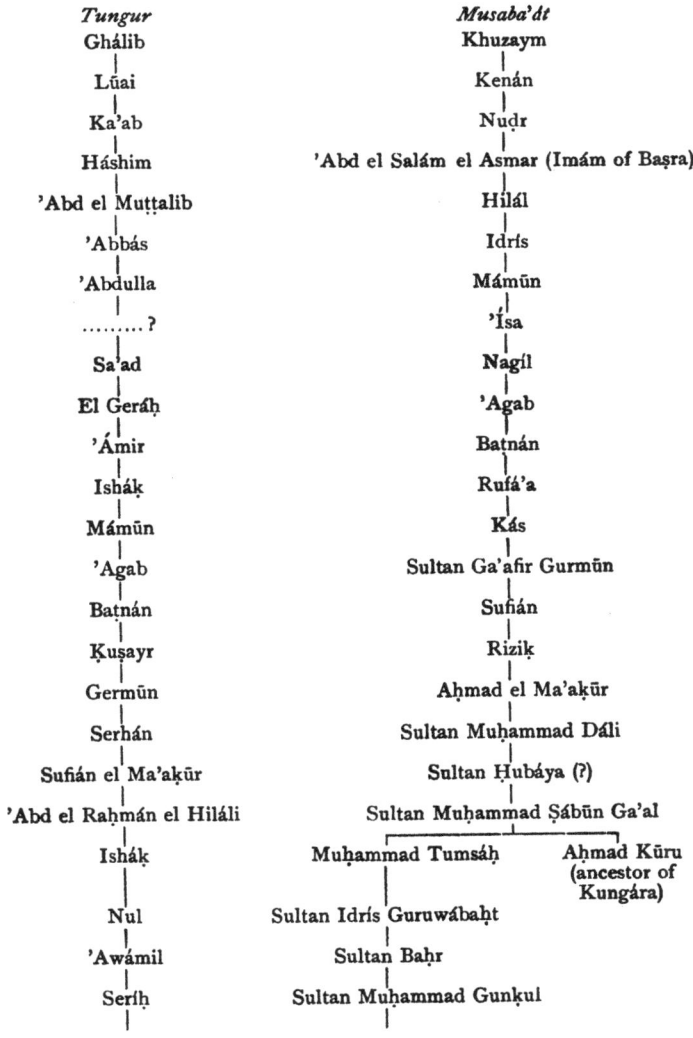

They say that Aḥmad el Ma'aḳūr was brother of Abu Zayd el Hiláli, but according to them the Tungur were in power in Dárfūr when the Beni Hilál invaded it. After Abu Zayd proceeded north leaving Aḥmad behind, the latter married the Tungur Sultan's daughter and his descendants were the Kungára (of whom the Musaba'át are a branch).

While the Tungur Sultan was absent fighting on a foray in the south Aḥmad was left as regent and took the opportunity to usurp the throne. He was succeeded by his son Muḥammad Dáli. Again the Takárír from the west have related to me that when the Arabs (including their own ancestors of course!) migrated south to Borgu they found the Tungur in power and drove most of them out: this, they say, was "before the time of the Beni Hilál and Aḥmad el Ma'aḳūr el Hiláli."

Yet again, the "Dongola nisba" says:—"the Tungur are of the Hilála, and ruled Dárfūr." It also adds that the Musaba'át are descended from the Hilála.

Now who were these Beni Hilál, and what grounds are there for supposing that they ever invaded Dárfūr, and what is their connection with the Tungur? The first question is easily answered, the second and third not so. The authentic Beni Hilál, in brief, were a great and famous Arabian tribe who invaded Africa in the eleventh century and warred for years

Tungur

Kun
|
Batt
|
Rufá'a
|
Sháu
|
'Amr
|
Ismá'íl
|
Bukr
|
Nūr
|
'Othmán
|
Náír
|
Yūsef
(present generation)

Musaba'át

Sultan 'Ísáwi
|
Sultan Háshim
|
Sultan Aḥmad el Ga'ali
|
Sultan Muḥammad Gabr el Dár
|
Sultan Ḥámid
(present generation)

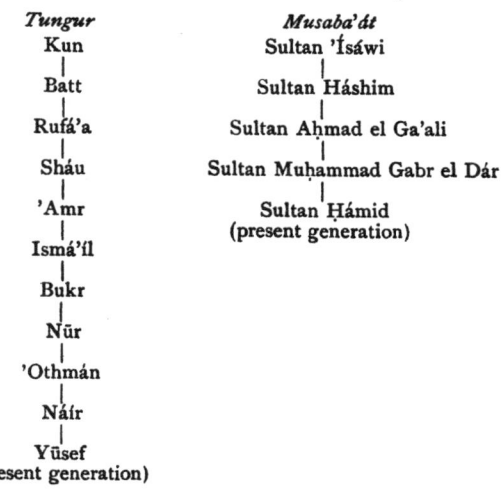

with the Berbers of the north. Their exploits under the hero "Abu Zayd" form a whole cycle of legends which were, till lately at least, rife all over Egypt[1].

I know of no historical evidence that the Beni Hilál ever came so far south-west as Dárfūr or Kordofán, but on the other hand the natives appear to believe that they did, and relate many stories of them and "Abu Zayd[2]." All these stories may be pure invention or echoes of the old Beni Hilál cycle of Arab legends, but the following is also perhaps a possible theory:—that a number of Arabs migrated westwards from the Nile and Upper Egypt about the fifteenth or sixteenth century or earlier, and that among them were a certain number of the ubiquitous Beni Hilál. That these Arabs, known at a later date as Tungur, passed through Kordofán and overcame the Dágu as described by Barth and others[3]. Having at first been probably a heterogeneous medley of many tribes they soon set about consolidating

[1] See E. W. Lane's *Manners and Customs of the Modern Egyptians*, Chap. 21, pp. 397–406, and Clément Huart's *Arabic Literature*, p. 405.

[2] These stories are given in Appendix 3. Escayrac de Lauture in his earlier work (1853) says that south of the deserts of the Tibbu, from the Senegal to the Blue Nile are the Arabs Abu Zayd ("Arab-abou-Zett"), whose ancestors according to universal tradition came from Yemen in Islamic days under Abu Zayd by way of the Red Sea, and crossed the White Nile, and spread over the Sudan. In this way were formed the Awlád Ráshid, Salamát, Rizayḳát, Beni Ḥelba [i.e. Baḳḳára tribes], and the Arab tribes of Senegal, Bornu, and Wadái; and also, in Kordofán, the Kabábísh, Beni Gerár, Habábín, Gawáma'a, Megánín, etc. However, in a later brochure published in 1855 Escayrac de Lauture recants somewhat and admits he laid too much stress upon Abu Zayd's wanderings: he has now discovered a fresh theory, viz. "que presque toutes les tribus arabes du Darfour, du Waday, du Baguermi, etc., sont d'origine koreychite," and their forbears found their way into Africa over the Red Sea. From these tribes "d'origine koreychite" he nevertheless specifically omits the Kabábísh, Ḥumr, Ḥamar, and Tungur and various others.

[3] Note that when the Sultan Sayf el Dín Ḳaláūn in 1287–9 sent an army to invade Nubia, there were a number of Beni Hilál among the troops (see Quatremère's *Mémoires* II, pp. 101 et seq.). Some of these may have settled in Nubia and pushed westwards at a later date. See also Chapter V, on the Gawáma'a. There is a large section of the Gawáma'a called Ga'afiría settled near Um Dam in Kordofán. There was a section of Beni Hilál called Ga'afiría; and there was an Arab tribe of the same name that settled between Esna and Assuwán after the Arab subjugation of the Nile banks. The connection between these various mentions of Ga'afiría may be more than coincidence and support the theory advanced as to the identification of Tungur and Beni Hilál. I know of no mention in any writer of a tribe of the name of Tungur or any name resembling it in Egypt or on the Nile or in Northern Africa at any time. Nachtigal judged the Tungur to be of Arab descent.

their power, and while intermarrying with the natives of the country, at the same time flattering their own vanity by inventing a noble lineage for themselves; and, on the strength of their including some Beni Hilál, members of a famous and noble tribe, they chose to usurp to themselves the pedigree of Beni Hilál. This device, common almost to generality, succeeded to the extent that to this day the invaders are known in Kordofán as Beni Hilál. There are a few local traditions that give colour to this theory, but not enough in any way to prove it: if it has any recommendation at all, it is that it might serve to account for and to reconcile some of the discrepancies in the different versions that are to be found of the origin of the Tungur and the Arab conquest of Dárfūr.

To specify these "local traditions":—

1. There is the desire of the Fūr and Tungur to prove that Aḥmad el Ma'aḳūr, the ancestor of the Tungur in Dárfūr, was a Hiláli, as has been mentioned. The Ḥawázma Baḳḳára, and the Takárír (as remarked) also speak of Aḥmad el Ma'aḳūr as a Hiláli.

2. Some 30 miles north of Bára, in Central Kordofán, is a small hill called Gebel el Zenáti: it is popularly supposed that the Beni Hilál under Abu Zayd here defeated a party of Zenáta Berbers under one "Khalífa[1]."

3. The people of Katūl, in Northern Kordofán, say that Abu Zayd and the Beni Hilál ruled Katūl for a time, and point out the house of the former (a rude rubble of stones) on G. Katūl.

4. The shallow part of the Nile south of Dueim has long been known as "Muḥaṭṭa abu Zayd[2]," and it is said that

[1] "El Zináti Khalífa" figures in the cycle of B. Hilál legends as the ruler of Tunis when Abu Zayd and the B. Hilál immigrated to the west. See Huart, p. 408.

[2] Cp. Petherick, *Travels in Central Africa...*, Vol. 1, p. 91:—"March 28 [1862] ...came to the ford Mochada [Muḥaṭṭa] aboo Zaet—so called from its having been crossed by Aboo Zaet, an Arab chief, who with his tribe from Arabia passed over, and formed a settlement to the West." Cp. also Escayrac de Lauture (p. 259), who says the "Arab-abou-Zett" crossed the Red Sea under "abou-Zett," "et suivi une route dont la trace semble être perdue, ils arrivèrent sur les bords du fleuve blanc; les eaux de ce fleuve étaient basses, ils le passèrent à un gué qui porte encore le nom de gué d'abou-Zett (Maadiat-abou-Zett)." It happens that the Bedayría, one of the oldest tribes in Kordofán, include a section called Awlád Hilál: I do not know if this is a reminiscence of the Beni Hilál or not.

Abu Zayd and the Beni Hilál crossed the Nile at that point. The various places at which they camped on their journey from the east can, it is said, be specified.

5. The Gawáma'a of Faragáb (east of Bára) say that the first Arabs to cross Kordofán were the Beni Hilál: they extirpated the Anag, or aboriginals, and were in their turn pushed westwards by the Fung dynasties of Sennár.

Now had so well-known a tribe as the Beni Hilál really invaded Kordofán and Dárfūr it is very probable that some record of the fact would be obtainable—but there seems to be none. Nor do travellers in Dárfūr appear to have heard of it: in addition the Tungur conquerors of Dárfūr are said to have been pagans. On the other hand local legends, as shewn, affirm that an Arab tribe did at some early date invade the countries in question from the east, before the immigration of the present tribes. Since we have some reason to believe that the Tungur were the tribe in question [see Barth], it is at least possible that many of the stories of the Beni Hilál and Tungur in Kordofán and Dárfūr relate to the same people.

A second and perhaps more satisfactory theory, that would be easily reconciled with both Barth's and Slatin's accounts of the Tungur, is that the Tungur were related not so much to the Beni Hilál as to the Berber and cognate tribes whom the Beni Hilál and other Arabs dispossessed of N. Africa in the centuries succeeding the invasion of 'Amr ibn el 'Ási. The Batálesa, from whom Barth says the Tungur split away, were, I believe, properly a section of the Zenáta Berbers[1], and it is undisputed of course that Arab and Berber not only fought but blended their races to a remarkable extent by intermarriage; and the subsequent tendency was invariably to claim an Arab rather than a Berber descent.

The Tungur then may represent a mixture of Zenáta Berbers and their Arab conquerors, the Beni Hilál (not to speak of other Arab or half-Arab people that may have been represented in the medley), and have migrated to Dárfūr either direct from the north or else by way of Dongola[2].

[1] See *Leo Africanus*, Hakluyt Soc. Edition, Vol. II, Bk III, p. 645 (note).

[2] Lejean thought the Tungur were Tibbu. See Keane, *Man*..., p. 71.

It is even possible that the Tungur were almost exclusively Zenáta and merely chose to claim connection with the Beni Hilál for their own glorification.

At present there are a few Tungur among the Musaba'át at Gikka close S.W. of El Obeid, and a few more near El Rahad[1]. These people mention the following among the subdivisions of the tribe:—

Karwa	Kirán
Karási	Būr Gelláb
Rishaydát	Nafar Baḥr
Ḥashim el Khalla	Nafar Abu Tarūs
Awlád Milayk	

PART III.

We will now turn to further mention of the Kungára and Musaba'át.

Dáli (or Delíl) has been mentioned as the first king of that composite race which is known generally as Fūr, and which sprang from the union of the Dágu and other old races and the immigrating Tungur. These Fūr very soon lost whatever little trace of the Arab they may have had in them[2]. They were divided into three large divisions, viz. Kungára, Karakrít, and Temurka: of these the first group provided Dárfūr with its Sultans[3]. With the Karakrít and Temurka we are not concerned; but from among the Kungára there rose into prominence the people called Musaba'át who later ruled Kordofán, until they gave way still later to their kinsfolk the Kungára proper. There are various stories of the rise of the Musaba'át, and these will be given.

After Dáli's death the country for some generations became a prey to civil war. Dáli had two grandsons[4] called Tonsam

[1] Some Zagháwa from Dárfūr say the Tungur were once great workers in iron, and it may be that some of the old iron-workings, whose sites are still to be seen in Northern Kordofán, are traceable to the Tungur. Iron smelting is now a forgotten art in N. Kordofán. Cp. p. 95.

[2] See Nachtigal (quoted by Ensor) and El Tunísí. The latter says that G. Marra was in his day (1803) inhabited by pure Fūr who were entire strangers to Arab language and customs.

[3] See El Tunísí.

[4] So Nachtigal. The Musaba'át say they were great-grandsons: see p. 55 (note).

and Kūru[1]; the former the ancestor of the Musaba'át, the latter the father of Sulaymán Solong and ancestor of the Kungára. The account of the separation of the Musaba'át from the Kungára, as given by the former is as follows:—The Sultan Muḥammad Ṣábūn, grandson of Dáli, had two sons, Muḥammad Tumsáḥ and Aḥmad Kūru. Great jealousy existed between these two brothers, and the ill feeling culminated when they met one day as the guests of a lady, who offered to Kūru red wine in virtue of his greater riches and power, and to Tumsáḥ gave white wine only. Tumsáḥ rose from the mat on which he was sitting, and swore he would no longer be in a position of inferiority, but would migrate eastwards to Kordofán. This intention he carried out. He collected a motley retinue from various Arab tribes and Kungára, and migrated east. The bulk of the people, who remained in Dárfūr, nicknamed Tumsáḥ's followers "Muṣabaḥát" (مصبحات) i.e. "people that go to the east" or "easterners"; and gradually "Muṣabaḥát" has become "Musaba'át."

A different account is that given by El Tunísí. He states that trustworthy people told him that Sulaymán Solong[2] had a brother Musabbá: these two shared the kingdoms of Dárfūr and Kordofán, which had originally formed one government, each engaging to respect the other's sphere of influence.

Nachtigal again (as quoted by Ensor) says that after the death of Delíl (Dáli) war broke out between Tonsam and Kūru, and that the former was at first successful, and drove Sulaymán "the son of Kūru" to the Musaba'át in East Dárfūr[3]. Sulaymán however returned and drove Tonsam from G. Marra [presumably to Kordofán], and "from this time dates the separation from the Furowi stem of the Messabát, who had lost their native language and adopted the manners and customs of the Arabs."

[1] "Tonsam" or "Tinsam" or "Muḥammad Tumsáḥ": "Kūru" (Barth's "Kūro") or "Aḥmad Kūru." See the Musaba'át "nisba" on p. 55. The forms Muḥammad Tumsáḥ and Aḥmad Kūru no doubt represent efforts to arabicize the older heathen names.

[2] El Tunísí calls him "Saloun or Soleiman"—the first ancestor of the true Sultans of Dárfūr. Cp. note 1, p. 53. Sulaymán may be an arabicized form of the name Seling or Saloun. Solong was a title applied to those who thought themselves of Arab descent (see Slatin, Chap. 2).

[3] I.e. Kordofán, no doubt.

Schurtz, finally, says[1] that after the fall of Dáli's government there was civil war, and Sulaymán Solong was the first to grasp the reins of government firmly and successfully. He had fled as a child to Wadái and "returned to war against his great-uncle Tinsam; established himself in the Marra Mountains, and from this point subdued and extended the territory of Darfur." Schurtz also says that the "Massabát" (Musaba'át) were a standing menace to Mūsa (the son and successor of Sulaymán—1637–82): "Their Sultan Djongol[2] laid claim to the throne on the strength of his relationship to the ruling dynasty." From now onwards Kordofán became more and more independent.

The Musaba'át were continually fighting against the Sultans of Dárfūr, who no doubt expected them to pay tribute. Their power probably fluctuated considerably, but did not reach its height for about a century after Sulaymán Solong's death.

Not only were the Musaba'át worried by Dárfūr, but in addition the rulers of Sennár on the east and south were periodically claiming Kordofán to belong to them. About the middle of the seventeenth century[3], after the death of Sulaymán Solong, Sennár had been particularly active in Kordofán, and the southern part of the country was made tributary to it, and about 1748 it made war upon the Musaba'át and conquered them. The rule of Sennár lasted nominally for over a decade, but in fact the Ghodiát gained the upper hand in the south about 1755. It appears that these Ghodiát were themselves more than half Fung by race originally, but had settled in Kordofán permanently and, so to speak, taken upon themselves the mantle of the Fung, when the latter fell into the throes of civil war in Sennár and abandoned Kordofán to a great extent.

The Ghodiát intermarried largely with the Musaba'át[4], now powerful in Northern and Central Kordofán. After the Ghodiát had been supreme, with intervals of struggle, for some thirteen years the chief power passed to the Musaba'át (i.e. about 1768).

[1] p. 544.
[2] Probably the Muḥammad Gunḳul of note 1, p. 55.
[3] For the following see Chapter 1, p. 8.
[4] So say the Ghodiát themselves.

It was about now that the famous Sultan Háshim el Musaba'áwi lived. He was the grandson of Muḥammad Gunḳul and direct descendant of Tonsam (Tumsáḥ). He was engaged in wars with the Fung or Ghodiát for some 17 years and was driven to Katūl[1], remained there for some years, and then returned to power when the power of the Fung was weaker. Finally he became involved in a war with Tiráb the Kungári Sultan of Dárfūr[2]. In 1785 he was defeated and expelled from Kordofán.

Tiráb however died the same year in Kordofán, and his successor, 'Abd el Raḥmán, retired to Dárfūr leaving a Kungári governor there.

About 1791 Háshim returned, ejected the governor, and for a further period of years continued a desultory war against the Kungára.

He was finally routed by the Kungári general and fled to Shendi, where he was eventually put to death.

Sennár being now rent by civil war, the Kungára remained as unquestioned rulers of Kordofán until the country was conquered by the Turks in 1821[3].

The capital El Obeid was then divided into quarters, the

[1] See Chapter VI, on the northern hills.

[2] For details see Chapter I.

[3] The tradition repeated by his descendants is that at Gebel Ḥinayk, whither Háshim had fled, he was well received by the Ḥasanía, but that the rest of the people raised the cry of a Fūráwi invasion and attacked him. He escaped over the Nile into the Gimi'áb country, and when they refused to let him pass he swore he would kill at least 100 of them. Accordingly he killed all he could, but on adding up the corpses found there were only 99; so he killed a dog to complete the number. Háshim then proceeded to west of the Sháíkía country to the "Gezíra Naṣri," where he married his daughter the princess Sheríffa to Malik Sabíl of the Sháíkía. After staying here for some years he proceeded to Metemma and married another of his daughters—the princess Ga'alía—to Malik Zubayr the Sháíḳi. Háshim now formed alliances with the Sháíḳía, Ga'alíín, and Danagla and at last decided to reconquer Kordofán. Accordingly he wrote to "the Effendína" in Egypt and requested their aid. Muḥammad 'Ali promptly sent the Defterdár who took El Obeid. Háshim, the story runs, unfortunately died at Metemma and so was never reappointed Sultan of Kordofán. As a matter of fact Burckhardt relates that Háshim after being ejected from Kordofán took refuge in the hills west of the Nile and south of Berber until, hard pressed by the Sháíḳía, he fled to Shendi, where after a time he was put to death by the "mek" Nimr on a charge of conspiracy. The tomb of El feki Abu Ḳurūn in El Obeid is said to mark the site of Háshim's house before his deposal.

remnant of the Kungára in one, the Musaba'át under Háshim's son Ádam Deballu in another.

In 1836 we hear from Holroyd that both the Kungára and the Musaba'át, "the tribe properly belonging to Kordofan," were very numerous; and two or three years afterwards Pallme could say the same: in the time of the latter the Kungára quarter was under Sultan Tayma, who was the official castrator and the proud possessor of two immense drums given him by Muḥammad 'Ali[1].

During the Turkish *régime* however many of them returned to Dárfūr, and in 1876 there were at El Obeid and the vicinity only a few hundred Kungára and Musaba'át left[2].

Their numbers have not increased since, and with the exception of a few small villages (e.g. at Gikka) and some scatterlings in El Obeid the tribe is almost confined to Dárfūr.

[1] See Pallme, p. 275.

[2] See Prout.

CHAPTER III

THE GHODIÁT, BIRGED, TOMÁM AND TUMBÁB

THE Ghodiát, Tomám, Birged and Tumbáb live, roughly speaking, between the southern Nūba hills and the latitude of El Obeid, and this topographical position, with Blacks to the south and mixed Arabs to the north, fairly accurately represents their ethnological place among the tribes of Kordofán.

In the Ghodiát the Arab blood is far from predominating. That they were in Kordofán before the arrival of the majority of the Arabs is certain[1], and though they no doubt contain some Arab and much Nūba and even Fūr blood, they, more than any other people in Kordofán, are closely allied to the Fung of Sennár, who from the sixteenth century until the latter half of the eighteenth were predominant in Southern Kordofán. They themselves say that the word Ghodiát is connected with the Arabic غُدَّة—a part or portion—since those Fung who first came to Kordofán split away from the rest of their people and settled there. They probably first entered Kordofán early in the sixteenth century, i.e. soon after 'Amára Dunkas had united the Fung and commenced his conquests, and they relate that they settled round Gebel Kurbág and Melbis close to the present site of El Obeid, the Nūba then being predominant and ruling the country from Gebel Kordofán and the surrounding hills. The Nūba "mek" they say was Kuldu, and from him Gebel Kordofán, and later the whole district, took its name, Kordofán being a corruption of "Kuldu fár (فار)," i.e. "Kuldu boiled with wrath[2]." The Ghodiát say they lived for a time in amity

[1] Every tradition admits it. See also Pallme, Petherick, and Prout.

[2] See Appendix I.

M.

with the Nūba and then enticed them from their hills to a "dilūka," cut off their retreat, and murdered them: after this the Ghodiát were supreme for a time[1]. They lived under the rule of a Sovereign called a "mangil": this term is said in Fung to denote an absolute ruler with the most complete autocratic powers, but a "mangil," it is added, was not honoured posthumously but relegated to oblivion as soon as dead: his successor became "mangil" while he himself after death was only spoken of as "sheikh."

As has been noted before, most of Southern Kordofán, including a large part of the "gebel" district, was for some time previous to the nineteenth century under Fung (or "Ghodiát") dominion, and at the present day several of the important "meks" in the eastern "gebels," such as Zeibak of Rashád have much Fung blood in them. During the sixteenth, seventeenth and eighteenth centuries Southern Kordofán was repeatedly invaded by the Fungs as a source of recruits and slaves, and no doubt the numbers of the Ghodiát and other tribes who had also immigrated—e.g. the Bedayría and Gawáma'a—were materially increased thereby.

In the northern parts of Kordofán, especially in the "gebels" of Kága, about this time and previous to the wars between Háshim the Musaba'áwi and the Fung, the Birged are said to have been supreme. At Kága and Katūl traces of their old dwellings on the hills are still to be seen. They were in part ousted by the Bedayría under the "Sultan Balūl" who was in his turn conquered by Háshim.

These Birged ("Birkit") are mentioned by Barth[2] as among the "negro" tribes near the frontier of Wadái with Dárfūr "in which country they are more numerous."

Dárfūr traditions[3] say that the ancestor of the Birged was a slave of one of the leaders of the Tungur invasion of Dárfūr.

In the eighteenth century the Fung were involved in wars with the Musaba'át of Dárfūr who were migrating eastwards in

[1] The remains of Ghodiát buildings on Gebel Kordofán point to their having made that hill one of their strongholds.

[2] See Barth, Vol. III, pp. 543 et seq.

[3] See Slatin, *Fire and Sword*, Chap. 2.

considerable numbers. Dilatory hostilities, as we have seen, continued for some years, but the Ghodiát, though so closely related to the Fung and though they no doubt favoured the Fung cause rather than the Musaba'át, are said to have intermarried with the latter very freely after the Fung had been finally expelled.

Closely connected with the Ghodiát are the Tomám: it is said that after one of the Fung attacks upon the country under the leadership of one Abu el Dís, and for a few years previous to the Musaba'át era, the Ghodiát and Tomám alternately paid the whole tribute required from the country to Sennár. This tribute was not paid in money, as there was none, but either in cattle or in iron "Ḥashásh Um Henána[1]."

[1] These "ḥashásh" are alluded to by Burckhardt (*Nubia*...) and by Pallme. The word means literally a hoe. Burckhardt says there was an iron currency in Kordofán (though "dura" and cows were the usual medium of exchange), and that these iron coins were made into spear-heads and other implements. Pallme writes that in addition to the Turkish currency "there is a small coin of iron, named 'hashias' in circulation, struck during the reign of the Sultan of Darfûr, which has continued in currency since that period: it is a small piece of iron, from two to three inches in length, and of the form of an obtuse bibrachial anchor. 150 of these pieces were formerly considered equivalent to one dollar; they subsequently fell in value to 250, and their present currency is 800 to the dollar, or one 'para' each" (see Pallme, p. 303). At first sight it would appear that Burckhardt and Pallme did not know the word "ḥashásh" for a hoe and that iron hoe-heads were merely used as a medium of exchange. I doubt however whether this is the only explanation, because some people still remember these "ḥashásh" being used exclusively as coins and some I have found at Gebel el Ḥaráza (see Chapter VI) were too small to have been any use for hoeing. It therefore appears that hoe-heads, which were chiefly of Dárfūr manufacture or made by blacks from Dárfūr who had settled in the northern hills where there is iron, were at first used as currency, and when the need for further differentiation of articles of currency arose, the people made smaller hoe-heads for use as coins exclusively and not of any use for cultivation, or in other words, in making their first coins they adhered to the shape of the familiar hoe-head currency instead of making round or square coins. Worthy of remark in this connection is the following quotation from Schweinfurth (Chapter IV)—"the 'loggoh Kullutty' is the circulating medium of the Bongo, the only equivalent which Central Africa possesses for money of any description. According to Major Denham, who visited the Central Sudan in 1824, there were at that time some iron pieces which were circulated as currency in Loggon on the Lower Shary, answering to what is now in use among the Bongo....The 'loggoh Kullutty' is formed in flat circles, varying in diameter from 10 to 12 inches. On one edge there is a short handle; on the opposite there is attached a projecting limb, something in the form of an anchor. In this shape the metal is stored up in the treasures of the rich, and up to the present time it serves as well as the lance-heads and spades for cash and for exchange...." The market appellation of these "loggoh Kullutty" was "melut." I believe the Jūr also

The Ghodiát by common consent are related by intermarriage to the Tomám, Birged, Bedayría and Tumbáb, but of the group the Ghodiát approximate most nearly to the Fung. The Bedayría have mixed most with the Arabs, and the Birged are the most closely related to the black races.

The days of Ghodiát predominance in central Kordofán were from about 1755 to 1768, but they had considerable power south of El Obeid until about the beginning of the nineteenth century and they claim that much of the land now occupied by those of the Gawáma'a who are in the south was granted to that tribe by the Ghodiát chief 'Ayád wad Um Bilayna[1]. This chief is said to have been a contemporary of the Abu el Dís mentioned above and to have resisted his invasion: he was overcome by him, but when Abu el Dís returned to Sennár, owing to internal dissensions there, he left 'Ayád as his regent over the tribes lying south of El Obeid[2]. The Turkish conquest in 1821 found 'Omar wad el Ḍow chief over these tribes, but complaints against him led to his deposition and the separation of the various tribes into distinct "'omadías" each under its own sheikh[3].

The Tomám are divided into fifteen sections, viz.:—

Fadirgin	Nafar el Fíl	Nafar 'Ali
Angūra	" " Nuṣr	" abu Ḥammad
Nar Fa'	" Sherba	" Bugl
Shōma	" Ḥasabulla	(2 others)
Nafar 'Ugla	" 'Omar	

to the present day use the "melut" both as a hoe and as a medium of exchange, in the latter case the "melut" being hoe-shaped but too small to be of use as a hoe. (For the phrase "Um Henána" see Chapter VI, on the Northern Hills.)

[1] Impressions from the great seal of 'Ayád are said to exist still in possession of some of the Gawáma'a to whom he granted land. His position seems to have corresponded to that of the "náẓir" or supreme arbitrator over the Ghodiát described by Pallme (p. 12).

[2] Abu el Dís is said to have been sent by "Muḥammad wad Ragab of Sennár, father of 'Adlán." The allusion is probably to Ragab wad Muḥammad, King 'Adlán's vizier, who, we saw, attacked Southern Kordofán between 1780 and 1788 (see Chapter I).

[3] The Ghodiát, Bedayría, Tomám, etc. have nominally remained separate, but the Ḥawázma Baḳḳára are at present very largely composed of a compound of them. Previous to the reoccupation of Kordofán in 1900 'Abd el Summad of the Bedayría was reckoned "náẓir" of so many of these tribes as had not joined the Ḥawázma or kept entirely separate.

The Ghodiát are divided into about twenty sections of which the following are some:—

Nafar el Marád	Nafar abu Khaḍra	El Ku'ūk
„ 'Omar	Salamát[1]	El Megabda[2]
„ Safei'	El Bŭrŭḥ	Serárír
„ Sa'īd	Idayrát	

The commonly accepted "nisba" for the Bedayría, Ghodiát, Tomám, etc. traces their descent to Kerdam the reputed ancestor of the Ga'aliín. Some say that Ḥámid and 'Ali the forefathers of the Ghodiát and Tomám respectively were sons of Samayra son of Serrár son of Kerdam; others say Tomám was the son of Kerdam, and Samayra the ancestor of the Ghodiát, Baṭáḥín, Ḳunăn and Ḳuṣáṣ, the Bedayría being descended from Samra the brother of Samayra, and the Gawáma'a and Gima'a from Mismár his other brother. The only allowable inference is that these various tribes are dimly related to one another[3].

In the "Mahdía" Eliás wad el Kunūna was "amír" of the Ghodiát and at the Khalífa's bidding took the bulk of the tribe to Omdurman.

At present the Ghodiát reside in practically the identical places which they occupied on their first advent to the country, namely round El Rahad and El Birka.

1 An offshoot of the Baḳḳára tribe of the same name in Borgu, Dárfūr, etc.

2 A section originally Bedayría by race.

3 See Chapter IV, on the Bedayría.

CHAPTER IV

THE BEDAYRÍA

THE Bedayría are a sedentary and debased tribe that have long inhabited Kordofán.

As the Ghodiát represent the old immigrant Fung stock, so the Bedayría are degraded offshoots of the once powerful Ga'aliín and Sháíkía of the riverain districts.

They claim that they and the Sháíkía are of common stock with the Ga'aliín, and the commonly accepted pedigree which shews the connection is as follows[1]:

[1] The extent to which the Ga'aliín and the Sháíkía themselves are descended from Arab and non-Arab elements respectively has been learnedly discussed by several travellers whose works are easily available, e.g. Hartmann held that they belonged in reality to a Nūba stock. The "Dongola nisba" notes "The Bedayría in the Sudan include some 'Abbásía [i.e. Beni 'Abbás] and some Anag" [i.e. Autochthons]. This probably is vaguely correct. It will be noticed that one Bedayr or Muḥammad Bedayr is given as the ancestor of the tribe. Some say this person is buried in Dongola. One wild story, from Dár Ḥámid, relates that Bedayr came as a Ḳádi with Abu Zayd el Hiláli when he drove the Zenáta Berbers southwards from North Africa.

Sir C. Wilson says the name of the tribe is derived from "Bedayr" the diminutive of "Bedr" (the full moon). The full moon, however, being to the Arab symbolical of beauty, the diminutive "Bedayr" is an obvious name to give to a child, and the argument is not advanced.

An earlier chapter in the "Dongola nisba" than that in which the note quoted above occurs, and written by a different hand, says: "The true Bedayría are descended from Badr son of 'Amr son of Gūía son of Ardhán son of Tha'aliba son of 'Adi son of Fezára, and they are a subsection of Fezára." (For Fezára see Chapters XV and XVIII.)

In the genealogical tree given, many names of persons and of tribes are omitted. It was made in Dongola for El Sayyid el Mekki the great religious sheikh who was among the Mahdi's foremost adherents. El Sayyid el Mekki was rightly not a Bedayri nor a Dahmashi, but of partly Takrūri origin; but since the Dahmashía of Dongola claim to be Ashráf (see Chapter VI), and there were some of them among the Bedayría living with El Sayyid el Mekki, he thought this a suitable connection to establish.

- 'Abbás (uncle of the Prophet)
  - 'Abdulla
    - Faḍl
      - Sa'ad
        - Ibráhím el Ga'ali[1] (ancestor of Ga'aliín, etc.)
          - Muḥammad el Yemeni
            - Aḥmad el Ḥegázi
              - Masrag
                - Harḳán
                  - Budá'a
                    - Abu el Dís
                      - Kerdam
                        - Delḥ
                        - Tomám (ancestor of the Tomám)
                        - Serrár[2]
                          - Samra
                            - Bedayr (ancestor of Bedayría)
                              - Dahmash
                                - ⋮ (18 generations to the present)
                            - 'Abd el Raḥmán abu Ishayḥ (ancestor of Shuwayḥát)
                            - Ṭerayf (ancestor of Ṭerayfía[3])
                            - Aḥmad abu Rísh (ancestor of Riásh)
                          - Samayra (ancestor of Ghodiát, Baṭáḥín, Ḳunan, and Ḳuṣáṣ)
                          - Mismár
                            - Sa'ad el Feríd (ancestor of Gima'a, Gawáma'a[4], Aḥamda, Gawábra, etc.)
                            - Rubáṭ
                            - Nebíḥ
                            - Ṣubuḥ abu Merkha
                              - Ḥammad el Akrat
                              - Ḥámid
                              - Ḥamaydán (ancestor of Sháfḳía, and Gamu'ía, etc.)

[1] Of Ibráhím el Ga'ali the author of the genealogical tree says, "As regards Ga'al [i.e. Ga'aliín] they belong to Beni 'Abbás and should not be called a tribe but rather one of the branches of Beni Háshim; and they are only known as Ga'al because their ancestor [i.e. founder] was known as Ga'al from the fact that he was a generous man, and in the time of the famine the feeble folk flocked to him, and he said to them جعلناكم [ga'alnákum, i.e. 'we have made you']; so they were surnamed Ga'al. Now the forefather of all the tribes of Ga'al was Kerdam son of Abu el Dís, and whoever is not among his descendants is not a Ga'ali: his home was in the land of Ḥegáz."

For notes 2—4 see page 72.

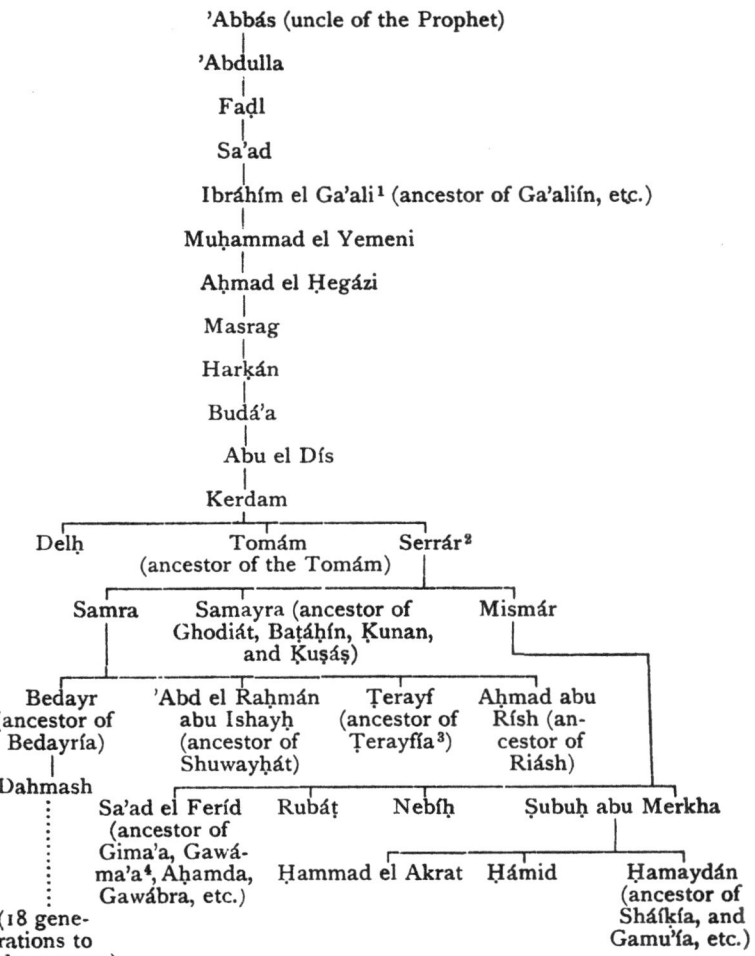

It is only certain that in the eighteenth century, on the river at least they were subject to the Sháíḳía; and so late as the outbreak of the "Mahdía," Sir C. Wilson spoke of them as "a Nuba people with an admixture of Arab blood, who still speak Rotana (i.e. Nuba) among themselves[5]." Many Ga'aliín and Sháíḳía (including the Bedayría, whatever their status may have been) and other tribes entered Kordofán either with or on the heels of the first Fung immigrants during the sixteenth and seventeenth centuries, settled round the present site of El Obeid, and largely intermarried with the Nūba. As a result we have the present Bedayría, Gawáma'a, and other smaller tribes.

Thus, too, among the Bedayría we find remains of other distinct tribes, as will be shewn.

The present Bedayría in Kordofán consist of two main sections, viz. the Dahmashía and the Awlád Na'amía:

The Dahmashía include

Awlád Ḥilayb	Shuwayḥát	Awlád Shiháda
Zenára	Riásh	„ Hilál
Ayadga	Kadūma	Ḥusaynát
Awlád Muḥammad	Awlád 'Ali	

The Awlád Na'amía consist of

Awlád Ḥamdulla	Awlád Melki	Awlád Mūsa
„ Mate'ye	Aynánía	

Of these sections more must be said:—

Many of the Dahmashía are said to be descended from Dahmash, great-grandson of Ghulámulla ibn 'Áid, who was the ancestor of a large part of the Rikábía, including the Dóálíb of N. Kordofán—i.e. they have Dongoláwi blood in them[6]: this is probable, as we know from Burckhardt and others that Bedayría were settled many years ago, as now, in Dongola.

[2] Serrár is said to have personally brought his family to Kordofán and to have given his name to Bír Serrár, a well and mountain a day's journey north of Bára, now belonging to the Gawáma'a (Awlád Murg).

[3] For the Ṭerayfía see Chapter V, on the Gawáma'a.

[4] See Chapter V. It will be noticed that the Gawáma'a themselves mostly say they are descended not from Sa'ad el Feríd but from Ṣubuḥ abu Merkha.

[5] See Burckhardt's *Nubia* and Sir C. Wilson's paper.

[6] See Chapter VI, on the Northern Hills. The genealogical tree given in the text inserts Dahmash as a son of Bedayr the ancestor of the Bedayría. This is probably an invention of the writer of the tree, for reasons explained above.

The Zenára are relics of a very old tribe, probably of Berber origin. Zenára are mentioned by Mas'ūdi[1] (d. 956 A.D.), and by Maḳrízi[2] (c. 1400 A.D.) and Ibn Khaldūn[3] (d. 1406) as nomad Berbers in Egypt and Morocco: the last named calls them a branch of the great Luáta section of Berbers. A parallel case is that of the Gellába Howára, who are an offshoot in Kordofán of the Howáwír, who again are of Berber origin[4]. The Zenára were also one of the minor tribes that with five others helped to form that section of the Ḥawázma now known as the Ḥalafa. The Shuwayḥát generally allege that they are closely related, but not subject to the Bedayría, and the "nisba" that is given above rather bears out their contention. The little "gebel" of Shuwayḥ in the "aḳaba" between Ḥashába and the river is named after them.

The Ḥusaynát are only Bedayría by marriage. On their father's side they belong to the Ḥusaynát on the Nile. One of them—'Abd el Raḥman—married the daughter of Mūsa el Ṣafí'a, the Bedayri chief whose grave is at El Obeid: their son was named Bedowi. The "naẓir" 'Abd el Summad[5], a famous Dervish, belonged to this section.

The Mate'ye are mentioned by Burckhardt among the principal tribes of Kordofán, but no one else, I think, mentions them.

The Bedayría are not by any means confined to Kordofán. There are still numbers of them on the river as far north as Assuwán. It will be seen from the "nisba" too that so closely are the Bedayría in Kordofán connected with the Gawáma'a and other tribes that it is hard to draw any distinct line between them. It is even said that the whole of the Ṭerayfía section of Gawáma'a and the Asirra section of the Ḥawázma, as well as many smaller families, should properly be classed as Bedayría.

Now Sir C. Wilson also says: "possibly at an early period some numbers of the Bedayriah tribe, now N.N.W. of Kordofan, may have established an overlordship, which was afterwards

[1] See Barbier de Meynard's translation, Vol. III, pp. 240 et seq.
[2] See Quatremère.
[3] See Ibn Khaldūn (de Slane), Bk I, pp. 9–11 and 235.
[4] See Chapter XIX, on the Howáwír and Gellába Howára.
[5] See Chapter III, on the Ghodiát, etc.

wrested from them by the Shagía." The Dárfūr boundary being now further west than it was at that time (c. 1885), "N.N.W. of Kordofan," i.e. E.N.Eastern Dárfūr, corresponds to the present N.N.Western Kordofán, and until some time not later than the middle of the eighteenth century the range of hills, in N.N.Western Kordofán, including Kága el Surrūg, Kága, and Katūl, was inhabited by blacks, partly Nūba and partly Birged. Then began a movement northwards by the Bedayría, who had previously been settled west and W.S.W. of the present site of El Obeid and had probably been under the Ghodiát overlordship. Their leader in this northern expedition was one Balūl. He conquered Kága el Surrūg and made his headquarters at G. Bishára Taib, that being a convenient base for raiding purposes. This "gebel" was in his time and for some time later known as Káb Balūl (Balūl's Fort). Now there were at this time no wells near G. Bishára Taib[1], and the people of Kága el Surrūg then, as now, drank from the stores of rain-water preserved among the rocks. The art of digging "ṣawáni'," i.e. wells cut through the rock stratum, had not been achieved, but was introduced by the Musaba'át shortly afterwards, as will be seen. Balūl therefore it is said made an arrangement whereby, in the dry season, daily relays of 100 camels brought water sufficient for his people from Abu Ḥaráz, nearly 150 miles to the E.S.E., there being no nearer wells then open.

While "Sultan" Balūl was thus ensconced with his Bedayría round "Káb Balūl," Háshim the chief of the Musaba'át moving eastwards from Dárfūr asked for permission to settle in these parts. Balūl presented Háshim with Kága el Surrūg, and the two chiefs swore an oath of brotherhood. This oath was abused by Háshim, who having gathered together large stores of arms at Kága el Surrūg, sent word to Balūl asking for assistance against an imaginary foe advancing from the west. Balūl at once set forth with his host, and pending the imaginary enemies' arrival, Háshim asked him to stay in his house and allow the Bedayría likewise to be each the guest of a Musaba'áwi.

In the night, the Musaba'át having taken the precaution of

[1] There were many fine wells at Fóga in the nineteenth century, close to the west of the "gebel." These are now dry: see Chapter XII, on the Ḥamar.

making all the Bedayría drunk, murdered them. Háshim now took possession of G. Bishára Taib and fortified it[1], and dug wells at Fóga.

He then moved further east and dug wells at Kága Sóderi, and other places[2]. After this it is said he pushed south and conquered El Obeid[3].

A number of the half-castes at Kága are descendants of refugees from Balūl's adherents and other Bedayría who settled thereabouts; e.g. the Serár Fár section of Kagáwis count themselves true Bedayría, and their claims are not denied by the Bedayría in the south. When, in the "Turkía," the district of Abu Ḥaráz, which was chiefly peopled by Bedayría, failed to pay its full tribute, the arrears were heaped upon Kága and Katūl: this is evidence of the fact that many Bedayría had migrated to the latter hills.

In 1882, on the first outbreak of the Dervish revolt, the Bedayría took the opportunity of attacking Abu Ḥaráz, whence they had been ousted by aliens from the river, and mercilessly butchered the inhabitants, including the government "'uhud," and the "náẓir" 'Abd el Raḥím el feki Bedowi the Ḥusayni.

The "amír" of the Bedayría in the times that followed was the 'Abd el Summad mentioned above: he and most of his tribe migrated to Omdurman, while the remainder stayed in Kordofán under 'Ebayd wad el Hág, Wad el Sangak, and El Nuṣri el 'Álim. The last mentioned was a notorious freebooter. These three were subsequently sent under the "amír" Abu 'Anga to the Abyssinian campaign, and only 'Ebayd returned alive. The present 'omda of the Shuwayḥát, Sulaymán el Záki, also acted as an "amír" over his people.

At present the Bedayría have a large number of villages close to the south, west, and north of El Obeid, and are much mixed with the Ḥawázma Baḳḳára.

[1] The stone fortifications, in the form of long stone walls are still to be seen, though ruined. Some attribute them to Balūl instead of to Háshim.

[2] See Chapter VI, on the Northern Hills. All the wells mentioned are "ṣawáni'" and the Arabs and Nūba reopen a number of them yearly. See p. 98.

[3] For his career in Kordofán see Chapter I.

CHAPTER V

THE GAWÁMA'A AND GIMA'A

PART I.

THE Gawáma'a are a much debased race and are flattered to an even greater extent than usual in the Sudan by the denomination of Arab. It is true they have Arab blood in their veins, but they have mixed so largely with other races that they are uniformly dark in colour and in their features present many characteristics of the blacks. This is due to the fact that their ancestors on the Arab side were among the first Arab or semi-Arab immigrants to Kordofán from the east, and being in a minority became largely absorbed by the indigenous races of their adopted country. In origin they claim to be 'Abbásía and allied racially to the Ga'aliín; but the latter tribe are themselves of very mixed descent and the pretentious pedigrees of both Gawáma'a and Ga'aliín have little to recommend their claim to accuracy[1].

It is admitted by the bulk of the more educated of the tribe that the name Gawáma'a (sing. Gáma'i) is derived from "gama'a" (جَمَعَ), "to collect," and signifies a collection of members of various tribes, just as on similar lines it is alleged that the origin of the word Ga'aliín (sing. Ga'ali) is from "ga'al" (جَعَل), "to make," and that one Ibráhím of the stock of the 'Abbásía in a time of famine expended his wealth in charity and so collected around him a medley of adherents who were "made men" through his generosity[2].

The Arab forbears of the Gawáma'a almost certainly immigrated into Kordofán in the sixteenth and seventeenth centuries

[1] See Chapter IV, on the Bedayría, and notes thereon. [2] Ditto.

"Gawáma'a 'náẓir' and sheikhs at El Obeid, 1906."

at the time when the power of the mixed race known vaguely as Fung was predominant in Sennár. This was a time of expansion and conquest westwards, and just as the Ghodiát of the present represent the Fung element in the invaders, so the Gawáma'a and other tribes, such as the Gilaydát, Gima'a, and Bedayría, may be said to represent the Arab allies of those Fung, with the addition at frequent intervals of batches of immigrants (probably Ga'aliín and other nondescript communities) from the river.

Fung and Arab, or Ghodiát and Gawáma'a etc. as they became, settled together in the neighbourhood of El Rahad and El Birka close to the north of the main ranges of the mountains of Southern Kordofán in a country suitable for cultivation and for rearing the cattle which they either brought with them or, as tradition relates, acquired from Felláta pilgrims coming from the west. They intermarried with one another and with the Nūba and gradually displaced the latter from what land they held north of Gebel Dáir and forced them southwards to the mountainous country which they still inhabit.

The Ghodiát seem to have been at first the controllers of the confederacy and the Gawáma'a subject to them, but before very long the Gawáma'a certainly became powerful enough to rank as their equals if not superiors, and the two races (together with other subsidiary and allied tribes) ruled as far north as the country held then, as now, by the Dár Ḥámid tribes; and when later immigrants arrived and wished to settle in Central Kordofán it was from either Dár Ḥámid or from the Ghodiát and Gawáma'a that they had to request a grant of land[1]. It cannot be said at what time the various people that went to form the Gawáma'a adopted that name, so to speak, officially, for themselves. Some of them at some time pushed westward and settled in the country of which the remainder was later overrun by the Ḥamar, and their descendants—called Gawáma'a (Ga'afiría section)—are still there, round El Sa'áta, in considerable numbers[2].

[1] See Chapter III, on the Ghodiát, etc. The Gellába Howára living N.E. of El Obeid obtained their land from the Gawáma'a: likewise various villages round Um Arba'a to the east of Gebel Um Shidera. There are many other cases also.

[2] These Gawáma'a mostly migrated to Dárfūr to the vicinity of Um Shanga in the eighteenth century and returned in the "Mahdía."

A few others established themselves east of Gebel Um Shidera on the S.W. borders of Dár Ḥámid near the present Um Arba'a; but the great bulk of the tribe, if tribe they can be called when one recollects the many diversified elements they contain, leaving the Ghodiát, Bedayría, and others a little to the west, and the Gima'a to the east, took up their abode in the comparatively rich lands that surround the present sites of Um Dam, El Taiára, and El Rahad, and have never been displaced. They and the Ḥamar now form the bulk of the sedentary inhabitants of the province.

The following are the divisions and subdivisions of the Gawáma'a at present: it will be seen that the tribe is divided into two main sections, the Ḥomrán and the Gima'ía, each of which is further subdivided:—

I.

Ḥomrán.

A. Awlád Gáma'i
1. Ashḳar
2. El 'Awag
3. El Bakhít
4. El Mulkáb
5. El Kerámsha
6. El Masíkh
7. El Dushásh
8. Awlád Sherayḳi
9. Awlád abu Sulaymán
10. Awlád Zídán
11. El Khátráb
12. El Ma'ináb
13. Awlád Nilayt
14. El Naḳármín
15. El Turḳab
16. El Masháikha
17. El Ferárín
18. El Shibráwín
19. El Belūḥ
20. El Kárko
21. El Hagu
22. El Tuk

B. El Ṭerayfía[1]
1. El Ḥarránía
(*a*) Awlád Sháíḳ
(*b*) El Ketátíl
(*c*) El Selímía
(*d*) El Timu
(*e*) Awlád Zayd
(*f*) Ferágía
(*g*) Awlád abu Mukhayra
2. El Zerázír (or Awlád Zarzūr)[2]
3. Awlád 'Imayr

[1] Some subsections of the Ṭerayfía trace descent to "'Ali Walad Ṭerayf" and some to his brother "Ma'alla Walad Ṭerayf." E.g. subsections number 8 and 12 claim descent from the former and numbers 5 and 17 and 18 from the latter. The greater number however say that 'Ali and Ma'alla's elder brother Sháíḳ were their ancestors.

[2] Awlád 'Aḳoi (Dár Ḥámid) by origin.

4. Awlád 'Abd el Aḥad
5. Um Gurṭa
6. El Na'amánín
7. Awlád Ábid
8. Awlád 'Ali
9. El Sheláliín
10. El 'Udūsa
    (*a*) Um Bárak Ḥerayḥír
    (*b*) Um Bárak Ḥammadowín
11. El Ḥiádba
    (*a*) Awlád Alwán
    (*b*) El Shadwánía
    (*c*) Um Tilayg
    (*d*) Um Tilayg Haydóbi
12. Awlád Mága
13. Awlád Siḥayl
14. El Hilayga
15. El 'Arada
16. El Kidil
17. Um Dóda
18. Um Wadíd
19. Awlád Sirayr
20. El 'Alayḳa
21. El Merázíḳ (or Awlád Marzūḳ)
22. El Osmániín
23. El Raḥáḥíl
24. Awlád Ḳásim
25. Awlád Miḳayl
26. Awlád 'Arūḳ
27. Awlád 'Afūna
28. Awlád Sherafía
29. Awlád Sherak
30. Awlád Tūtū
31. Awlád Gamí'
32. El Nimráía
33. Awlád Nūr
34. Um Ádam
35. Awlád abu Gin

C. El Serayḥát[1]

1. El Deḳashma
2. Awlád Mūsa
3. Awlád abu Gindía
4. Awlád abu Sunnud
5. Awlád abu Ghulmán
6. El Ḳura'án[2]
7. Awlád Gimay'a
8. Awlád Gamá'a
9. El Balūliín
10. El Habaysía
11. Awlád Ferag
12. Awlád Baḳḳári
13. Awlád el Ḥurr
14. Awlád el Sheikh
15. El Ḳelálím
16. Awlád Ligám
17. El Hamdánía
18. Awlád 'Awáli
19. El Shibláwiín
20. El Busáṭ
21. Awlád Um Ḳót
22. El Meráḳíb
23. El Kadobsi
24. El Ba'áshím
25. Nas el Aḥmar
26. El Gedádín
27. El Gabrinín
28. El Ramaḍáni
29. Awlád Habíla
30. Um Ismá'íl
31. Awlád 'Agūb
32. Awlád Rufá'a
33. Um Kilmán
34. Awlád abu Sin
35. Awlád Surūr
36. Awlád 'Alwán
37. Awlád abu Howa
38. El 'Aríḍ
39. Um Tidim

[1] *For note see page* 80.
[2] Blacks from N.W. of Dárfūr. See Appendix 4.

D. Awlád Murg[2]
1. Um Kelayb
2. Um Barakát
3. Um Dhiáb
4. Um Fáris
5. El Nugára

E. El Gamría[2]
1. Awlád Malik
2. El Biday
3. Awlád abu Timám
4. Ebay'a
5. Awlád Ḥasan
6. El 'Adlán
7. 'Abd el Gibár
8. Abu Ḥalíma
9. Awlád Sūḳ
10. Awlád Mūmin
11. El Ḳeráfít

[1] The following is given as the genealogy of the Serayḥát:—

Ṣubuḥ abu Merkha (said to have been buried at Gebel Arashkól on the White Nile)
| Ḥamaydán
| Muḥammad Ghánim
| Idrís
| Serayḥ (ancestor of the Serayḥát)
| Maḥmūd
| Muḥammad 'Áid
- Sellama
  - Manṣūr (ancestor of subsections 7 and 8)
    | Mūsa (ancestor of 2 and 5)
    | Bukr
    | Duḳshum (ancestor of 1)
    | Issayd (the first to settle inland from the river, i.e. near Um Dam. His fathers lived on the river)
    | Raḥma
    | Muḥammad
    | Manófal (died 1830)
    | Muḥammad (died 1865)
    | Raḥma (see Chapter I)
      - 'Ali
      - 'Abd el Ḳádir
  - Bugha (ancestor of subsections 3, 9, 10, 13, 14, 15, 18, 19, 23)
  - 'Abd el Raḥím (ancestor of subsections 4, 22, 24)
  - Raḥma (ancestor of subsection 25)
- Náṣir
- Nuṣr (ancestor of subsections 11, 12, 16, 17)

For Ṣubuḥ abu Merkha, see Chapter IV, on the Bedayría.

[2] The Awlád Murg and the Gamría were originally a subtribe of the Serayḥát or of the Awlád Gáma'i: opinions differ on the point. The Awlád Murg live north of Bára on the confines of Dár Ḥámid. The Gamría are S.E. of the Awlád Murg round Baharía.

F. El Ghanaymía[1]

1. Awlád Ṣáliḥ
2. Awlád 'Ísa
3. Um Shiḳil
4. El Merámra
5. El Magidía
6. Awlád Ḥammayd

G. El Faḍaylía

1. El Ba'ígáb
2. Awlád Tūri
3. El Faṭaháwi
4. El 'Abídía
5. El Maḥmūdi
6. El Tunuwi
7. El Bedlawi
8. El Tibráwi
9. El Beráḳít
10. El Magaylisáb
11. El Halímab
12. El Azayriḳáb
13. El 'Agáki, or, 'Agágík

II.

El Gima'ía.

A. El Ga'afiría[2]

1. Awlád 'Adi
2. Awlád Um Raḥmán
3. El Nália
4. El Boṭránía
5. El Ḥawámda
6. Awlád Ḳadím
7. Awlád Zuayd
8. El Geráráb[3]
9. El Masíkháb[4]
10. El Shikayt
11. El Shíbaylía
12. El Nuḳária
13. El Ridaysáb
14. Zurḳáb
15. Awlád Rahūda
16. Awlád Merri'i
17. Awlád Ḥáshim
18. El Danaksi

[1] The Ghanaymía were originally a subtribe of the Faḍaylía. It is said that they afterwards joined the Ṭerayfía. They are now independent of either.

[2] The Ga'afiría section claim descent from the same Ṣubuḥ abu Merkha whom the Serayḥát claim as ancestor; thus:—

Ga'afir (great-grandson of Ṣubuḥ abu Merkha)

Bishr					Muftáḥ			
Ḥasabulla (ancestor of sub-sections 4, 8, 12)	Ḥámid (ancestor of 5)	Náli (ancestor of 3)	'Adi (ancestor of 1)	Zuayd (ancestor of 7)	Haysinna (ancestor of 19, 20)	Rahūda (ancestor of 15)	Háshim (ancestor of 17)	Merri'i (ancestor of 16)

For the Ga'afiría settlement on the Nile banks from Esna to Assuwán see Burckhardt's *Nubia*. The original Arab Ga'afiría appear to have been a subdivision of the Beni Hilál (see Lane, *Manners and Customs*..., Chap. XXI, pp. 397–406). Cf. note 3, p. 57.

[3] The name "Geráráb" is derived from جرّ "to drag":—the ancestor of the section found a dead body and dragged it along the ground and buried it. He was accused of being the murderer (and probably was). The origin of the name of the tribe Beni Gerár is similar.

[4] The Masíkháb are called after their ancestor who was مسيخ "a bully." He was the only boy among a family of girls and used to bully his sisters.

19. El Haysinna
20. El Ḳoṭáḳíṭ[1]
21. El Muftáḥ
22. El Bishr
23. Awlád Ḥáshi
24. El Ḥantūshi

B. El Gemámla

1. Awlád Maṭlūt
   (*a*) Awlád Raḥayma
   (*b*) Awlád Mūsa
   (*c*) Awlád Ádam
   (*d*) Awlád Muḥammad
   (*e*) Awlád Timsáḥ
   (*f*) El Ṣubayḥ
   (*g*) Awlád 'Abd el Ḥamíd
2. Awlád el Feki el Aṭrash
   (*a*) Awlád 'Abdulla
   (*b*) El Gaḳímía
   (*c*) El Helaywín
   (*d*) Awlád el Mulūk
   (*e*) Awlád Shákhi
   (*f*) El Adhūna
3. El 'Abi
4. Awlád abu Sharr
5. El Sha'álibi
6. Awlád Bishára
7. Awlád el Hósh
8. Awlád Habūd
9. Awlád Gafūn
10. Awlád Rikáb
11. Awlád 'Afán
12. El Dishaynáb

C. Awlád Bíka

1. El Tuaymát
   (*a*) El Fatáḥa
   (*b*) Abu Áshay'
   (*c*) 'Aṭítulla
   (*d*) Awlád Manna
2. El Ghubaysháb
3. El 'Anáḳar
4. Awlád Shayn
5. El 'Atūr
6. Um Kūdi
7. Awlád Masakh
8. Um Shenab

The above sections of the Gawáma'a with very few exceptions probably all belong originally to the same group—namely that comprising the Bedayría, the Ga'aliín and the Gima'a, but they are very loosely connected[2]. Some say the Ṭerayfía section of the Ḥomrán are properly Bedayría—some that they belong to the Gamu'ía section of the Ga'aliín.

The Serayḥát too are said once to have been Serayḥáb—i.e. Ga'aliín from round Metemma. According to their account their ancestor Serayḥ lived fourteen generations ago and was a

[1] So called because they used to squabble like wild cats.

[2] The exceptional degeneracy of the Gawáma'a is mentioned by Prout (1876): he says "with them no girl has the right to marry until she shall have presented to her brother a child as his bondman. The father of this child she chooses when and where she will..." (p. 34). This custom is now in disuse, but until a few years ago it was said in excuse of a girl who bore a child before marriage "عانت خالا" (lit. "she has helped her uncle"), and her brother used to take the child.

descendant of that same Ibráhím who was "father" of the Ga'aliín; and the division of the Serayḥát into subsections appears to have been several generations subsequent to him. It is also said that the Serayḥát all lived on the Nile banks until six generations ago. As regards the Ga'afiría, it is not improbable that they are an offshoot of the powerful tribe of that name who at the conquest of the Nile banks by the Arabs settled between Esna and Assuwán.

The Tuaymát section of the Awlád Bíka were originally Kawáhla but it is unknown at what date they joined the Gawáma'a.

So soon as the Mahdi proclaimed himself the Gawáma'a joined him and when, after the fall of El Obeid, he marched to Omdurman, it was the Gawáma'a who formed the main bulk of his force. They remained at Omdurman during the time of the Khalífa and lost very heavily in numbers. Their best known amírs were Idrís Tindía (of the Gimá'ía), 'Omar Ḥowár el Sheikh (of the Ḥomrán), Raḥma Muḥammad Manófal (of the Serayḥát), Shámi Habbáni (of the Awlád Bíka), and Ḥámid el Dakhayri (of the Ghanaymía).

They have now returned to their old villages and resumed their occupations as cultivators and collectors of gum. In El Taiára district and at Um Arba'a the gum forests provide them with an unfailing source of wealth.

PART II.

The Gima'a, as appears from the genealogical trees of kindred tribes, are closely connected with the Gawáma'a: the composition of the two tribes is probably similar, though the Gima'a in appearance and way of life shew more traces of Arab blood. They may have immigrated rather later than the Gawáma'a.

The Gima'a country lies to the east of that of the Gawáma'a and near to the White Nile, and is rich in gum forests. They have been larger breeders of cattle than the Gawáma'a, and their dances and their methods of hairdressing have been imitated from the true cattle-owning Baḳḳára.

In 1876 Prout assessed their numbers at about 25,000. At the close of the "Turkía" they were under 'Asákir abu Kalám, and when 'Abdulláhi, the future Khalífa, and his father moved from the west on their way to perform the pilgrimage to Mecca, shortly before the rise of the Mahdi, they were guests of the great Gima'a sheikh for some months. 'Abdulláhi's father died during the visit and was buried by 'Asákir at Sherkayla[1].

During the Dervish days again 'Asákir was their chief "amír" for they had joined the Mahdi very early in his career; but when in 1885 they were summoned by the Khalífa to Omdurman they shewed some reluctance to comply with his orders. Accordingly 'Asákir was imprisoned and the amír Yūnis wad el Dekaym was sent to compel them to obedience.

Most of their wealth, which was in kind, was confiscated and some 7000 men of the tribe with their families were forcibly transported over the river to Wad el 'Abbás opposite Sennár, leaving Dár el Gima'a deserted, and compelled to submit to the Dervish *régime*[2].

'Asákir abu Kalám was released and reinstated, but some six or seven years later he dared to disparage the Khalífa's methods and was again thrown into chains, and exiled to Regáf[3].

Since the reoccupation the remnants of the Gima'a have gradually filtered back to the west bank of the White Nile. The tribe is mainly sedentary, and with the partition of the White Nile province from Kordofán early in 1905 came under the jurisdiction of the former.

A small number of them, chiefly of the 'Abaysáb section, are camel-owning nomads under Kordofán province, and spend the year with the Dár Ḥámid section of the Kawáhla.

The following sections are represented in Kordofán at present:—

'Abaysáb (Kabūiáb and Sayláb)	El Rowashda
Mesadáb	Huluf
Dár 'Awáb	Tína

[1] See Slatin, Bk 1, Chap. IV.
[2] See Slatin, Bk 2, Chap. XI.
[3] See Slatin, Bk 3, Chap. XVI.

CHAPTER VI

THE NORTHERN HILLS

AT the present day the only hills in Northern Kordofán that are inhabited are El Ḥaráza, Abu Ḥadíd, Um Durrag, Kága[1], Katūl, Abu Tubr, and El 'Aṭshán. The last named is inhabited by Zagháwa, and is mentioned in treating of that tribe. Gebel Mídób to the west lies in Dárfūr, and is dealt with separately. In earlier days many other hills were inhabited, and ruins of old stone villages are to be seen as far north as Gebel Nisab el Ḥuṣán, and as far west as Um Badr[2]; but the gradual diminution of the water supply and the retaliatory measures taken by the Arabs who suffered from the depredations of these thievish communities of hillmen, has caused the abandonment of all but the hills specified[3].

In addition it is indicative of the increased security that whereas until a few decades ago the villages were invariably perched upon the sides of the hills or hidden in the recesses, where they could be easily defended, they are now with very few exceptions built in the open near the foot of the hills and

[1] Kága includes Kága el Surrūg on the Dárfūr frontier, Kága el Ḥufra, Kága Sóderi, and, according to many, a number of the uninhabited hills lying between the places mentioned.

[2] There are said to be ruins on a large scale at Abu Sofián north-west of the Wádi el Melik, but I have not seen them.

[3] The Kabábísh of the third to the seventh generations from the present are said to have exterminated many of the Nūba from the most northernly hills.

As there are no signs of wells having been dug,—and in fact the hard nature of the ground would make it difficult—it is probable that the people of such hills as were once populated, but are so no longer, subsisted on rain-water stored in "gulut" up in the rocks.

among the cultivation. It is uncertain whether at any time a single homogeneous race inhabited all these hills. As has been mentioned earlier the Anag are almost unanimously said to have formed the aboriginal population in these parts. In the lack of more data it is hard to say whether there is good foundation for the tradition, or whether the name Anag has been borrowed from elsewhere and become by habit synonymous with aboriginal: or again it is possible either that the whole of these hills were inhabited by Anag, or that Anag lived at El Ḥaráza, though not in the more westernly hills. It is commonly said that the ancestors of the present inhabitants, as distinct from the aboriginal Anag, who are extinct, were Nūba of the same race as those in Southern Kordofán: the term used by the Arabs to designate the people of all these hills is always Nūba: and finally, in many cases, and in fact more usually than not, a native of El Ḥaráza, Kága, etc., if asked his race will at once say Nūba: (the terms Kagáwi and Katūláwi are also used). The stalwart physique of the southern Nūba is noticeably absent in the north however.

It is probable either that in the old days before the Nūba had been driven from the Nile, these hills and their environs were conquered by the Nūba from another race, or that they were seized by such other race from the Nūba, and in any case remained in the hands of the conquerors, who no doubt became fused with the conquered, until the Arabs arrived.

The Arabs then exterminated all whom they could, and drove the remainder to take refuge in the larger hills, where they have remained until the present, though again and again modified in race by alien infusions of blood[1].

To this day there exist, though in less numbers each year, "Kugura" (sing. "Kugūr"), i.e. rainmakers, in all the inhabited northern hills, with similar functions to those of S. Kordofán.

[1] Prout (1876) speaks of "colonies of negroes" from the south at Kága, Katūl and Gebel Kón (in El Taiára district to the east of El Obeid). Rüppell (1829) says the inhabitants of El Ḥaráza, Um Durrag, and Abu Ḥadíd are "a mixture of Nūba with Ethiopian or Dongoláwi." Note that Lepsius while holding that the Nubians of the Nile valley were originally homogeneous with the Nūba of Southern Kordofán, suggests that the name Nūba has incorrectly been extended to the population of all those regions which provided negro slaves for the inhabitants of Egypt.

At Kága, Katūl, and El Ḥaráza they have very little power and only appeal to the most ignorant of the people. At Um Durrag and Abu Ḥadíd, however, until a few years ago the "mek" who was also the rainmaker of the "gebel" was deposed at once if the harvest was a failure.

It will be as well to give here an account of what little is known of the Anag.

Before 1286 A.D. we have no historical mention of them, though they may have existed for centuries.

In the year mentioned[1] ambassadors bearing a complaint against the King of Dongola came to Egypt from "Ador King of the Gates and of the princes of Barah (Bazah), Al Takeh, Kedrou, Denfou, Ary, Befal, Anedj and Kersah[2]," and the following is an incident in the course of the second expedition sent by the Sultan Ḳaláūn against Shemamun King of Dongola in 1269 A.D.:—"les Musulmans trouvèrent au bord de cette eau des hommes qui leur apprirent que le roi Any étoit parti depuis deux jours, pour se retirer du côté d'Anedj. Ils le poursuivirent encore quelques temps et retournèrent sur leurs pas, chargés de butin, après avoir partout sur leur route massacré les Nubiens.... Le roi Any échappa...La disette d'eau empêcha les Musulmans de l'atteindre. D'ailleurs le pays qu'ils auroient eu à traverser étoit un désert affreux, qui servoit de retraite aux éléphans, aux singes, aux sangliers, aux giraffes, et aux autruches...." So rife are mentions of the Anag in the hills of Northern Kordofán that it is possible that it was there that the folk known as Anag dwelt and that Any sought refuge.

At the same time, on the Nile and east of it Egyptian temples and Coptic monasteries, tumuli and wells, are all freely ascribed to the Anag,—a fact which merely proves that Anag existed in the neighbourhood and that nothing is known about them. Mr Crowfoot found families at the Shablūka cataract and in the Mesallamía district on the Blue Nile who were

[1] See Quatremère, Vol. II, pp. 100, 101.

[2] Some of these places are identified by Mr Crowfoot in a paper read before the British Association in August 1907 as follows:—The Gates = Kabūshía near the ancient Meroe; Barah (Bazah) lies to the east of Kabūshía; Al Takeh = Kassala; Kedrou = Kadaru, a little north of Khartoum; Kersah lay between the White and Blue Niles.

supposed to be Anag[1]. He also mentions that learned Arabs have told him that the Anag were akin to the Nūba of Kordofán.

Popularly connected in some very vague way with the Anag is a race called Abu Ḳona'án. I am told that in Sennár and at Gebel Ginis are a people who call themselves Anag and Abu Ḳona'án indifferently: thus too there are to be found at El Ḥaráza, Um Durrag, and Abu Ḥadíd, but not at Kága nor Katūl, numerous rings of stone (granite felsite and sandstone) and hollow conical ornaments (or implements—no one could tell me the use of them[2]) which have been found on the sites of old settlements and hung up as curios or amulets in the huts, and which are called "Ḥaggar Abu Ḳona'án" or Anag relics indiscriminately. Similar stones have, I believe, been found in the "Island of Meroe."

As these stones are not found at Kága and Katūl they are presumably the work of a people who settled at El Ḥaráza, Abu Ḥadíd, and Um Durrag, but not at Kága and Katūl; and this settlement would be prior to the coming of the Buḳḳera, Shabergo, Maṭara, etc. (of whom more later), because these tribes are distributed more or less evenly over all the five hills mentioned, and, in addition, know nothing of the origin of the stones. The shape and workmanship of these stones, as will be seen from the accompanying illustrations, suggest northern and Egyptian rather than southern and negroid influences. In fact it is not unlikely that they represent somewhat crude attempts to imitate, so far as circumstances permitted, the bead ornaments that were in fashion among the more civilised people of the north until mediaeval times.

The tale at El Ḥaráza is that the Abu Ḳona'án lived "in the days of the prophets," i.e. before Islam, and were a rich and very godless folk who amassed wealth galore, but a great famine

[1] See Mr Crowfoot's paper referred to above. In January, 1909, Mr Currie hearing tales of the Anag ruling the Gezíra till about 1400 A.D. from their capital at Góz Bakhít, visited that place and found a large non-Moslem burying ground and many remains which are said to be Anag.

[2] Dr Seligmann suggested to me that they might be ceremonial mace heads. One native at El Ḥaráza averred that they were used by the aborigines in order to avert lightning.

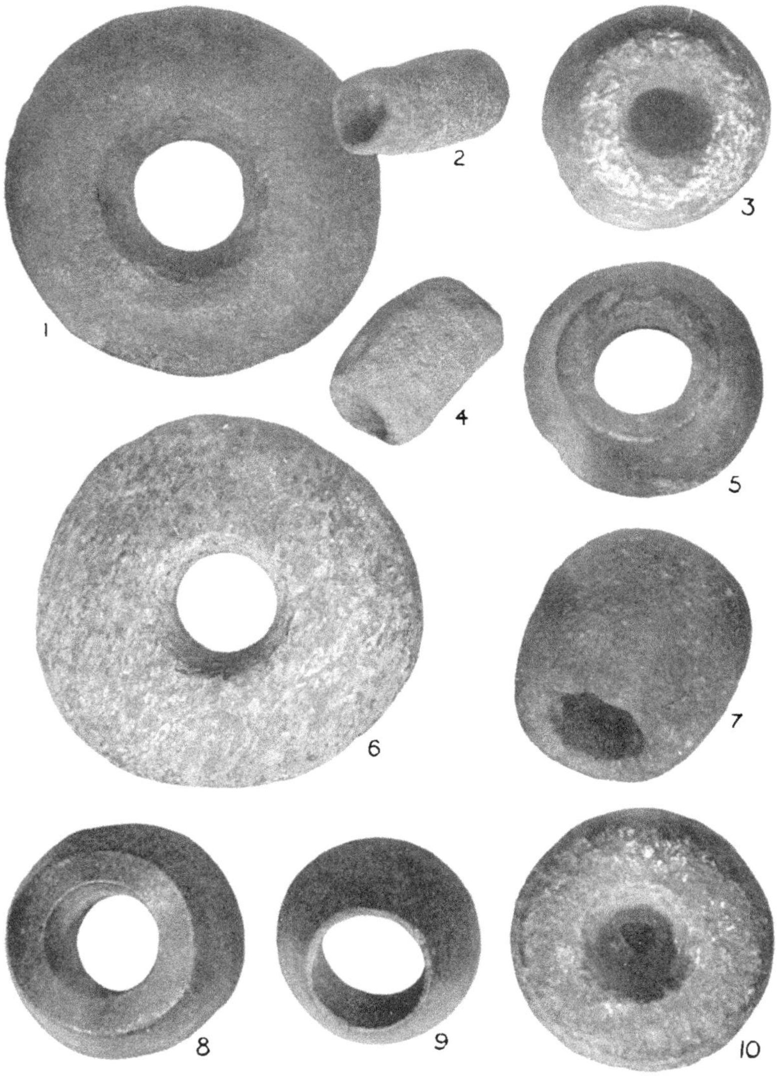

"Stones from Gebels el Ḥaráza and Um Durrag."

1. Felsite. 2 and 4. Soft yellow sandstone. 3. Hard sandstone ($1\frac{1}{2}$ inches deep, unfinished). 5 and 8. Granite. 6. Dioritic gneiss (a stone of like shape in red sandstone, $2\frac{1}{2}$ inches in diameter, also found). 7 and 10. Fine grain sandstone. 9. Hard red sandstone.

(*Illustrations two-thirds of actual size.*)

came upon them, and the price of corn was its weight in gold: finally they perished of hunger and became extinct.

Now there are at El Ḥaráza examples of rock pictures belonging to different periods[1]: firstly, there is at Gebel Shaláshi highly finished work full of life and movement, representing men, horses, giraffes, and hyaenas portrayed in white or red pigment: these resemble the "Ḥaggarát Maktūbát" of N. Africa. Secondly, there is at Gebel Karshūl a rough and inartistic form of conventional pictography almost exactly corresponding to the common "Libyo-Berber" rock pictures found over the greater part of North Africa and the Tuwarek country[2]. Thirdly, at Gebel Kurkayla there are pictures of animals very roughly chipped on lumps of granite. It is true that rock pictures of a similar nature are to be found almost all over Africa, but it is more probable that those at El Ḥaráza should be connected with a non-Nūba race than with the Nūba.

Both the Blemmyes (the Beja of the middle ages, and probably the Bisháriín etc. of the present) and the ancestors or precursors of the Berber and Tibbu tribes of the deserts roamed the country round El Ḥaráza in past days. The former, for instance, in 200 A.D. were settled on both sides of the Nile, and were assisted in their raids on Egypt by the Nobatae (Nūba); and, as regards the latter there can be no doubt that the Bayūda desert and Northern Kordofán, which together roughly formed what used to be known as the desert of Gorham or Goran, was once the home of roaming tribes probably connected on the one hand with the ancient Garamantes and on the other with the Tibbu and Eastern Tuwarek,—part descendants of the old nomad Berbers[3].

It is just possible that there may even be a connection between the names Gorham (Goran) and Abu Ḳona'án. It is to these old nomads of the desert that I am inclined to attribute the rock pictures at El Ḥaráza which are said to be the work of Anag or Abu Ḳona'án.

[1] See article "Rock paintings in Kordofán," in Vol. XXXIX (1909) of the *Journal of the Royal Anthrop. Institute.*

[2] Similar examples are found at Gebel el Afárít close to Gebel um Shirsh in Dár Ḥamar. The Shaláshi pictures were seen by Lejean (see Hartmann, *Nigritier*, p. 41).

[3] See Appendix 4.

Whether Anag and Abu Ḳona'án are identical or not; whether either includes the other or not, cannot be said. The Anag are said to have come from the north and settled for the most part in the now unpopulated country north of the Wádi el Melik: they are also said to have been a fair-haired race, and it is curious that occasionally there is born at El Ḥaráza, but nowhere else that I know of in Kordofán, a yellow-haired, pink-skinned child from parents living in the mountain. Such children are said by the people themselves to be a survival from a fair race of ancestors who came from the north and are spoken of as Ḥūr (حور)—a name used for the Turks not only here but in Asia. These children are generally delicate. In 1909 I saw a boy about seven years old and another of about 18 months, of this description: both had curly flaxen hair and grey-brown eyes. The fathers in each case were said to be Dóálíb and the mothers "Nūba." Whether this is merely a case of albinism or whether it is a xanthochrous type similar to that still found recurring among the Berbers in Morocco and the Atlas, I am quite unable to say[1]. Evidence that the Anag are connected with the old Berber tribes is to be found in the theories put forward in *Les Origines Berbères*, by L. Rinn. This author is a strong advocate of linguistic and ethnological affinities between both the Turanian stock and also the Soudras and Aryans of India on the one hand and the Berbers on the other,—and indeed the resemblance between Vedic and Berber tribal names is remarkable,—and holds that the latter immigrated to Africa from the east. The great god or goddess of the Turanians was An (Enn, Enni, Anou) and Anou likewise was an ancient Numidian deity whose name survives in several mountains in Barbary. Rinn discovers this root An in a most surprising number of words—in fact in almost every proper name containing an "n," e.g. Luna, *μην*, Diana, Dionysus, Britain, Caledonian, Erin, Aquitain, Hun,

[1] "The Egyptian monuments of the fourteenth and fifteenth centuries depict the Libyans (Berbers) as pink complexioned, blue eyed, and fair or red haired"......—"the occasional fair haired and light or grey eyed families found among these people" [Berbers]. These two quotations are both from Dr Brown writing in the Hakluyt Society's edition of *Leo Africanus* (Bk I, pp. 202 et seq. note), and seem pertinent to the question under discussion.

Hellene, Aino, Annam, Menes (the Pharaoh) and Canaan[1]! Had Rinn come across the word Anag he would have been delighted and undoubtedly added it to his list, and seized upon the fact that in the quotation given above from Quatremère with the Anag is mentioned Kedrou, and that Kadrou was one of the daughters of Brahma and the personification of the people of the mountain.

Another and perhaps more reliable fact in support of the connection between the primitive inhabitants of El Ḥaráza and the old desert nomads is that there are still traces of matrilinear descent being reckoned at El Ḥaráza, Abu Ḥadíd and Um Durrag, as it was among the tribes of the eastern deserts. For instance, the present "mek" of Abu Ḥadíd was chosen because his mother was the daughter of a previous "mek": she married a Zagháwi, but the son counts his connection with the Zagháwa as less than that with the "Nūba" of Abu Ḥadíd. Again, the mother of the "mek" of Um Durrag was daughter of a "mek," but his father was of no rank at all.

Another ancient people is also spoken of at El Ḥaráza, viz. the Ḥenána. This may possibly, though it is by no means likely, be a corruption of Hilála and relate to the fabled invasion of Abu Zayd and the Beni Hilál[2]. Nothing whatever is known of the Ḥenána beyond the fact that they were later than the Anag and Abu Ḳona'án; and the name is only used in one connection, viz. to call the old iron implements (chiefly hoes and arrowheads) which are occasionally found "Hadíd Um Ḥenána[3]."

To turn now to later times; what little can be learnt is as follows:—

[1] According to Rinn, Galla, Baḳḳára, Teḳali, Dárfūr, Wadái and Bornu are all Berber names! Certainly the -ag of Anag may well represent the Tuwarek prefix meaning "son of."

[2] See Chapter II.

[3] A superstition prevails now that if the iron implements are allowed to lie on the land they will attract the strong north wind and the corn will be overwhelmed by the sand: in consequence they have diligently been collected and with due formalities stowed away by "fekis" in deep fissures in the rocks: it was here I unearthed a lot of them, covered by stones.

I notice that in El Mas'ūdi's *Meadows of Gold*... (translated Sprenger, 1841), the Zang (a name commonly used for all the black races) are said to be under the astronomical influence of Saturn and "to him lead and iron are sacred," or, probably a better translation, "he is the enemy of iron." May this have any connection with the above-mentioned traditions of El Ḥaráza? Cp. Chapter III, note on p. 67.

In the early parts of the eighteenth century a small colony of Rikábía from Mundera near the Blue Nile migrated to El Ḥarâza and expelled most of the previous inhabitants; and intermarried with the remainder. In the latter part of the same century the kinsmen of these immigrants on the river fought with the Sháíḳía and were badly defeated. Accordingly 70 or more of them joined their relations at El Ḥaráza. Thus the present inhabitants, so far as any hard and fast line can be drawn, are a mixture of Rikábía and the earlier races[1].

The Rikábía claim to be Ḥusaynía Ashráf, and therefore claim relationship with the Nuráb Kabábísh, the Shabwáb Danagla at El Ṭawíl and El Bashíri, and the Arab element in G. Abu Tubr.

They are now called "Dóálíb" after Muḥammad Dólíb one of their ancestors, and are a particularly acute and capable clan; and it will be remembered that Dóálíb were largely employed by the Turks after the conquest as tax-collectors.

The following is a family tree shewing their alleged descent[2]:—

'Ali = Fáṭima (daughter of the Prophet)
|
Il Imám Ḥusayn
|
Zayd el 'Abdín
|
Muḥammad Tughi
|
Muḥammad Naghi
|
Muḥammad Turki
|
Ḥasan el 'Askari
|
'Ali el Riḍḍa
|
Muḥammad el Bághir
|
Ga'afir el Ṣádiḳ
|
Mūsa el Káthim
|

[1] It was probably of these immigrants that Browne wrote "the inhabitants of El Ḥaráza are idolaters of mixed complexion, but most of them of a reddish hue." He twice mentions that the people of El Ḥaráza (and Abu Ḥadíd) were neither Arabs nor Muḥammadans. (See Browne, App. 6, p. 566.)

[2] As my informant considered himself the 35th in descent from 'Ali the son-in-law of the Prophet, there are several generations left out in the pedigree.

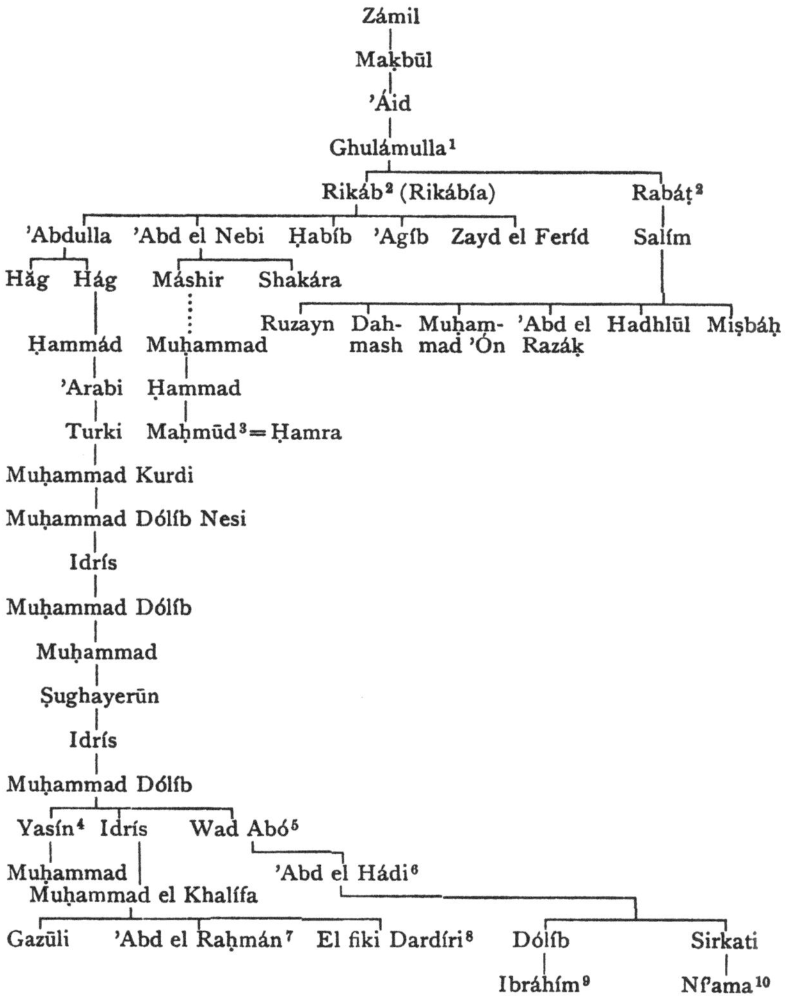
Zámil
Maḳbūl
'Áid
Ghulámulla[1]
Rikáb[2] (Rikábía)
Rabáṭ[2]
'Abdulla
'Abd el Nebi
Ḥabíb
'Agíb
Zayd el Feríd
Salím
Hăg
Hág
Máshir
Shakára
Ruzayn
Dah-mash
Muḥam-mad 'Ón
'Abd el Razáḳ
Hadhlūl
Miṣbáḥ
Ḥammád
Muḥammad
'Arabi
Ḥammad
Turki
Maḥmūd[3] = Ḥamra
Muḥammad Kurdi
Muḥammad Dólíb Nesi
Idrís
Muḥammad Dólíb
Muḥammad
Ṣughayerūn
Idrís
Muḥammad Dólíb
Yasín[4]
Idrís
Wad Abó[5]
Muḥammad
'Abd el Hádi[6]
Muḥammad el Khalífa
Gazūli
'Abd el Raḥmán[7]
El fiki Dardíri[8]
Dólíb
Sirkati
Ibráhím[9]
Nï'ama[10]

[1] Author of the first part of the "Dongola nisba." He is said to have been the first of his family to come from Arabia to Africa.

[2] The various sons and grandsons of Rikáb and Rabáṭ according to the "Dongola nisba" were ancestors of the following people:

Hăg ancestor of the Dóálíb.
Hág (or Hagág) ,, ,, El Ashíbáb in Dongola.
,, some Kawáhla at Teḳali.
,, the El Hadáhíd on the river.
,, ,, El Ginána ,, ,,

These Dóálíb at El Ḥaráza are at present easily distinguishable from the rest of the population by their sallow complexions, but they are intermarrying to such an extent that the same may not be true a few generations hence.

Of the tribes into which the people of El Ḥaráza divide themselves an account will be given later; but before leaving El Ḥaráza some account of its natural features may be given. The range known generally by this name measures in all about 17½ by 13 miles as the crow flies, and is by the natives themselves commonly divided into two parts, of which the western is called Kailūm and the eastern El Ḥaráza, the most easternly part of the latter again being differentiated under the name of Kobé. Again, each of the scores of peaks comprised in the

Hág (or Hagág)	ancestor of	the	El Simriab on the river.
	,,		some families incorporated with the Sháíḳía.
Máshir	,,	the	El Ṣádiḳáb on the river.
Shakára	,,	,,	El 'Abídáb ,, ,,
	,,	,,	El Nūráb (Kabábísh).
Habíb	,,	,,	El Sabábía in Dongola.
'Agíb	,,	,,	El Ḥalimáb ,, ,,
Zayd el Feríd	,,	,,	El Shabwáb at Khor Ṭawíl and El Bashíri in Kordofán.
	,,	,,	El Akázáb in Dongola.
	,,	,,	El Tamaráb ,, ,,
Ruzayn	,,	,,	Awlád Ḥabíb Nesi.
Dahmash	,,	,,	Bedería Dahmashía in Dongola and Kordofán.
	,,	,,	Awlád el fiki 'Ali Manófal in Dongola.
Muḥammad 'Ón	,,	,,	Awlád Gábir in Dongola.
	,,	,,	El Kenánía ,, ,,
'Abd el Razáḳ	,,	,,	Awlád el Sheikh Ḥasan Belíl in Dongola.
	,,	,,	Awlád Da'ūd at G. abu Tubr in Kordofán.
Hadhlūl	,,	,,	Awlád Maḥmūd at G. el Ḥaráza.
Miṣbáh	,,	,,	Awlád walad Da'ūd with the Kabábísh.

[3] This Maḥmūd was the leader of the first Rikábía immigrants from Mundera near the Blue Nile. He married Ḥamra of the Shabergo section at El Ḥaráza. His grandson was the contemporary of Wad Abó.

[4] The "Sheikh Masháikh" and "muowin" mentioned in Chapter I.

[5] Wad Abó was the leader of the second Rikábía (Dóálíb) immigration.

[6] Pallme met 'Abd el Hádi and says he had 24 children living at the time (1838). His people were employed in thieving and hunting giraffe (see Pallme, pp. 96 and 240).

[7] The present "'omda" of Bára (1910).

[8] One of the heads of the Tigánía "taríḳa" in the Sudan and a very holy man.

[9] Present "'omda" of El Ḥaráza (1910).

[10] Present "náẓir" of Kága and Katūl.

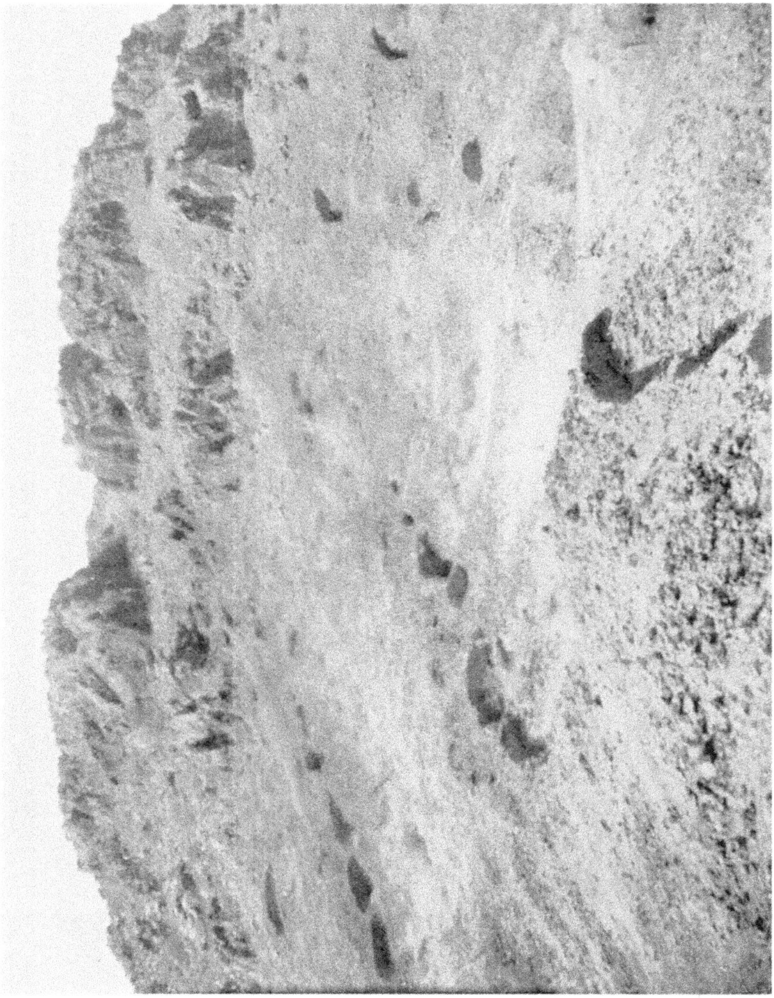

"Old iron-workings on G. el Ḥaráza."

whole has its own particular denomination. The nomenclature of the "gebels" is generally non-Arabic, and the proportion of foreign to Arabic names probably roughly represents the relative proportion of non-Arab and Arab blood in their inhabitants. Good examples of the former are Atki, Ang-al, Kalūdi, Karshūl, Turelli, Fandung, Kuriddi, Kurkayla, Tutu, Artōzĭk, Arangóg, Kaysay, and Tŭgŭngăndŭ. Old ironworks are still to be seen. It is not known if these date back to the Ḳura'án (see App. 4), or the Tungur (see p. 60), or only to the Kungára. Some are at Arangóg on the south of El Ḥaráza; others at Kaysay: the former are at the foot of the mountain in an inlet, the latter are some 400 feet above the plain and the old stone village, in a high pass in Jebel Kaysay. The backwalls (which are of fine burnt brick and two feet high) are arranged in tiers like the seats of a circus, each higher up the slope than the other, and in the form of a shallow semicircle. This backwall is in each case about 20 yards from point to point, and consists of four or five smaller consecutive concave divisions, each of which was presumably used by a different person. The refuse was thrown on to the top of the backwalls. The ground is strewn with cylinders of very hard burnt clay, one end of which obviously rested among the molten iron, and to the other the bellows were presumably applied. These cylinders lay horizontally side by side on a low brick rest built with a series of hollows on its upper surface, into which the cylinders fit. There are similar ironworks at Kobé at the east end of El Ḥaráza: the village beneath them in no way differs from half a score of others which are dotted about the range. It is situated as usual in a deep narrow ravine in the hills and built of loose boulders; a khor flows through it, and the entrance to the ravine was defended by a rampart (single, double, or treble) of piled stones. Until the last few years the people still resided on these old sites, and built huts of stone mortared with mud. They have now ventured out into the open and build straw huts.

The water-supply of the mountains is very varied. Firstly and best there are two very fine "ṣawáni'" wells of 100 feet cut through the rock stratum by the Dóálíb to the N.W. of the "gebel." Secondly, there is one ordinary well of 20 or 30 feet dug yearly near the foot of Gebel Gózi down to the rock stratum (which elsewhere prevents the opening of wells except after great trouble). Thirdly, there are two springs, one called Shegmál, on the south of Kailūm, and the other Shungul, on the north side of G. Sighi. These two springs are in the nature of "gulut," i.e. they are large holes of 6 feet to 10 feet deep in among the rocks at the foot of the "gebels." The herds water at them daily, and they are said to refill themselves at any time of the year within one day.

Fourthly, there is "Khashim el Leban," a wonderful great well in G. Kobé, which some former people cut through rock stratum for over 100 feet. It lies in a funnel surrounded by high rocky hills, and the usual approach to it is by jumping from rock to rock for half a mile. The water when I saw it was only 40 feet down, but later in the year the drift is cleared out of it down to 90 feet. Even so the bottom is not reached, there being no need for this since some 15 feet down a side of the well seems to have fallen in and formed a great chamber with a wall of rocks and stones.

Fifthly, there is Belbelday in G. Kobé—a shallow "tumut" of about 10 feet in a "khor" fed by the rocks all round it: but this supply sometimes fails in summer if the flocks have watered much from it. Sixthly, there are numerous waterholes or "ḳulut" up in the rocks all over the "gebels" and dependent on the rain for their water, and not lasting over the summer months. The largest of these is called Koi, and is a great hole at the top of Gebel Kailūm.

The system adopted for watering the flocks from one of the last mentioned "ḳulut," viz. El Tūba, is most extraordinary. The water is some 150 feet up in the mountain, in a hole on the top of a precipitous mass of rock which rises at an angle of about 80 degrees. A man climbs up this sheer face of rock, draws the water, and then pours it like a waterfall over the edge. So much of the water as is not wasted forms a small pool in the earth at the foot of the precipice, and is there drunk by the goats. In the dryest part of the year this method is discontinued as slightly wasteful.

Now whereas the foreign elements at El Ḥaráza, and probably (though in a less degree) at Um Durrag and Abu Ḥadíd, came from the north and east, it was from the west that many of the immigrants to Kága and Katūl arrived. From their position near the Dárfūr border it was only natural that the black races of Dárfūr should spread to them.

However, the names of the various clans in all these hills are alike: some of them may represent names of old races; some of tribal divisions, either original and authentic, or formed by imitation of the surrounding peoples. They are as follows:—

1. Maṭara, chiefly at El Ḥaráza.
2. Dugága „ „ „
3. Udungía „ „ „
4. Derham „ „ „ (closely related to the Buḳḳera).
5. Beringirri „ „ Abu Ḥadíd.
6. Dugarós „ „ „
7. Kerrak „ „ „ (the ruling family).
8. Asadáb „ „ Um Durrag and Katūl.
9. Beni Hilál „ „ Katūl.
10. Shabergo, now chiefly at Kága and Katūl: there are also some at Abu Ḥadíd and Um Durrag. These people are said to have come from the river, before the advent of the Dóálíb, under one Ṣaláḥ. It is said there are still some of them at Wad Medini on the Blue Nile. Ṣaláḥ found the Buḳḳera at El Ḥaráza and fought with them: eventually he married one of their women and his people spread westwards. It will be remembered that when the Dóálíb immigrated their leader married a Shabergo woman in similar manner, and no doubt for the same political reasons. There are now a number of them in Dárfūr[1].
11. Serár Buḳḳer (i.e. "the cattle aristocracy") or Buḳḳera. Chiefly at Kága and Um Durrag.
12. Serár Fár (i.e. "the rat aristocracy"). Chiefly at Kága and Katūl. Their subdivisions are: Um Dow; Um Gu'; Serár Ghoráb (i.e. "the crow aristocracy"); Abu Khayrín; Abu 'Umría. They are said to be a remnant of the Bedayría who were with Balūl at Káb Balūl and after his defeat by Háshim[2] to have fled to Kága and settled there. Their camel brand (i.e. the "uṣbū'a") is similar to that of the Bedayría.
13. Serár Ghanam (i.e. "the sheep aristocracy"). Chiefly at Kága.
14. Serár Khashab (i.e. "the wood aristocracy"). „ „ „

[1] They are said to be connected with the Ṭowál section of Kabábísh. Their camel brands are similar.

[2] See Chapter IV, on the Bedayría, etc.

15. Serár Khayl (i.e. "the horse aristocracy"). Chiefly at Kága.
16. Berangōl. Chiefly at Kága. They are of Bedayría origin.

There appear to have been numerous settlements of aliens at Kága and Katūl. Kungára, Birged, and Kerobát[1] from Dárfūr or west of it, and Bedayría from Central Kordofán have all settled there and intermarried at different times. The last named came about the middle of the eighteenth century, and shortly afterwards Háshim el Musaba'áwi attacked Katūl, cut off its supplies, killed a large proportion of its people, and sold many more into slavery. It was Háshim too who after killing Balūl went to Kága and there opened a number of wells through the rock at Sóderi, a feat said to have not previously been effected. He is also said to have cut wells through the rock at Fóga, Mazrūb, Katūl (bír Tinní), Kugum (by G. abu Fás el Mufettiḥ) and El Magaynis[2].

A curious custom found at Kága is worthy of notice: this custom is non-Arab, but it cannot be said to what element in the population it is more especially ascribable:—

At the time of the threshing of the corn the general desire is for sufficient wind to blow away the chaff from the grain, and it is customary to raise a wind in the following manner:—One of a pair of twins, whether male or female, takes a stick and with it rummages in the holes of the field mice, the idea apparently being that the prevalent sand-charged wind has its home therein, and may be annoyed or released into activity. After doing this the twin proceeds to the village dustheap, and beats upon it with a stick until there is a plentiful supply of powdered ash, etc., and then casts up handfuls of it into the air—as a lure to the wind to come and whirl it away. A second plan is also adopted for the same purpose of raising a wind. A live hen is ducked into water and then released: its frantic

[1] A Dárfūr race: they only settled temporarily. They are mentioned by Barth (Vol. III, p. 543) among the Arabs of Wadái.

[2] Ḥámid Gabr el Dár lineal descendant of Háshim, living in El Obeid, actually sold his well, thus inherited, to the Nūba of Kága in 1908.

The wells at the places mentioned were certainly cut through rock: the present generation until 1911 were too lazy to do more than open wells in softer ground or else find and reopen the site of old "ṣawáni'" (sing. "ṣáni'a," i.e. a well cut through rock). In 1911 a new ṣáni'a was dug at Mazrūb. El Magaynis is now waterless.

"Girls from Katūl at 'Id el Asóda, 1911."

shakings with a view to drying its feathers are considered likely to induce a wind to blow.

In the Turkish days El Ḥaráza, Um Durrag, and Abu Ḥadíd were all under the Dólábi 'Abd el Hádi, but Kága and Katūl were not. It is said that the yearly tribute of Katūl was £260.

The first "náẓir" or "'omda" of Kága of whom there is record was Aḥmad Surūr. In his day El Dow was "'omda" of Katūl, but when El Dow died Katūl was placed under Aḥmad Surūr. It soon became independent, however, and since 1841—i.e. for 70 years—has been under Tamar Ágha, the nephew of El Dow, and said to be son of a Turkish official who visited Katūl[1].

Aḥmad Surūr was succeeded at Kága by Sálim wad el Kír, who was followed in succession by El Ṣáfi Sigayr and El Ṣáfi abu Gambil. The last named was in power at the outbreak of the "Mahdía."

Ibráhím Dólíb, descendant of 'Abd el Hádi, was left as "'omda" of El Ḥaráza at the reoccupation: his brother Yasín was at the same time made "'omda" over the "meks" of Abu Ḥadíd and Um Durrag; and Ní'ama Sirkati, another descendant of 'Abd el Hádi, was sent in a similar capacity to Kága (excluding Surrūg) and Katūl. Ibráhím Ḳarrad, a rascally and cunning dwarf, was made "'omda" of Kága el Surrūg.

At present Ibráhím Dólíb and Ní'ama Sirkati still hold their respective positions, Yasín Dólíb was deposed and his "gebels" are under the control of their own "meks," and Ibráhím Ḳarrad has been succeeded by a less dishonest Kágáwi.

The natural features of Kága and Katūl are as follows:—The rain-water from the hills at Kága, which are only some 200 feet in height, drains into the "Wádi" of Sóderi which runs along their southern face. In this "Wádi" the water usually lasts in pools until about January, and is much used by the Arabs on their way back from the north-west grazing grounds to Central Kordofán. The Kabábísh also use Sóderi

[1] Tamar Ágha remained at Katūl till 1885, then spent seven or eight years as a Dervish in Dárfūr. He was wounded at the battle of the Atbara with Maḥmūd, and at the reoccupation was reinstated at Katūl.

wells in the dry weather. The ground rights belong exclusively to Kága[1].

When the rain-water dries up, the old wells are reopened at depths curiously varying according to the uneven level of the hardest rock stratum beneath.

Until 1910 there were no other wells at Kága, but in that year the Kabábísh found water at El Gibaylát on the north side of it at a depth of only 40 feet. They opened between 100 and 200 wells, which lasted them from the beginning of the year until the rains of July.

In addition to the well supply there are many natural tanks slightly adapted in past ages by human agency, and known as "ḳulut" (sing. ḳelti) in fissures up in the hills. These are filled by the rains and hold a great deal of water.

Katūl, about 23 miles E.S.E. of Kága, is a rather higher and much more solid "gebel." It is provided with "ḳulut" in the same way as Kága, but most of the flocks water at Girgil, Tefallung, 'Id el Asóda, and Bír Tinní, all close to the mountain; while others are sent farther afield to El Gemáma, Um Náwi, and Sóderi. The area that has been dug for wells at all these places except the last two belongs exclusively to Katūl.

Kága el Ḥufra, a range of low hills, with a high drift of sand on its west side, is so called from a large depression in the plain to the east of the hills. This depression fills after heavy rain and provides water for the neighbours and for nomad Arabs coming south-eastwards, until about the end of the year. If the rains are not very heavy El Ḥufra is dry by the end of October, and the people have to fetch their water from Sóderi or Abu Agága[2]. Occasionally a deep well or two yields water for a short time after the standing water has dried up.

Kága el Surrūg lies farther west, on the present Dárfūr boundary. Its water during the dry season is almost entirely

[1] By local custom the Arabs have free rights of watering so long as the rain-water stands, but so soon as the mouths of the old wells appear they leave the place to its owners, or pay for such water as they take. Exceptions are only made when circumstances of great amity prevail.

[2] The name Abu Agága comprises the site so marked on the maps and all the country up to G. Bakalái. Wells are sometimes dug at Abu Agága proper, sometimes at El Shwayb near G. Bakalái, but they never last long.

from "ḳulut" in the rocks, but wells are occasionally opened at El Ḳáshṭa to the north.

Um Durrag and Abu Ḥadíd lie between El Ḥaráza and Katūl. Between them they have a scanty water supply from 'Id el feki and some "ḳulut" in the rocks.

The names of some of the peaks at these hills are curious, e.g. Kuburkunkur, Síkí, Sí, Tegmálidid, Kilmán, Selingáwar, Dási, Karshennad, Maynanni, and Sillig. Close to the S.E. of Um Durrag and the N.E. of Abu Ḥadíd is a large and rich salt pan known as El May'a.

Abu Tubr is a pair of small hills covered with boulders, lying to the S.E. of El Ḥaráza and overlooking the open country which lies to its south.

The Nūba of Abu Tubr contain some elements of the same Dongoláwi blood as is found at El Ḥaráza, but are a dark and evil-featured people, with characters to match. Until lately Abu Tubr was no more than a nest of brigands.

The non-Nūba element there is connected with the Magídía.

CHAPTER VII

GEBEL MÍDÓB[1]

THE "gebel" of Mídób lies almost due west of Omdurman and covers about 27 miles east and west and 37 miles north and south, according to the French service maps[1]. Round about it are scattered a considerable number of villages of which the inhabitants cultivate crops of "dukhn" in its season, and for the rest of the year tend their herds of sheep, which are very considerable. The depression on the west side of the "gebel" and known as El Málḥa contains valuable deposits of "naṭrūn" (rock-salt) lying one or two feet below the surface of the water: it is said to be about half a mile or more square.

The nearest neighbours of the people of Mídób are,—on the east the nomad Kabábísh Arabs, on the north the Zagháwa, and on the west and south the Berti of Dárfūr. The "gebel" and its various watering places have for the most part both an Arabic name and a native name; e.g. the native name for "gebel" Mídób itself is "Tiddi ór," a Mídóbi is "Tiddi," the watering place known to the Arabs as El Serayf ("Zerrif" on the French maps) is "Kundul" to the Mídóbis.

The subdivisions into which the people of Mídób divide themselves are as follows:—

Kágeddi	Turkeddi
Urrti	Usutti
Torrti	Ordarti

[1] The writer has not visited Gebel Mídób. It lies in the territories subject to the Sultan of Dárfūr. The information given was obtained from Mídóbis who came to Kordofán to trade in sheep or work for hire and who understood Arabic sufficiently well to render conversation easy.

They speak of themselves as an ancient colony of Maḥass and Danagla from the Nile, but have no idea at what date their migration westwards occurred.

They say that some of them who have visited the river have found that the language of Mídób greatly resembled the dialect of the Maḥass or the Danagla, and give as an example the word "Kósi" meaning a wooden bowl (for eating from) both in the tongue of Mídób and of the old inhabitants of Dongola.

The names of a number of the peaks in gebels El Ḥaráza, Um Durrag and Abu Ḥadíd closely resemble Mídóbi words, and it is undoubted that immigrants of cognate race to the ancient inhabitants of the country round Dongola have settled in the three hills mentioned, as they are alleged to have done at Mídób.

The common prefixes Ka, Kur, Kar, found in the names of several of the peaks in El Ḥaráza and Um Durrag—e.g. Karshūl, Kuriddi, Kurkayla, Kalūdi, Karshennad—may correspond to the Mídóbi word "Kărr" meaning a village.

On the other hand the word "Tiddi" at once suggests the Teda (or Tibbu) who to a large extent include the Zagháwa; the Zagháwa language appears to resemble that of Mídób[1]; the Zagháwa are close neighbours of Mídób; and there is no doubt that the nomad Tibbu used to roam the country including Northern Kordofán and the Bayūda desert, and known in the middle ages as the desert of Gorham or Goran[2]. These Tibbu are themselves of partly Berber stock, as are many of the inhabitants of Dongola and Maḥass, and herein perhaps may be found the source of the alleged migration of Danagla and Maḥass to Gebel Mídób.

The Mídóbis themselves disclaim all relationship with the Zagháwa and say they do not understand their language. It is quite possible they are in some way connected with the mysterious Anag[3] who are fabled to have inhabited Northern Kordofán.

[1] A number of notes on the language of the Zagháwa of Dárfūr and the people of Mídób were sent by me to the *Royal Anthropological Journal* for publication and will probably appear about the end of 1912.

[2] See Appendix 4.

[3] See Chapter VI.

At present, in addition to the village headmen they have a supreme "mek" or "náẓir" (Arabic) over them. Their tribal customs shew traces in certain points of an old system of matrilinear succession such as was in vogue among the ancient nomad tribes on either side of the Nile (e.g. the Beja) thus:—It is said that if a "mek" dies, the succession passes not to his sons but to his sister's son, or, in default, to his maternal aunt's son; and again if A murders B, B's relatives take vengeance in the first instance upon A; but, failing him, upon his sister's son or his maternal aunt's son. On the other hand, in the case of inheritance the sons are given two shares to the daughter's one. I have heard Arabs say that they can remember a time when Mídób was under a female ruler.

Before any enterprise is undertaken a soothsayer is consulted for omens. This soothsayer is always a woman and is called "tódi." She takes seven cowries and throws them down together at random on the ground: from the position in which they lie relatively to one another the "tódi" deduces good or bad luck for the venture in hand.

NOTE. Having regard to the possible connection of the people of G. Mídób with the tribes to the west of them, it is worth remarking that Maydóbi (or Mídóbi) is a common place-name in Hausaland and Bornu; and that, similarly, all over the western Sahára "Gar" is a common prefix denoting a mountain or village, and so may be connected with the prefix Kar (etc.) mentioned on p. 103.

CHAPTER VIII

THE ZAGHÁWA[1]

It is undisputed that the Zagháwa are closely connected with the Tibbu (or Teda) family, but discussion has at times arisen as to whether these Tibbu are of a negro or Hamitic descent.

As regards the Zagháwa at any rate examination of some of the allusions to them by writers of various ages help to prove that they contain large numbers of both negroes and Hamites, as Professor Keane holds. Professor Keane in his article in the *Encyclopaedia Britannica*[2] in speaking of the Hamitic and Semitic stocks as superimposed on a negro race in the Sudan, classifies as Hamitic the Fulah[3], the Tibbu, and the Berbers, but allows that the Hamitic peoples have more readily mixed with the negro than have the Semitic peoples. He rejects Müller's assumption that the Tibbu are negroes, but, as regards the Zagháwa, calls them and the Ennedi a mixture of Tibbu and negro. Cust, however, while admitting the affinity of the Zagháwa to the Tibbu ("Teda") classes the Tibbu with the negro on linguistic grounds[4].

That the Zagháwa actually are a blend of Hamitic Tibbu, and negroes, seems to be borne out by the allusions to them in the pages of the old Arabic writers, but it will also appear, I think, that they contain other elements as well, and that the term Zagháwa was often used to include a large number of the tribes of north-central Africa: it will also be seen that "Zagháwa" is derived from the town or principality of Zagháí,

[1] See p. 103, note 1.

[2] See Article "Sudan."

[3] I.e. Felláta.

[4] See Cust, Vol. 1, p. 253.

the name being also used for the people inhabiting Zaghái; and that this term Zaghái was of very wide and indefinite use.

One of the first mentions of the Zagháwa is to be found in the geography of Idrísi, written in 1154: he says:—"the two most important residences of the Zagháwa are Saḳwa and Sháma. There is there a nomad tribe called Ṣodráya who pass as Berbers[1]." These Ṣodráya, he says, resemble the Zagháwa in their habits and customs, identify themselves with them racially, and are commercially dependent upon them. He also mentions a mountain called Lūḳiyya in the Zagháwa country, and lays peculiar stress upon the fact that the Zagháwa do not eat serpents. Witness is borne to this connection of the Zagháwa with the Berbers by Ibn Khaldūn (1332–1406) who, in speaking of the Tuwarek ("mulethamín"—"veiled ones") says they are a section of the Sanhága Berbers, who include the kindred tribes of Lamtūna, Zagháwa, and Lamta, and have frequented the tracts separating the country of the Berbers from that of the blacks since a time long previous to Islam[2].

Sultan Bello (c. 1816) says "adjoining to it (i.e. the country of the Mósí) on the north side the province of Sanghee lies. Its inhabitants are remnants of the Sonhaga (Sanhága), wandering Arabs and the Felateen[3]," and Cooley holds that the situation and features of "Sanghee" as described by Bello are sufficient to identify it with the Zaghái of Ibn Khaldūn[4].

So much for the Berber affinities of the Zagháwa. Now Mas'ūdi includes the Zagháwa among the descendants of Cush the son of Canaan and among the tribes whom he vaguely designates "Ḥabsha." He says that after the deluge the Zagháwa and the Demádem went westwards, separating from their kinsfolk the Nūba, Beja, and Zang[5].

[1] See Jaubert's translation.

[2] See Ibn Khaldūn, Bk II, p. 64. The Almoravides who conquered part of N. Africa and Spain were chiefly Lamtūna Berbers, though they were assisted by many Arabs. Various Arab writers declare the Sanhága were originally Himyarite Arabs from Yemen. Ibn Khaldūn (Bk II, p. 105) quoting Ibn Sa'íd speaks of the Zagháwa as Muhammadans and including a section called "Tadjua" (Dágu?).

[3] See Denham, Clapperton and Oudney. Sultan Bello succeeded his father 'Othmán Dan Fódio, the founder of the Fellála dynasty, in 1816. See also Davis.

[4] See Cooley, pp. 97 et seq.

[5] *For note see next page.*

Makrízi too, or Ibn Sa'íd from whom he copies, says that all nations between Abyssinia (to the south), Nūbia (to the east), Barka (to the north), and Takrūr (to the west), are called "Zagháí[1]." Takrūr itself, roughly about 1040, was the first principality to be converted to Islam, and it was apparently known as Zágha (a word presumably connected with Zagháí) to Ibn Baṭūṭa, since his description of the place and its conversion to Islam could only apply to Zagháí[2]. This supposition is confirmed by the statement of Ibn Khaldūn, who heard in Egypt from the Mufti of Ghána that his people used the name Takrūr to designate the Zagháí[3].

Leo Africanus also states that the "Sungai" (i.e. Zagháí) language was used in five states[4].

In still later days Muḥammad Masíni, the follower of Sultan Bello, speaks of a tribe of "Sokai," dwelling under the rule of a king on the mountains near the western source of the Niger above Timbuctu, and also in the desert among the Tuwarek between Kághó and Sokkatū. Muḥammad Masíni's "Sokai," it can hardly be doubted, is, as Cooley says, the same as Zagháí, when one calls to mind the previously mentioned connection between the Tuwarek and the Zagháwa and the similarity of the names Sokai and Zagháí.

[5] See Mas'ūdi, Vol. III, p. 1, where the following occurs:—

لما تفرق ولد نوح فى الارض صار ولد كوش بن كنعان نحو المغرب حتى قطعوا نيل مصر ثم افترقوا وصارت منهم طائفه متيمين بين المشرق والمغرب وهم النوبه والبجه والزنج وصار منهم فريق نحو المغرب وهم انواع كثيرة نحو الزغاوى والدمادم. . . .

[1] See Hamaker, p. 209. Ibn Sa'íd's date is 1214–1286 A.D., Makrízi fl. c. 1400.

[2] See Cooley, pp. 97 et seq. The various negro kingdoms were converted at dates which different accounts fix at various times. See Leo Africanus (Pory) in which 208 A.H. is given as the date when "all the Kingdomes of the negros adioyning vnto Libya received the Mahumetan law" (Vol. I, p. 163).

Barth (Vol. IV, pp. 407 et seq.) writing subsequently to Cooley and after discovering Aḥmad Bába's history of Songhay deduces from the latter that Tilután the Lamtūna chief adopted Islam and converted the negroes about 837 A.D.; and that Zá-Kasí early in the eleventh century was the first Muhammadan king of Songhay.

Ibn Baṭūṭa's date was 1302–1377. See Vol. IV, p. 441.

[3] Bk II, pp. 105 et seq.

[4] See Cooley, pp. 97 et seq.

In view of the above and the racial complexity of the various peoples whose offshoots seem after further fusion to have been known as Zagháwa, it seems vain to dogmatize on the subject of the original race to which the Zagháwa belong, and one can only regard them as a blend of negro and Hamite taking both words in as broad a meaning as may be admissible.

Whether Barth is correct in identifying those ancient Garamantes who used to hunt the Troglodytes of Egypt in chariots, as Herodotus describes, with the Tibbu who used to reside in Fezzán till they were forced southwards, or whether Mr E. T. Hamy is more correct in identifying the Tibbu with the Troglodytes, rather than with their oppressors, there is cause to suppose that some at least of the ancestors of the Zagháwa have inhabited the country where they are at present for thousands of years, and equal cause to assume that they have suffered very great racial modifications and admixtures during that time[1].

To come to more recent days:—

According to both Maḳrízi and Abu el Fidá, in the latter half of the fourteenth century the Zagháwa were subjugated by the great tribe of Bulála (who were themselves probably related to the Tibbu), and earlier in the same century, according to Barth, Mansa Mūsa the king of Melle had subjugated Zágha, Songhay, and other neighbouring states[2]. From then onwards there is little known of their history, and it may be assumed to be much the same record of "blood and thunder" as that of their neighbours.

About the end of the eighteenth century they emerge as a vassal state in Northern Dárfūr under practically independent rulers[3], and we also hear of some of them as trading with caravans from their station at Bír el Melḥ[4]. During the following century

[1] See Cust, Vol. I, p. 253. The reference to Barth is Bk IV, pp. 168 et seq. Müller in his edition of Claudius Ptolemaeus (Bk IV, p. 743) identifies the Garamantes with the Tibbu ("Teda"). For the opposite view see *L'Anthropologie*, Vol. II (1891), in which Hamy speaks of Nachtigal's having found in Tibesti the caves of the "Toubous, descendants directs des Ethiopiens Troglodytes, qu'Hérodote représentait comme les victimes des Garamantes."

[2] See Barth, Vol. III, Ch. 51, p. 428; and Vol. IV, pp. 407 et seq.

[3] See El Tunísi.

[4] See Browne, p. 205. On p. 566 (Appendix VI) Browne speaks of "Zerawy" (between G. abu Ḥadíd and Shershár) as being reported to be neither Arabs nor

they are mentioned as being rich in flocks and living quietly in N. Wadái and N. Dárfūr[1], while others were probably pursuing the more congenial occupation of alternately pillaging and guiding trading caravans between Fezzán and Bornu[2].

It was probably early in the eighteenth century that a party of Zagháwa first immigrated to the hills that lie close to the north of Kagmár in Kordofán, and settled there. According to their own account their leader was El feki 'Obayd the son of one of the smaller Zagháwa "meks" of Dárfūr, and the cause of their migration was a family quarrel; but the Dár Ḥámid tribes say that one of the Sultans of Dárfūr sent a body of Zagháwa and Ḳura'án to assist 'Abd el Ḥamayd, the sheikh of the Awlád 'Aḳoi, who was acting in place of Kirialo the Mermeri chieftain of Dár Ḥámid and the temporary holder of the tribal "nahass," in the work of collecting his tribe and bringing them to Tendelti (El Fásher): they say that 'Abd el Ḥamayd after leading these Zagháwa and Ḳura'án into Kordofán, won them over to his cause by bribery and force combined, and never having had any intention of returning to Dárfūr, he settled the Zagháwa round Kagmár, enslaved the Ḳura'án, and himself went to Sennár.

It is possible that there were two distinct immigrations. The Zagháwa say that on their arrival in Kordofán they found the Magídía in occupation of the Kagmár hills, and drove them eastwards to Sheḳayḳ. As the present generation is said to be the seventh in descent from El feki 'Obayd, we may count this as having occurred about 1700 A.D.

At some later time in the same century, or the beginning of the next, when the Zagháwa had increased in numbers and power, they quarrelled with the Awlád 'Aḳoi about the watering rights at Kagmár, which had originally been possessed by the latter. The Zagháwa say that the Awlád 'Aḳoi demanded tribute, which was refused: the Awlád 'Aḳoi say the Zagháwa

Muhammadans: he apparently did not connect these "Zerawy" with the Dárfūr Zagháwa, though his informants no doubt were referring to the Zagháwa colony near Kagmár.

1 See Barth, Vol. III.

2 See Carette, pp. 312 et seq. It is only the Tibbu who are specifically mentioned but no doubt Zagháwa were among them.

tried to prevent their watering at Kagmár. At any rate a fight ensued, the respective leaders being Merágha (Awlád 'Aḳoi) and El mek Manṣūr[1] (Zagháwa), and "99" of the Zagháwa were slain. The Zagháwa went and complained to the Fūr ruler at El Obeid who gave judgement. Both parties again differ as to what the judgement was: the Zagháwa say that he decreed that either "99" of the Awlád 'Aḳoi should be executed, or that they should hand over Kagmár to the Zagháwa in satisfaction; and that the Awlád 'Aḳoi chose the latter alternative: they add that the boundaries then fixed for the Zagháwa were as follows:—

South—Gebel el Milaysa
East —Um Gurfa
North—Khor el Ẓull[2]
West —El Showa

The Awlád 'Aḳoi of course deny this and say that the Sultan ordered them to pay "día" (blood-money), and that after much haggling they agreed to give Gebel el Fília and Gebel el Sirayf in settlement, and did so, stipulating at the same time that the Zagháwa should abandon all rights to Kagmár and Gebel el Gehanía, though by kind leave of the Awlád 'Aḳoi they were allowed to water at the former. The best comment on these stories is that the Zagháwa were certainly not ousted from Kagmár, as they must have been had the facts been as the Awlád 'Aḳoi state, and the Awlád 'Aḳoi do not at present so much as claim any right west of Um Gurfa.

Very soon after the Turkish conquest of Kordofán, the Zagháwa at Kagmár were attacked by the nomad Kabábísh Arabs from El Ṣáfia, but a settlement of the matter was arranged amicably. The Kabábísh since that date have had the right of watering at Kagmár, though for long the Beni Gerár nomads were also claimants. The latter have now retired but the feud between the Kabábísh and Zagháwa is not yet dead.

For the greater part of the Turkish *régime* the Zagháwa round Kagmár, inhabiting Gebels El Roy'ián and El 'Aṭshán, were officially reckoned as subject to Dólíb 'Abd el Hádi the

[1] The fourth generation from 'Obayd.

[2] Spelt الظل but pronounced El Dull.

Dólábi who from Gebel El Ḥaráza ruled over the northern hills, and paid their tribute through him. Shortly before the outbreak of the "Mahdía," however, they made themselves independent, and their "mek" El Tóm Muḥammad paid direct to government.

These Zagháwa at Kagmár are now entirely cut off from their western kinsfolk and none of them can so much as speak a word of any language but Arabic, nor name a single Zagháwi of Dárfūr: in fact they have taken unto themselves the following pedigree:—

Khálid el Guhani[1]
|
Zayd
|
'Aṭá
|
Aḥmad el Deráwísh
|
'Ali el Mukáshif
|
Ḥásan el Maḳdūb
|
Ibráhím Dellum
|
El feki Ḥasan
|
El Sultán Aḥmad Doura
|
Ḥasan Kurai
|
'Omar
|
El feki 'Obayd[2]
|
Aḥmad Kókó
|
'Agūb
|
Ḥabíb
|
Manṣūr[3]

Muḥammadáni — 'Agūb — Hadhlūl, Muḥammadáni

Muḥammad — El Tóm[4] — Muḥammadáni[5]

[1] The usual faked "nisba" of Northern Kordofán tribes begins with "'Abdulla el Guhani." Feeling the need of making some slight distinction between themselves and the Arabs, the Kagmár Zagháwa have adopted "Khálid, brother of 'Abdulla" as their ancestor.

[2] Said to have brought the Kagmár colony to Kagmár.

For notes 3—5 see next page.

Of the Zagháwa they say there are nine sections represented in Kordofán, viz.:—

Awlád Doura	Awlád Butra
Awlád Sheríf	El A'iláwi
Awlád Takarnu	El Milís
Awlád Kuayn	El Bedayát
El Mirra (Mirĕra)	

Of these the Bedayát are not in a sense true Zagháwa by origin, but only by adoption[6], and the only sections known by name to the few Dárfūr Zagháwa that I have questioned are the Awlád Doura and the Mirra: the remainder are probably sections that have been formed since their migration to Kordofán.

The following sections were mentioned by the Zagháwa from Dárfūr as composing their tribe; but no doubt the list is very incomplete:—

Awlád Diḳayn	Awlád Sherra (Sharira)
Artayt[7]	Awlád 'Ádi
'Agába	Kalíba
Mirra (Mirĕra)	Dangari
Nĕgri	Bŭg'a
Kourra[8]	Kóbera
Kaitinga	Tobá[9]
Awlád Doura (i.e. the Kagmár people)	

From the facility with which the Dárfūr Zagháwa speak Arabic and the apparent prevalence of Arab customs and

[3] "Mek" at the time of the fight with the Awlád 'Aḳoi.

[4] "Mek" at the time of the quarrel with the Kabábísh. He succeeded Hadhlūl since the latter had only one child, which died.

[5] The present "mek" at Kagmár.

[6] So say the Kagmár people, but the Dárfūr Zagháwa say they and the Bedayát are all one and the same race. Note that the Zagháwa call the Bedayát "Tobá," i.e. Tibbu.

[7] The following quotation from an article by D. A. Cameron, Esq. (*Journ. Archeol. Instit.*, Feb. 1887) is especially interesting:—"Hamdany relates that Kenan the son of Ham married Arteyt the daughter of Benawyl ibn Ters ibn Yafeth. She gave birth to Haká and El Asáwed, and the Nouba and Koran and Zendj and Zaghawa, and all the tribes of the Negroes."

[8] The Zagháwa in their own tongue speak of themselves as "Korra" or "Kourra," and Dárfūr as "Korra dár."

[9] I.e. the Bedayát. An account of the Bedayát and some of their strange customs will be found in Slatin, Chap. III.

"Zagháwa from Dárfūr."

manners it is evident that they are rapidly becoming arabicized[1]. They do not however like to be called Arabs as yet, and when asked, for instance, to what race the Dágu (whom they despise) belonged, they said they (the Dágu) were "only Arabs," and that their own (Zagháwa) ancestor was a slave (عبد) from the East called Mi'amía. However they said that all their names for men and women were Arabic, and I found none with a non-Arabic name.

They all professed strict Muhammadanism, stated that the only written language of their people was Arabic, and that religious "fekis" were more numerous in their country than in the countries to the east of it.

Adam and Howa (Eve) represented to them, as to the Arabs, the forefathers of mankind.

According to Muhammadan custom a corpse for burial is laid facing the east, and is placed at full length on the right side with the head to the south and the feet to the north. The corpse of a murdered person, however, is placed with the head to the east and the feet to the west. No reason for this could be elicited. The grave is in two sections: a broad hole is first dug to a depth of about three feet; at the bottom of this a narrow hole, just sufficient to take the corpse, is hollowed out, and the body put in it, wrapped in its cerements. Over this second cavity, which contains the body, logs of wood are placed close side by side so as to form a roof to the second cavity and a floor to the larger one above. Earth is then heaped over the wood and the upper hole filled up. A stone is erected at the head and the foot of the grave, and sometimes a circle of small stones is put all round. No objects of any sort are buried with the dead man; and he is apparently considered to have no further existence now or hereafter.

As regards inheritance and marriage;—a man is succeeded in the first instance by his sons, beginning with the eldest. If he had no sons his brothers inherit. If he had no brothers the inheritance goes to the Sultan. Daughters get nothing under

[1] I can give no full account of the Zagháwa of Dárfūr, since my only informants have been young men who have come to Kordofán to work for hire, and I have had no opportunity of seeing the people in their own country.

any circumstances. Women are regarded as an unfortunately necessary evil, and not to be encouraged.

An ordinary prosperous man marries four, five, or six wives. A great man has ten or more: a very poor man only one or two.

The dowry is paid in kind by the man (generally in the form of sheep).

The usual blood money for killing a man is 100 bulls; for killing a woman 50 bulls; for killing a slave about 20 or 30 bulls payable to the master.

The murderer when caught is tied up until his relatives are thought to have had sufficient time in which to pay the blood money: if undue delay occurs the murderer is knocked on the head.

In case of theft no penalty is exacted by custom provided the stolen goods are returned. If the local ruler, however, catches the offender, he fines him: if the Sultan catches the offender he either puts him to death, or cuts off his right hand and left foot.

A man found in adultery pays a cow or eight sheep to the injured husband each time he is caught in the act.

There are a large number of rainmakers ("hógi[1]"). The means employed by a "hógi" to cause rain are said to be reading (the Ḳurán) and spitting repeatedly on his rosary. These "hógi" are popular and respected, and not, apparently, held in any fear. It is said that when they cause rain to fall, they can so arrange that they themselves and the place whereon they stand is left entirely dry.

Various sections of the Zagháwa in Dárfūr are under separate "mulūk," who act as deputies of the Sultan of Dárfūr: the following are the names of some of these "mulūk":—

Section	*"Malik"*	*Section or Tribe of "Malik"*
Awlád Doura Awlád 'Agába Awlád Diḳayn	Muṣṭafa Wad Baḥr	Awlád 'Agába
Kaitinga	Ḥasan wad Kunjuk	Fūr
Artayt (subject to Kaitinga)	Ṭaha wad Nūrayn	Kaitinga
Mirra	Hasáb Tór Jikayl	Mirra

[1] "Hógon" is the word used on the Hombori plateau (Upper Niger) for a rainmaker or sorcerer.

"(*from left to right*) ''omdas' of Megánín, Gilaydát, Habábín, Nawáhia, Gawáma'a (Gamría and Ghanaymía), and Gellába Howára."

CHAPTER IX

DÁR ḤÁMID

DÁR ḤÁMID are a composite tribe, and the name is commonly used to include the following communities:—

Feráḥna	Nawáhia	Gilaydát
Habábín	Awlád 'Aḳoi	Megánín[1]
Merámra	'Aríffa	

The sections generally assumed to possess the most exact right to the title of Dár Ḥámid are the Feráḥna, the Habábín, the Merámra and the Nawáhia. The remainder, excluding the Megánín, are regarded by all except themselves as of inferior distinction and as later accretions. On the other hand all tribal genealogies, chiefly out of compliment, shew a certain relationship between all the eight tribes, but it will always be found that each of the eight tribes has so adapted the "nisba" as to suit its own convenience or glory. This factor and the lack of reliable records have caused great confusion, and though the same names occur in each "nisba" they appear in various orders, and the father in one "nisba" is the son or brother in another. The following are a few of the various "nisbas" collected from the heads of the tribes:—

I. The 'Aríffa version is:—

'Abdulla el Guhani[2]
|
Dhubián
|
Ḥámid el Afzár
|

[1] The Megánín are sometimes inaccurately spoken of as separate from Dár Ḥámid.

[2] See Chapter I.

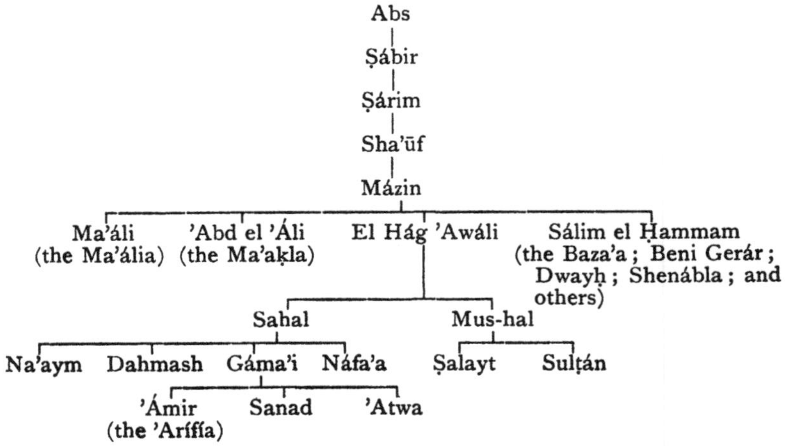

2. The Ma'ália say Ma'áli their ancestor was son of Sahal.

3. The Megánín give the following two versions, of which the former is the more usually followed:—

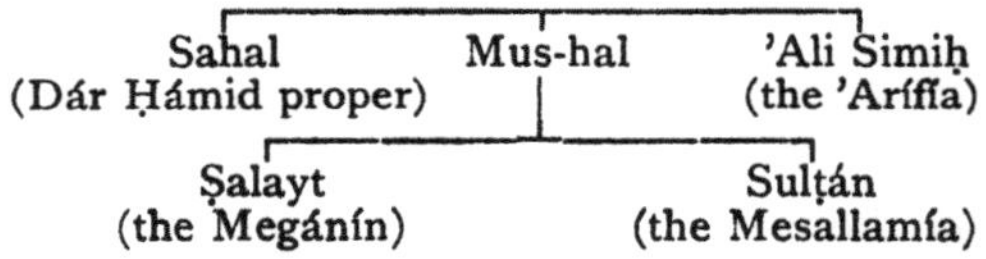

or else

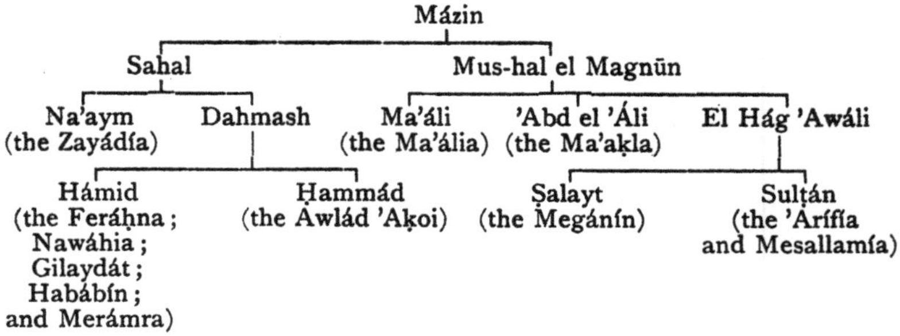

The former Megánín tree, at least as regards Sahal and Mus-hal and their descendants, is in closer agreement with the "nisbas" of other Dár Ḥámid tribes.

The Merámra and Feráḥna arrange the tree thus:—

'Abdulla el Guhani
|
Dhubián
|
Sofián
|
Ṣárim
|
Ṣábir
|
Mázin
|
El Hág 'Awáli
|
Sahal
|
Dahmash
|
Na'aym
- Ḥámid (Dár Ḥámid proper)
- Ḥammád (Awlád 'Akoi)

Turning to the genealogies provided by other tribes we find, for instance, the Ḥumr Felaita (Baḳḳára) giving the following table:—

'Abdulla el Guhani
- Dhubián
  - Aḥmad el Agdum (the Baḳḳára)
  - Ḥámid el Afzár (Dár Ḥámid)
- Sofián

and the Ta'áísha (Baḳḳára) the following[1]:—

Shaker
- Aḥmad el Agdum (the Baḳḳára)
- Ḥámid el Afzár
  - Ḥámid (Dár Ḥámid)
  - Ḥamar (the Ḥamar)
  - Zayád (the Zayádía)
  - Ma'ála (the Ma'ália)

[1] See *Handbook of the Sudan*; and compare the table given in Dr Helmolt's *History of the World*, p. 585, chiefly on the authority of Nachtigal, viz.:—

Mohammed el Hauri
|
'Abdalla el Dja'ânis, ancestor of the Djôheina
- Hammed el Afzer, ancestor of the Fezára, who are among the oldest Arab colonists of Africa (Ziâdîya, Kurumsîya, Qâsârina; Mâlîya, Aulâd 'Abdûn, Ma'aqila; Habbâbîn, Djelledât, Mejânîn, Aulâd Igoi, Beni Umm Rân, and Beni Djerrâr)
- Hammed el Ajzem
  - Djunêd
- Shâkir
  - Dahmesh
    - Bedr, ancestor of the Bedrîya
- daughter

The generations beyond Hámid are as confused as those following him, in the "nisbas," and the names used are merely echoes of half-forgotten traditions.

In fact though the eight tribes of Dár Ḥámid may be closely connected by origin in antiquity and certainly are so by intermarriage in later times, it is likely that their grouping together under a common designation was due in the main to their occupation of a single tract of country under the leadership of a single chieftain. Thus "Ḥámid" (known as "El Khuayn"—"the cunning rascal") probably had as his immediate *entourage* the closely-connected families of Feráḥna, Habábín, Merámra and Nawáhia, and at the call of his "nahass" could count on the support of the other four tribes (if not others such as Ma'ália and Ma'aḳla).

The usual form in which the traditions are couched is that the Feráḥna and Ḥabábín were Ḥámid's descendants by one wife, the Nawáhia by a second, and the Merámra by a third.

The only clue to the date at which Ḥámid lived is afforded by the "nisbas." According to these he is about the 12th, 13th, or 14th progenitor of the present generations—i.e. he lived from about 300 to 500 years ago. The fact that he is generally called a descendant of 'Abdulla el Guhani is quite unimportant, since 'Abdulla is indiscriminately named as ancestor by nearly every tribe in Kordofán.

The people of Gebel Katūl say that when Ḥámid came from the north he asked the advice of Abu Zayd el Hiláli as to where he should settle. Abu Zayd replied that Dárfūr would be unsuitable, for it was "dár 'abíd wa meli kibdak" (a land of slaves and belly-filling); that Southern Kordofán was also useless since "kán maṭarat inmuggat, wa kán yibisat inshekḳat" (if there is rain it becomes a swamp, and if it is dry

As regards this table, of course "'Abdalla el Dja'ânis" is 'Abdulla el Guhani. Most of the tribes said to be descended from "Hammed el Afzer" are at once recognizable as the present sections or subsections of Dár Ḥámid tribes. There are Beni 'Omrán ("Beni Umm Rán") living among the Bedayría ("Bedrîya") at present, whatever their origin; but they are regarded generally as a Dárfūr race with little Arab blood in them. The children of "Djunêd" and the tribes of the Baḳḳára descended from them will be found in Chapter XI on the Baḳḳára. For "the Fezára" see Chapter XV on the Kabábísh.

the ground cracks): he therefore recommended the Khayrán (where Dár Ḥámid chiefly reside at present) since it was "merkaz saláṭi; magerr buáṭi" (the land always chosen by rulers to settle upon; a rich land of waters). Ḥámid followed Abu Zayd's advice. As not only the fact that Ḥámid and Abu Zayd were contemporaries is doubtful, but even the existence of Abu Zayd at all, this does not greatly help matters. According to the usual Dár Ḥámid account Ḥámid came with his brother Ḥammád through Egypt along the Nile, and settled west of the present site of El Fásher in Dárfūr at a place called Um Dufun: here he married and begot his children. The mother of the Feráḥna and Habábín was Feraḥána, a woman from Gebel Mídób. Ḥadaya, a woman of the wild Bedayát of N. Dárfūr was mother of the Merámra, and Um Kassawayn of the Nawáhia. This Um Kassawayn was a woman from Baghdád, and was found by Ḥámid (some say in Upper Egypt, and some in Dárfūr or Kordofán) wandering about with a small child astraddle her hip: Ḥámid married her and became by her ancestor of the Nawáhia: the child found with her later became father of the Baghadda[1], of whom there are numerous villages in Kordofán.

Ḥámid's brother Ḥammád was ancestor of the Awlád 'Aḳoi. The Gilaydát are said by some to be descended from the union of Ḥámid with a slave woman, by others to have been slaves of Dár Ḥámid from time immemorial: they will be alluded to later.

The story of the Dár Ḥámid "naḥás"—the war drum, the possession of which invests its holder with the chieftainship, is complicated and confused, but it is clear that the right was not hereditary in practice, but fell to the most powerful chief in the confederation.

It is said that the first to hold the "naḥás" after Ḥámid's death was his son Muḥammad Mermer or Meraymir (so called from the cooing noise he made as a child when crawling about on the ground). Muḥammad Mermer was nicknamed Kirialo, and it is by this name that he is generally known, though it is from the other that the Merámra take their designation. This is what appears from the Merámra "nisba," but

[1] Singular Baghdádi.

it is quite likely that Muḥammad Mermer is a legendary name invented to account for the name of the tribe, whereas Kirialo is a genuine and more modern personage. At any rate, Kirialo was at some date at the head of the Dár Ḥámid tribes in Dárfūr, and at this time they were all nomad, and not mainly settled in villages as at present. Unfortunately he fell foul of the Sultan of Dárfūr[1], who either distrusting the Dár Ḥámid or else wishing the more easily to levy impositions upon them, gave orders to Kirialo to collect his scattered nomads and settle them round the capital. Kirialo demurred and was cast into prison. Before his imprisonment however he had been warned by one of the Maḥámíd Arabs who was high in the Sultan's councils what was likely to be the result of his attitude, and had found time to send for his sister's son 'Abd el Ḥamayd, chief of the Awlád 'Aḳoi, and to hand over to him the "naḥás" and suggest to him the best line of conduct to observe. Whether this transfer of the "naḥás" was absolute or whether 'Abd el Ḥamayd was merely appointed as Kirialo's agent and *locum tenens*, is still discussed with interest by the Merámra and Awlád 'Aḳoi.

Kirialo was never released from prison, but he pretended repentance and diverted all suspicion from 'Abd el Ḥamayd, whom the Sultan trusted and sent to enforce his previous orders. With Abd el Ḥamayd the Sultan sent a body of Zagháwa and Ḳura'án[2], Tibbu (or Teda) and negroid people from N. Dárfūr, to assist him in collecting the Dár Ḥámid tribes.

'Abd el Ḥamayd led these troops into Kordofán, where many Dár Ḥámid were settled on their present sites, and then partly by force and partly by bribery won them over to his cause, and settled the Zagháwa round Kagmár (where there is now a colony of them) and enslaved the negroid Ḳura'án.

[1] It is impossible to say which Sultan is alluded to. If, as appears later, he was nearly contemporary with Ba'adi abu Shilluk of Sennár he may have been any one of the following:—Muḥammad Doura (1722–32); 'Omar Lele (1732–39); Abu el Ḳásim (1739–52); Muḥammad Tiráb (1752–85). But if Kirialo was really the son of Ḥámid who, according to the "nisbas," lived 12 to 14 generations ago, then all these Sultans are too recent. It is far more probable that Kirialo was a chieftain in the eighteenth century, far recent to Ḥámid, but connected with him in vulgar report in order to add lustre to his name.

[2] See Chapter VIII.

This done, 'Abd el Ḥamayd went to Sennár to ask for protection from the "mek" of that country against the Sultan of Dárfūr: this was a natural step to take because Dárfūr and Sennár during the whole of the eighteenth century were constantly on bad terms, and Central Kordofán passed from the domination of one to the other repeatedly, Southern Kordofán being more permanently subject to Sennár and Northern Kordofán to Dárfūr. 'Abd el Ḥamayd was favourably received by the Fung ruler, said to have been Ba'adi abu Shilluk, but had to promise in return to give his allegiance to Sennár and pay tribute. This was agreed to, and most of Dár Ḥámid moved from Dárfūr to their present position in Central Kordofán. After a few years the Fung, it is said, invaded Kordofán, and remained in power till Háshim the Musaba'áwi from Dárfūr ejected them: the invasion of Kordofán here alluded to probably took place about 1748[1].

On the death of 'Abd el Ḥamayd the "naḥás" passed to his descendants in a direct line for three generations, the three holders being El Nūr, Merágha, and Yūsef: the last named is the great-grandfather of Muḥammad Ibráhím 'Áif, one of the present "'omdas" of the Awlád 'Aḳoi. Now until the time of Yūsef the Awlád 'Aḳoi had been sufficiently powerful to withstand the demurs of other claimants, but now the Merámra, Feráḥna and Habábín all disputed his rights and elected Um Beda wad Simáwi the sheikh of the Habábín to hold the "naḥás" as being the richest and most powerful sheikh in the confederacy. As might have been expected the Merámra and Awlád 'Aḳoi both dissented from this arrangement and seceded for a time from the league: the former at this time were under 'Ebayd wad Ḥamdūk.

From Um Beda the "naḥás" passed to Tumsáḥ his son, and afterwards to Simáwi wad Tumsáḥ. This Simáwi was head sheikh of all Dár Ḥámid at the close of the Turkish rule, and became a prominent "amír" under the Mahdi and the Khalífa. He served in Kordofán and Dárfūr under 'Othmán Ádam and finally died a natural death in Dárfūr in 1891[2].

[1] See p. 10, note 2, for this date.

[2] He is generally called Simáwi Um Beda, or "Giraygír."

After the Dervish revolt the Habábín reasserted their right to the "naḥás" over the whole of Dár Ḥámid, but at present each of the various tribes is independent of the others and admits no allegiance to any save its own particular sheikh. However, when the sheikh of the Megánín, whose tribe has increased very largely and remained more nomad than the rest, got himself a "naḥás" for the Megánín alone in 1906, he was generally regarded as very presumptuous, and his own tribe would not let him use it, even for ceremonial and pacific objects.

Some attention must now be paid separately to the tribes composing Dár Ḥámid.

At present the most numerous of the Dár Ḥámid tribes is the Feráḥna. They have about 60 villages, own rich flocks and herds and hold most of what is certainly the best land in Kordofán, viz. the "Khayrán" (sing. "Khór") or low-lying cultivable basins that stretch from north to south from near Shershár to the vicinity of Bára. The water in these basins is sufficiently near the surface to permit of irrigation by "sáḳia" and "shádūf." It has already been mentioned that they derive their name from Feraḥána the Mídóbi wife (or concubine—some say) of Ḥámid; but it is also stated that their name is connected with Fara'ón (Pharaoh) and that they are mainly descended from Egyptian traders who filtered up the Nile, pressed inwards to Kordofán, and settled and intermarried with other tribes to the north of Bára[1]. The subdivisions of the Feráḥna are as follows:—

El Sherama	Awlád Ḥizma	El Na'ūmía
El Tursha	El Kerimía	El 'Awámra
El Aḳáríb	El Berayḳát	El Showál
El Rubshán	El Filíát	

In the latter days of the "Turkía" the most prominent sheikhs of the Feráḥna were 'Omar Muḥammad Ḳash, the late "'omda," who was the official "'uhda" of the tribe, and 'Azra 'Abdūl. In the "Mahdía" 'Omar became an "amír," and on Simáwi Um Beda's death in 1891 succeeded him as head "amír" of Dár Ḥámid under 'Othmán Ádam, pending the

[1] Compare—"the mongrel race now inhabiting the valley of the Nile is contemptuously named by Turks and Arabs 'Jins Firaun' or 'Pharaoh's breed'"—Burton, *Pilgrimage to Al Medina...*, Vol. I, p. 10, note 1.

"'Omar Ḳash ''omda' of the Feráḥna, Khor abu Dullum, 1911."

coming-of-age of Simáwi's son Tumsáḥ. Rizayḳa 'Ali was another of their "amírs" in the "Mahdía." From the fact that they are seldom if ever mentioned by travellers it may be inferred that they have been less nomadic in their habits, if not less important also, than most of the other Dár Ḥámid tribes:—in fact they are "nouveaux riches."

Allusion has been made to the descent and former power of the Habábín. At present they reside on the north-west side of Dár Ḥámid round Um Ḥashím. They have some twenty-five villages, but a large proportion of them are nomad for a great part of the year. Jealousy and territorial contiguity has now converted the close sympathies between them and the Feráḥna, based on their supposed common stock, into mutual distrust. Their subdivisions are as follows:—

Nás el Sheikh	Abu 'Amár	Nás Ḥamír
Awlád Ánis	Awlád Wasík	Feláta
Awlád 'Awăna	El Kirán	Awlád Milayt
Awlád Sakíran	Awlád Bilál	Nughūra
Awlád Zagháwa	Awlád Ḥámid	Kakko
Awlád Nakūr	Awlád Selmán	Awlád Muḥammad
Um Sa'adūn[1]	El Fás	Awlád Dáir

Rüppell mentions them as one of the chief tribes of Kordofán about 1829, and as having lately moved to Dárfūr together with the Megánín, Ma'ália, and Gilaydát to avoid the oppression of the Turkish governor at El Obeid[2].

Werne seems to have confused them with the Habbánía, a tribe of Baḳḳára, with whom they have no connection[3].

Pallme does the same. Mansfield Parkyns by Habábín denotes the whole of Dár Ḥámid including Megánín, Feráḥna, etc.: the explanation is that in his day the Dár Ḥámid "naḥás" was held by Simáwi wad Um Beda the Habbáni.

The Nawáhia claim descent from Muḥammad Náhi son of Ḥámid by Um Kassawayn. Their subdivisions are as follows:—

Awlád Muḥammad
- (*a*) Awlád 'Egayl
- (*b*) Rushdána

[1] The Um Sa'adūn reside among the 'Aríffa.

[2] It must be remembered that the boundary between Kordofán and Dárfūr was then more to the east than now. See p. 21, note 1.

[3] "Habbáni" is the singular of both "Habbánía" and "Habábín."

(c) Awlád Sa'ad
(d) Ḳanáfíd
(e) Awlád Keraym
El Bilálía
(a) El Berabísh
El Gamū'ía
Mufettiḥ
Ḥamdána
Awlád Gima'án
(a) Abu 'Alwán
(b) Awlád Ferayḥa
Awlád 'Abd el Dáim
Um Burūr
El Nuṣáría
Awlád Ma'áfa

They have about 35 villages in Bára district and others to the east in Um Dam district: they also own one or two of the "Khayrán." In the past they have never been of any great importance and have been generally unnoticed.

At the close of the "Turkía" their official "'uhda" was Sa'ad abu Sáil. Prominent sheikhs under him were Abu el Ḥasan Belíla, father of the late "'omda" Belíla abu el Ḥasan, Aḥmad abu el 'Abbás, and Ḥámid Manófal. In the "Mahdía" their chief "amír" under Simáwi Um Beda in Kordofán was Ibráhím Takrūri who is at present "'omda" of the Nawáḥia in Um Dam district. The present "'omda" of the tribe in Bára district is Ismá'íl Zeyátía.

The Merámra are still largely nomadic in their habits and have only about 12 villages in Bára district and about the same number in Um Dam round Gebel Maghanus. They, like the Habábín, own none of the "Khayrán." Their country is to the east of that of the other Dár Ḥámid tribes and to the south of the Awlád 'Aḳoi. Small colonies of them also are to be found in other tribes, viz. among the Gawáma'a (in the Ghanaymía section) and the Ḥamar (in the Beni Badr section of the 'Asákir). The subdivisions of the Merámra are as follows:—

Samnía
(a) Nás Hadhlūl
(b) Nás Ma'áfa
(c) Nás Nuṣar
(d) Sellám

(*e*) Awlád Ḥátim
(*f*) Nás Biḥayl
(*g*) Gezay'i
(*h*) Abu Tinaytim
(*i*) Dowashna

Mesábíḥ

(*a*) Turku

Dár el Ba'ag

(*a*) Rubshán
(*b*) Nás abu 'Ali
(*c*) Kurumusía[1]

At the end of the "Turkía" the head sheikh of the Merámra was Muḥammad Manṣūr the brother of the late tribal feki Mud'ak Manṣūr and father of the present "'omda" Ḥámid Muḥammad. The latter and Belal Aḥmad were their chiefs in the "Mahdía," the former under Simáwi Um Beda in the west and the latter in Omdurman with the Khalífa. In 1906 the tribe split into two portions, those in Bára remaining under Ḥámid Muḥammad, and the Merámra of Um Dam district (chiefly Mesábíḥ) choosing Aḥmad Belal, son of Belal Aḥmad, as their "'omda."

The Awlád 'Aḳoi, as has been seen, are not descendants of Ḥámid but of his brother Ḥammád: they are thus in the position of cousins to the true Dár Ḥámid. Most of them live to the east in Um Dam district, but a number of them are at Um Gurfa, a rich tract of land in the north-east of the Dár Ḥámid possessions in Bára district. A portion of them are nomad and wander farther to the west under an "'omda" called Muḥammad 'Abdulla.

There are a few of them among the Gawáma'a, viz. the Zerázír subsection of the Ṭerayfía section.

Their chief sheikhs at the close of the "Turkía" were Ibráhím Zerátía, Ishayra, and Daḳíḳ. In the "Mahdía," most of them with El Kír Muḥammad and Aḥmad Dukka as "amírs" resided in Omdurman: the rest, with Ishayra, a "low fellow of the baser sort" served under Simáwi Um Beda. Ishayra died before the reoccupation: the other two ex-"amírs" are still

[1] Note that the Kurumusía ("Kurumsíya") are mentioned as a distinct division of Fezára in the genealogy quoted in note 1, p. 117. Others of them are among the Zayádía, to whom they are closely related.

alive. About 1906 Aḥmad Dukka made an abortive attempt to supplant El Kír as "'omda" of the Awlád 'Aḳoi in Um Dam district. The subdivisions of the Awlád 'Aḳoi are:—

Awlád Ḥamayd	Awlád Gámi'a	Awlád Ḥammūd
Faḍlía	Awlád Gamū'a	El Turshán
Muglán	'Utug	Awlád Rays
Ḥugag		

The 'Arífía sojourned for long in the countries west of Dárfūr and are probably only loosely connected with Dár Ḥámid originally. They are much mixed in blood with the natives of Borgu. Their villages number about 25 and their lands lie in a central position to the south of Dár Ḥámid and contain a few of the "Khayrán." The 'Arífía explain their name by saying that their ancestor Gáma'i as a boy wore a long tuft of hair on his head and was therefore called "Abu 'Uruf"; and his descendants 'Arífía. They also own some gum gardens west of El Gleit.

Ádam Wad el feki Muḥammad was their chief sheikh and "'uhda" at the close of the "Turkía," and with him were 'Abd el Salám abu Gebarulla and 'Omar Sulṭán father of the present "'omda" Aḥmad 'Omar. In the "Mahdía" Aḥmad 'Omar succeeded his cousin Ádam as "amír" and served under Simáwi Um Beda. The subdivisions of the tribe are as follows:—

'Áamir
- (*a*) Awlád Ramaḍán
- (*b*) Nás Um Birsh
- (*c*) El Khansūr

Sanad
- (*a*) Abu Su'ūd
- (*b*) Nás el Ḍow
- (*c*) Nás Kiddu
- (*d*) 'Abd el Sálim
- (*e*) El Hág
- (*f*) Abu Ḥammád

'Atwa
- (*a*) Nás Belal
- (*b*) Nás Balūl
- (*c*) Nás Bilayl
- (*d*) Abu Kusayra
- (*e*) Abu el Roy'ián[1]

[1] The 14 subsections here given are only of recent origin, i.e. from four, five or six generations back. The three main sections are older and more clearly defined.

The Gilaydát are an interesting people and were, after the Nūba, undoubtedly among the earliest inhabitants of Kordofán. It is probable that they immigrated with those now debased tribes such as the Ghodiát and Gawáma'a who apparently crossed from Sennár soon after that kingdom had seen completed the blend of Fung and Arab and had attained to power on the Blue Nile. On arrival in Kordofán they settled south of the present site of El Obeid and on the northern fringe of the southern mountains, and were no doubt overcome by later hordes of Arabs who had not mixed with the aborigines to a like extent. Hence the disdain with which the Gilaydát are sometimes spoken of, though a sense of loyalty has ascribed to them the paternity of Ḥámid. At present they live round Gebel Um Shidera (or Shagera) on the south-west borders of Dár Ḥámid and south of the Ma'aḳla and Ma'ália of El Gleit: others of them are in Dárfūr. They have some 25 villages and own some gum forests. The only watering places owned by the Gilaydát are in the valley known as Sheḳ el Gilaydát, viz. at Um Keraydim and El Gebír. They also own baobab trees near Um Shidera and use them for water storage. They were known by name at least to Burckhardt, Rüppell, Parkyns, and Prout. Their subdivisions are as follows:—

Rudána	Awlád Erbūd	Um Bádiría
Naṣírát	Awlád Wálid	Ḥarbía[1]
Akáshía	Awlád Defín	

Góda Edóma was their head sheikh in Turkish times and was succeeded by his son Bukr Góda. Bukr and his brother 'Ídám were their "amírs" in the "Mahdía," the former in Omdurman, the latter in Kordofán under Simáwi Um Beda. 'Ídám's nephew Málik Bukr succeeded his brother Muḥammad as "'omda" soon after the reoccupation.

As regards the Meganín:—When Baron J. W. von Müller visited Kordofán between 1847 and 1849 he found some Meganín settled at Ḥashába and thought that he had discovered an unknown race of Arabs[2]. He says they wore long curled hair

[1] A number of the Ḥarbía who were entirely nomad at the time of the reoccupation were then placed under the "'omda" of the nomad Ma'ália.

[2] See *R. Geogr. Journal*, Vol. XX.

plaited into tresses behind the ear; traded in gum; grew dukhn; and were "entirely isolated." There are still Megánín at Ḥashába but the bulk of the tribe is, and always has been, farther to the west and is mainly nomad.

Being now practically cut adrift from Dár Ḥámid they are somewhat chary of allusion to the time when they were subject to the Dár Ḥámid "naḥás."

Their name is to be found in any list of the important tribes of Kordofán in the nineteenth century.

At present their winter and summer headquarters are round El Mazrūb and Ḍelíl and Shabūḥa and Shiḳayla on the western side of Dár Ḥámid. El Mazrūb is the only watering place they possess since El Magaynis has run dry, but they have rights at Girgil and by arrangement with other tribes are allowed to water at various places such as El Rákib and Um Gemári. At Ḍelíl they own some hollow water-bearing baobabs. In the rains they nearly all move north-west with the other nomads. In latter Turkish times their chief sheikhs were Leban of the Tibo' section, Guma'a of the Awlád Máḍi, and Ḥammad Belíla; while the Mesá'íd, not then subject as now to the Megánín[1], were under Sulaymán Dardáb and Um Beda Sulaymán (the father of the present sheikh Naṣrulla Um Beda).

In the "Mahdía" they had three chief leaders, viz. Ḥammad Belíla, who died in Omdurman soon after the Khalífa's accession; Gema'án 'Ali, the brother of the present "'omda" Muḥammad 'Ali el Akhayḍer and successor of Ḥammad Belíla; and 'Agabna Guma'a the father of sheikh 'Ali 'Agabna of the Awlád Máḍi section. 'Agabna remained in Kordofán and served under Simáwi Um Beda.

The origin of the curious name "Megánín" or "madmen" is said to be as follows:—The children of Sahal and 'Ali Simiḥ (see the genealogical tree) used to squabble together after the wont of children and one day Ṣalayt (or Mus-hal according to another account) interfered and took the part of one child against another. Sahal reproved him for taking part in a children's quarrel at his time of life, and called him "magnūn" ("madman"). Ṣalayt (or Mus-hal) said he did not care if

[1] Until 1883 they paid their tribute of £214 odd separately (see Stewart).

he was "magnūn"—he would do what he pleased;—and as "magnūn" he was henceforward known, and his descendants as "Megánín."

The following are the sections of the tribe:—

1. 'Aiádía
   (*a*) Awlád Gimí'a
   (*b*) Awlád Gima'a
   (*c*) Awlád Gámi'
2. Ḥamaydía[1]
   (*a*) Awlád Geray'u
   (*b*) Awlád abu Zayd
   (*c*) Tagūla
   (*d*) Raywát
   (*e*) Awlád Gam'ūn
3. Tibo'
   (*a*) Nás el feki
   (*b*) Nás Rakūba
   (*c*) Nás abu 'Agūb
4. Awlád Máḍi
   (*a*) Nás Muḥammad
   (*b*) Nás Ḥammatulla
   (*c*) Awlád el Ḥamman
5. Awlád Rūmía
   (*a*) Nas Kitra
   (*b*) Awlád Muḥammad
6. Hayádira
7. Ghadiánát
8. Awlád Sá'id
   (*a*) Awlád Ráḍi
   (*b*) Nas 'Omára
   (*c*) Awlád abu 'Isayla
9. Awlád Faḍála
   (*a*) Abu Rishayd
   (*b*) Markūk
10. Mesá'íd
    (*a*) Awlád Harrán
    (*b*) Awlád abu Diḳayna
    (*c*) Awlád Mindik
    (*d*) Awlád Gám'i.

[1] The Ḥamaydía trace their descent thus:—

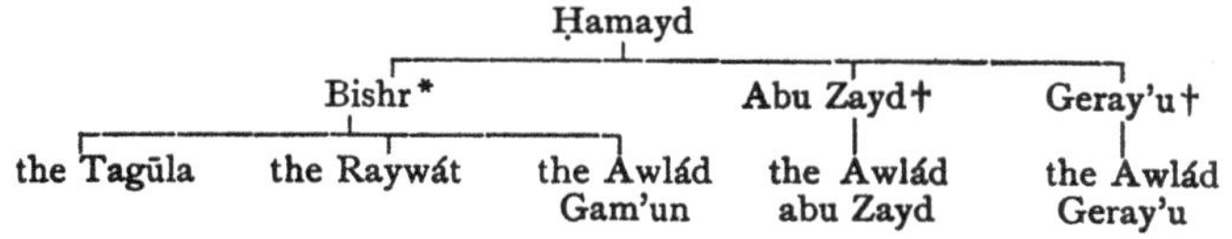

* By one wife. † By another wife.

The present "'omda" Muḥammad 'Ali el Akhayḍer gives his pedigree thus:—

Sahal
⋮
Edḥaymer wad Tabi'oi
|
Ḥasan
|
Mũsa
|
Kitr
|
Gama'alla
|
Gerári
|
Gima'a
|
Gótulla
|
'Ali

Leban — *Muḥammad* — Guma'a — Guma'án

(sons of *Muḥammad*:) Aḥmad — Muḥammad — Faḍl el Síd — 'Ali — Gád el Rub

To leave the Megánín and revert to Dár Ḥámid as a whole:— Among some of the northern nomad tribes are to be found a number of families who originally belonged to Dár Ḥámid. Notable examples are the large Dár Ḥámid section of the Kawáhla, and the Dár Ḥámid section of the Kabábísh in Dongola province.

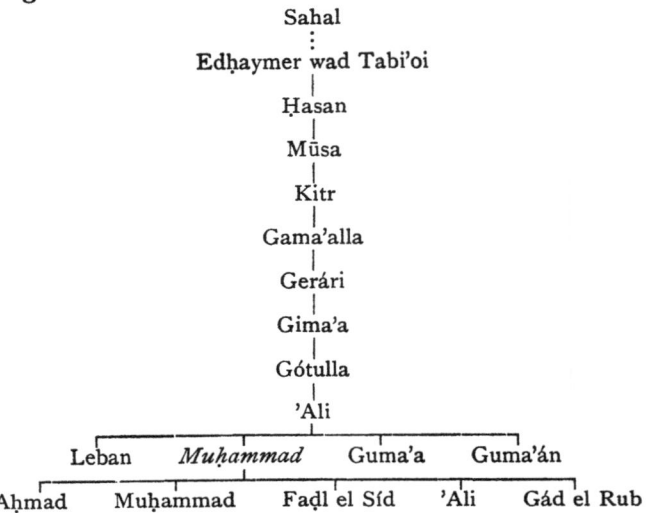

The Kawáhla are an eastern tribe and quite distinct from all the other Kordofán tribes, being related to the Bisháriín and 'Abábda etc., but until the outbreak of the "Mahdía" a great number of them were enrolled among the Kabábísh: to these Kawáhla there attached themselves a large body of Dár Ḥámid tribes, chiefly Megánín of the Awlád Máḍi and Awlád Faḍála sections, and when the Kawáhla broke away from the Kabábísh, most of these Dár Ḥámid went with them and became a section of Kawáhla: others remained behind as a section of Kabábísh in Dongola. To this day the tribal camel-brand of the Awlád Faḍála is the same as that of the Nás wad 'Omára subsection of the Dár Ḥámid Kawáhla; and the Awlád Máḍi generally use the "dámi'" and "ḳiláda" that distinguish practically all the Dár Ḥámid Kawáhla camels. Of course these Dár Ḥámid who are Kawáhla or Kabábísh by adoption neither own nor claim any rights at present to the lands of the Dár Ḥámid proper; but are as much "strangers in the land" as the rest of the Kawáhla are, in spite of the fact that they graze their herds for a large part of the year in Dár Ḥámid territories.

CHAPTER X

THE MA'ÁLIA, MA'AḲLA, AND ZAYÁDÍA

PART I. THE MA'ÁLIA.

THE Ma'ália are related to the Dár Ḥámid tribes and both parties generally claim Ḥámid el Afzár and Sahal among their ancestors[1]. However the Ma'ália were not among the actual descendants of Ḥámid el Khuayn though they are said to have been subject to his authority and that of some of his successors. Most of the Ma'aḳla, whom the Ma'ália choose to include among their subtribes and in their genealogies, are of a distinctly different stock, as will be seen; but they were for a long time subject to the Ma'ália.

The following is the pedigree of the head sheikh of the Kordofán Ma'ália according to himself:—

Sahal ("descendant of 'Abdulla el Guhani, and ancestor of the Zayádía and Dár Ḥámid")

Um Ḥammád married (1st) Ma'áli married (2nd) Um el Ḥatásha

- (by Um Ḥammád): Muḥammad el Keraym; 'Uḳál (ancestor of Ma'aḳla)
- (by Um el Ḥatásha): Khabūr (ancestor of Khawábír); 'Aláḳ (ancestor of 'Alayḳa)

Muḥammad el Keraym
|
Ḥamdulla
|
'Awanulla
|
Gamīl
|
Elū
|
Farag
|

[1] E.g. in the *Handbook of the Sudan*, Ḥámid, Ḥamar, Zayád and Ma'ala are quoted on the authority of a Ta'áíshi sheikh as being the four sons of Ḥámid el Afzár.

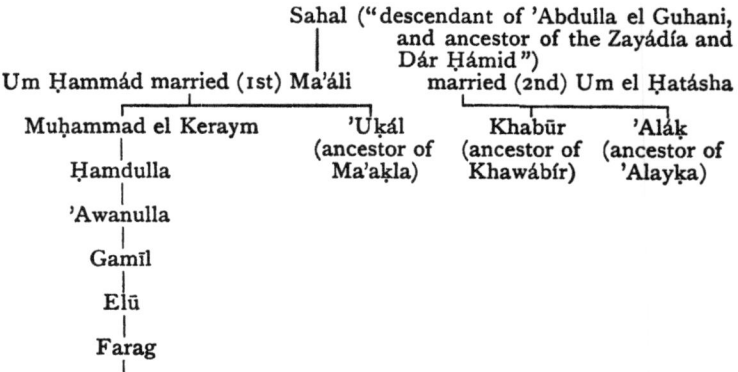

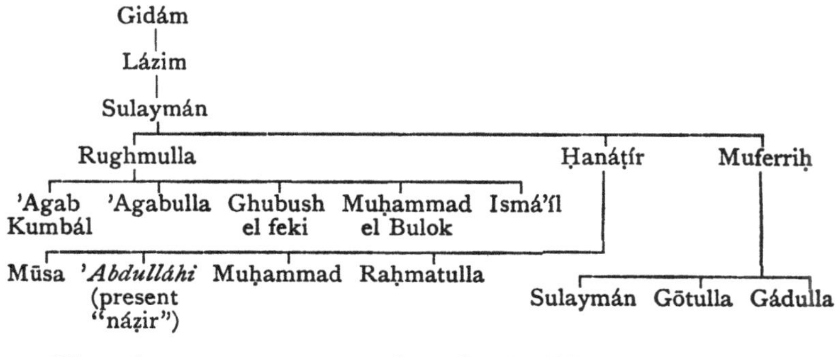

Though one can assume that the Ma'ália are related to the Dár Ḥámid tribes and migrated with them from the north or north-east to Dárfūr and Kordofán, little else is known of their early history.

They are widely scattered in Dárfūr and Kordofán now, and the same was the case under the Turkish *régime*. Burckhardt mentions them among the principal tribes of Kordofán and gives their habitat as between El Obeid and the Shilluk country, i.e. south-east of El Obeid: he also mentions that they supplied incense to the markets[1]. A certain number of the Ma'ália still reside in this direction, in El Taiára district; but we hear from Rüppell that many of them, soon after Burckhardt wrote, were driven to Dárfūr by the oppression of the Turks: they no doubt joined the bulk of their kinsfolk there.

In 1876 Col. Prout put the number of the tribe (whom he calls Mahalia) in Kordofán at about 2000, and describes them as wandering, as they still do, from south-west of Abu Ḥaráz as far north as Kága. That the bulk of them were in Dárfūr is shewn by the fact that in 1883 they were assessed for tribute at £1450 in Dárfūr as against £149 odd in Kordofán.

The Ma'ália in S. Dárfūr were held in great contempt by the Baḳḳára, as being drunken and immoral[2].

At the first outbreak of the "Mahdía," 'Ali wad Ḥigayr, who had been appointed sheikh of the Southern Ma'ália in Dárfūr by Slatin Bey, remained loyal, but the bulk of his people

[1] See Burckhardt, *Nubia*....

[2] Slatin, *Fire and Sword*, Bk 1, Chap. 5.

revolted in company with the Rizayḳát and Habbánía; and in 1882 'Ali was killed by the Rizayḳát.

Muḥammad abu Saláma the sheikh of the Northern Ma'ália in Dárfūr, who had been made a bey by Gordon, also remained faithful at the very beginning of the revolt; but seeing most of his people joining the Dervishes, and Slatin Bey hard pressed by the Rizayḳát, he concluded an alliance with Madibbo the sheikh of the latter tribe.

Practically all the Ma'ália were converted to Mahdiism before the end of 1882, though it is true a few fought on Slatin Bey's side at Um Waraḳát. Ḥanáṭír Sulaymán, a Ma'áli sheikh in Kordofán in Turkish days, was a prominent "amír" in the "Mahdía," and it was he who was sent by the Khalífa with Wad Nubáwi of the Beni Gerár to try and persuade Ṣáliḥ Bey Faḍlulla of the Kabábísh to come to Omdurman and make his peace.

Ḥanáṭír succeeded his elder brother Rughmulla in the sheikhship: he is said to have married 84 wives and to have had over 100 children. He is still alive, though his second son 'Abdulláhi is at present head sheikh of the tribe in Kordofán.

The Ma'ália are very scattered still: apart from those in Dárfūr there are colonies of them near Sherkayla, Sungukai, El Oḍaya, G. abu Sinūn, and El Gleit. Though they have numerous villages many of them remain nomad. Their chief wealth is in camels and sheep.

At El Gleit among the Ma'aḳla and at Um Serír among the Gilaydát they have some eleven villages, but they are not reckoned by other tribes as the original owners of the land.

The following are some of the subsections of the Ma'ália, descended from Um Ḥammád and Um el Ḥatásha respectively (see above in the genealogical tree):—

1. *Um Ḥammád*
   - A. Mukraym[1]
     - (*a*) El Aḳáriba (including Nás Farag)
     - (*b*) Um 'Egayli („ El Ḥarbía[2])

[1] I.e. descendants of Muḥammad el Keraym (see genealogical tree above).

[2] The Ḥarbía are really more Gilaydát (Dár Ḥámid) than Ma'ália. This list of tribes was given by the Ma'áli "'omda," and since some of the Ḥarbía are subject to him he counts them Ma'ália. See Chapter IX, on Dár Ḥámid.

(*c*) Dár el Khádim
(*d*) Awlád Um Gima'a
(*e*) Awlád Khayára
(*f*) Awlád 'Aṭáalla
(*g*) Awlád Um Ḥamda
(*h*) El Surūría
(*i*) El Rishaydát
(*j*) (others)
B. El Ma'aḳla[1]
2. *Um el Ḥatásha*
A. Khawábír[2]
(*a*) Um Felaḥ
(*b*) Guayl
(*c*) Awlád Rishdát
(*d*) Ḥidayba
(*e*) Khawábír el Ḥumr
(*f*) Genábla
B. 'Alayḳa
(*a*) Abu Ḳuṣayer
(*b*) (others)

PART II. THE MA'AḲLA.

As has been remarked, the Ma'aḳla are of a quite different stock from that of the Ma'ália, but their previous incorporation with that tribe accounts for their having escaped the notice of travellers.

In Kordofán they are roughly divided into Samá'ín[3] and Bishária, each under its own "'omda," but the two sections are dovetailed into one another and the subdivisions of both are in the list which follows given all together.

Samá'ín	Awlád Ḥasabulla
'Abádía	Dár Wálid (closely connected)
Amámir	El Sherak (closely connected)
Shĕăla	El Ribaydát (closely connected)
Um Selmán	El Na'asna (closely connected)
Bilál	El Kĕlăba (closely connected)
Nás Lázim	Kenákíl[4]

[1] It has been explained that the Ma'aḳla are not really by birth Ma'ália at all. Their subsections are given later.

[2] There are no Khawábír in Kordofán and I do not know if they are really Ma'ália at all. In the "Mahdía" they generally acted in conjunction with the Míma (see Slatin, *Fire and Sword*...). They live in Dárfūr.

[3] From Ismá'íl, pronounced Ismá'ín.

[4] This section is not in Kordofán but in Dárfūr.

Doura	Kagábíl
Tarūm	Awlád Ḥarayz[1]
Nas Sellám	Awlád Gima'a
Awlád Ḍáhir	Awlád abu Ḥammad
Shilaymát	Um Zayáda
Bishárfa	'Abd el Ḥabíb
'Aiál Shambūl	El 'Alowna
Bishára	Gharayr

Now the Samá'ín despise the Bisháría because the ruling family of the latter traces its descent to the founder of the tribe through a woman only:—that is to say that Khaḍra the "mother" of the Bisháría, and herself a Ma'aḳlía of sheikhly blood, was married to El Ḥág Bishári a feki from the East, and the present head sheikh[2] is descended from their union.

We may perhaps see traces here of the old matrilinear custom of the eastern tribes such as Bisháriín and 'Abábda[3]. When we find among the subsections both "Bisháría," "Bishára," and "'Abádía," the idea of connecting many of the Ma'aḳla with the tribes of the Eastern Sudan is strengthened. In addition too most of the Bisháría say that many of their kin are in the eastern deserts, and many admit frankly that by origin they are not Arabs at all, but Bisháriín who have migrated westwards and intermarried with the Ma'aḳla and other tribes.

It is curious that a large proportion of the Bisháría Ma'aḳla can read and write and are counted fekis: of hardly one of the Samá'ín, however, can this be said, and the fact of this difference is no doubt due to the difference in their origin.

The head sheikh of the Bisháría says the Ma'aḳla are the sons of two persons called Ḳáli and Wáli, but is vague as to further details[4] and fights shy of over-close enquiries.

The stereotyped account of the origin of the Ma'aḳla is, as usual, that their ancestors were 'Abdulla el Guhani and his descendant Sahal, and that they are therefore closely related to Dár Hámid, the Ma'ália, and the Zayádía.

[1] This section is not in Kordofán but in Dárfūr.

[2] El Ṣáfi Sulaymán.

[3] See C. B. Klunzinger's *Upper Egypt*, pp. 257 et seq., and Sir G. Wilkinson's *Modern Egypt and Thebes*, p. 386, etc. For the Beja matrilinear system see Quatremère's *Mémoires...*, Vol. II.

[4] Ḳáli is said to have had two sons, Ḥubaysh and Ramaḍán.

In the Turkish days there were few Ma'aḳla in Kordofán, and they were much scattered. At present there are some 15 villages of Samá'ín and allied subsections round El Gleit in the west of Bára district, and about the same number of Bishária etc. round El Sa'áta to the south-east of El Gleit.

A number of Ma'aḳla too are still residing near Shakka in Dárfūr, and in the gum-picking season many of these latter visit their kinsfolk in Kordofán and rent "gardens" from them.

The Samá'ín etc. in Kordofán were until 1906 under the Ma'ália and paid tribute through the Ma'áli sheikh. In 1906 they broke away and were allowed to appoint an "'omda" of their own—viz. Bashír Ḍow el Bayt.

Two years later they were subjected to taxes in place of tribute, much to their disgust.

Bashír Ḍow el Bayt was succeeded by 'Othmán 'Ali in 1910.

PART III. THE ZAYÁDÍA.

There was a tradition told in Dárfūr that Zayd the ancestor of the Zayádía was a slave of the first Tungur immigrants to that country[1], but perhaps the tale emanated from a hostile source for the Zayádía, though not a great or famous tribe, to judge by appearances have at least as much claim to be considered Arabs as the great majority of the so-called Arabs of the Sudan.

They are mentioned by Burckhardt[2] as being in his day one of the principal nomad tribes of Kordofán and Dárfūr, but the greater part of the tribe has always lived in the latter country and roamed the northern "wádis" with their camels, or accumulated wealth as breeders of horses[3].

In the tribal genealogies they are grouped with the Dár Ḥámid tribes and especially with the Megánín, for both tribes claim descent from Sahal. The Zayádía state that Sahal had two sons, Dahmash and Na'aym, the former ancestor of the Zayádía, the latter of Dár Ḥámid[4]. Those in Kordofán say

[1] See Slatin, Chap. II. [2] *Nubia*....

[3] Ensor who met some of them at Um Badr in 1875 also mentions some of them as settled at El Fásher.

[4] See Chapter IX, on Dár Ḥámid.

that the tribe is divided into three main divisions and many subdivisions: the following are said to be their names:—

Awlád Girbu'
- (*a*) Nás Ḥasan
- (*b*) Nás Adrag
- (*c*) Nás Shók
- (*d*) Nás Sherri
- (*e*) Nás abu Ḥammám
- (*f*) 'Aiál Sulaym
- (*g*) El 'Ísáwía[1]
- (*h*) Nás el Tóm
- (*i*) Nafá'ía
- (*j*) Nás Kirtūb
- (*k*) Um Deráwa
- (*l*) Awlád Fáris
- (*m*) El Imayría
- (*n*) El Misámír
- (*o*) El Getárna
- (*p*) El Kurumusía[2]

Awlád Mufaḍḍal
- (*a*) Awlád 'Awanulla
- (*b*) Awlád Imáma
- (*c*) Awlád Baybush
- (*d*) Awlád Zayn
- (*e*) Awlád Wáfi
- (*f*) Awlád Shaḥáwín
- (*g*) Awlád 'Awáda
- (*h*) Awlád 'Awádía
- (*i*) Awlád Um Gam'ūn

Awlád Gábir
- (*a*) 'Aiál Sabt el Nūr
- (*b*) 'Aiál Riḳay'a
- (*c*) 'Aiál abu Mis-him
- (*d*) Awlád Tátūn
- (*e*) Awlád abu Ma'áli
- (*f*) Awlád Ḥammūd
- (*g*) Awlád Gubarát
- (*h*) Awlád Zayd
- (*i*) Awlád Berbūsh (or "Berábísh")
- (*j*) Nás Um Gema'a

[1] There are some other 'Ísáwía living on the west side of the Nile and tributary to the Kabábísh "náẓir." The 'Ísáwía with the Zayádía and those with the Kabábísh are related.

[2] Other Kurumusía are with the Merámra (see Chapter IX), but it is to the Zayádía that they are more closely related.

" Zayádía, 1907."

At the close of the "Turkía" practically the whole tribe was in Northern Dárfūr[1]. They were not among the first tribes to revolt, but late in 1883 they and the Mahría became disaffected and shortly after joined the Dervishes.

After the reoccupation a number of them gradually found their way into Kordofán and settled among a scattered colony of Gawáma'a at Um Arba'a to the east of Gebel Um Shidera on the borders of the lands of the Gilaydát and 'Aríffa sections of Dár Hámid and to the north of the Baza'a. In 1906 they were allowed to elect Mu'azib Idrís[2] as "'omda" over themselves and were collected and allocated lands for cultivation at Um Arba'a. They own no gum forests however[3]. The majority of the Zayádía are still in Dárfūr, nomadic in habits, and intimate with the Zagháwa and other neighbouring peoples.

[1] In 1883 their tribute in Kordofán was only £55 odd, whereas those in Dárfūr were assessed at £2500 (see Stewart).

[2] Mu'azib immigrated with a considerable following about 1904. He is of the Nás Ḥasan subsection of the Awlád Girbu' and traces his descent thus:—

Girbu'
|
Mufaḍḍal
|
Sálim
|
Ḥasan
|
Idrís
|
Um Beda
|
Selmán
|
Idrís
|
Mu'azib

[3] With one exception, viz.:—the Gawáma'a of Um Arba'a, having gained a few gum "gardens" at the expense of the Baza'a, gave them to the Zayádía in Nov. 1911.

CHAPTER XI

THE BAḲḲÁRA TRIBES

PROFESSOR BUDGE remarks in his *History of the Sudan*[1] that the Baḳḳára of Kordofán "are undoubtedly the descendants of the terrible Menti of the Egyptian inscriptions."

This remark can hardly be taken in any but a highly metaphorical sense: the Menti may have lived in much the same country as that now inhabited by the Baḳḳára, and probably bred cattle for that reason—the conditions being eminently suitable; but this fact and a truculency common to both peoples is hardly sufficient foundation for an assumption of common descent. The Baḳḳára, though they have in their veins a deal of black blood, are at least predominantly Arab,—which the Menti presumably were not.

From their traditions and those of other tribes it appears that they came to their present position from the north[2] through the old kingdoms of the blacks, and only contain in their ranks comparatively few Arabs from the river and eastwards.

A very large number of them are still farther west than Kordofán.

A few travellers who have met them in Dárfūr and westwards have given fragmentary notices of them: thus Muḥammad el Tunísi who went to Tendelti (El Fásher) in 1803 speaks of

[1] See Vol. II, p. 397.

[2] The Arabs invaded Egypt under 'Amr ibn el 'Ási in 641 A.D. and extended their conquests over the northern fringe of Africa at the expense of the Berbers in the succeeding centuries. As the Berbers were swept away by or coalesced with the Arabs, further migrations southwards by the Arab tribes took place in increasing numbers (see Barth and Fournel).

"Blue Messiría" (Messiría Zurruḳ) as camel-owning nomads in Dárfūr, and mentions the difficulties the Sultan Muḥammad Faḍl experienced in getting tribute from the Rizayḳát and Messiría Ḥumr.

Barth also[1] mentions that in his day the Messiría were the third largest tribe of Arabs in Wadái, had their headquarters at Domboli, and were divided into Messiría Zurruḳ and Messiría Ḥumr: he found other cognate tribes, e.g. Awlád Ráshid, Salamát, Awlád Ḥamayd, Ziūd, etc. in Kánem, and Salamát close to the south of Lake Chad.

PART I. MESSIRÍA AND ḤUMR.

The Messiría and Ḥumr are really members of the same tribe. The true Messiría are divisible into Zurruḳ and Ḥumr; but in Kordofán the two divisions have become so distinct that the Ḥumr have ceased to rate themselves Messiría at all[2].

The subdivisions of the Messiría are as follows:—

A. Awlád Um Sálim
  1. Awlád Sulaymán
  2. Awlád Ḥammūda
  3. Awlád abu Zaydán
  4. Awlád Muṣbáh
  5. Awlád Ebdó

B. El Ghazáya
  1. Awlád Um Raydán
  2. Awlád Khayr
  3. Awlád Bilál
  4. Awlád Agmán
  5. Awlád 'Awaḍa
  6. Awlád Mismár
  7. El Ku'ūk
  8. Awlád Um Kerábíg

C. El Dirávi
  1. Awlád Kudum
    (a) Awlád Faḍla
    (b) Awlád Delóṭ
    (c) Awlád Gháli

[1] See Vol. III, Chap. 40.

[2] I have used the term Messiría throughout in a sense exclusive of the Ḥumr except where the contrary is stated.

2. Awlád Serír
   (*a*) Abu Khorays
   (*b*) Awlád Bokhát

D. El Enenát
   1. Awlád Ḥeglíga
   2. Awlád Kidayba
   3. Awlád Hilál
   4. El Ḳurūn
   5. El Shukría
   6. Awlád Nuṣár
   7. Awlád Um Fáris

E. Awlád abu Na'amán
   1. Awlád Mahádi
   2. Um Ḥayūb
   3. Awlád Ḍow

F. El Zurruḳ
   1. Awlád Ghánim
   2. Abu Alwán
   3. El Diraymát
   4. Beni Sa'īd
   5. Awlád Ḥinayḥi
   6. Awlád Ḳá'id
   7. El Kurbág
   8. El Genaḥát

G. Awlád Ḥaybán
   1. Awlád 'Ísa
   2. Awlád Gabríl
   3. Awlád el Sháib
   4. Awlád Faṭr
   5. Awlád Óda

By the middle of the eighteenth century the Messiría, pushing eastwards, had occupied lands to the east of the present Dár Messiría and were paramount between Dár Ḥumr and El Birka, El Rahad, and Sherkayla. Gradually however the Ḥawázma allied themselves with such tribes as the Bedayría, Ghodiát, Tomám, Birged, etc., and drove the Messiría back towards their present position.

Since then the Ḥawázma have been entirely separate from the Messiría, but, as will be seen, have absorbed much of the foreign blood of their allies.

During the earlier years of the "Mahdía" many of the Messiría remained loyal: in 1880 they had assisted Slatin Bey against the Sultan Hárūn in Dárfūr, and later a contingent assisted him at Um Waraḳát in 1882. In 1883 the Beni Ḥelba revolted and under Bishári Bey wad Bukr fell upon the loyal Messiría who resided round Dára under 'Abdulla Um Drámo and killed many of them. Stress of circumstances forced 'Abdulla to join the Rizayḳát in the same year at the siege of Dára, but he kept up his communications with Slatin Bey until the evacuation of Dárfūr[1].

In subsequent years a considerable portion of the tribe contrived to avoid obeying the Khalífa's orders to the tribes to join him on the river, and in consequence they rendered themselves liable to frequent raids and forced levies.

After the fall of Omdurman in September 1898 a number of the Messiría under Muḥammad el Faḳír wad Gabūri[2], their present "náẓir," employed themselves in looting the disbanded Dervish forces who were retiring pellmell to their homes in the west.

Though not a large tribe, in Kordofán, they are comparatively rich, especially in cattle and horses; but they labour under a great disadvantage in the smallness of their territories and have insufficient room for normal expansion: the result is, naturally, continuous quarrels with their neighbours. Their cultivation is chiefly round El Sinūt and Mafūra, and their flocks and herds water in the Wádi el Ghalla.

The Ḥumr are divided into two separate divisions, viz. Agaira and Felaita.

[1] See Slatin, *Fire and Sword*.

[2] Muḥammad el Faḳír is of the Um Sálim section. His pedigree is as follows:—

Sulaymán
|
Ramaḍán
|
Ḥasan
|
Muḥammad
|
'Othmán Aygal
|
El Gabūri
|
Muḥammad el Faḳír
|

Aḥmad	Ádam	'Abd el Raḥím	Bashír	Fáṭima	Bakhíta	Um Bukhayn	Um Adaz	Fáṭima

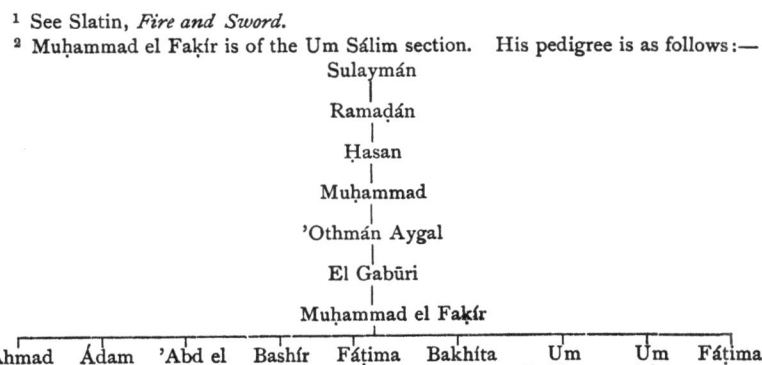

The subdivisions of the Ḥumr Agaira are[1] :—

A. Awlád Kámil

1. Kalabni
2. Dár Muta
3. Dár Um Shayba
4. Dár Sálim
5. Awlád Kimayl
6. El Mizagina
7. El Fayarím

B. Awlád 'Omrán

1. Awlád Ghigidayr
2. Awlád Nigayr
3. Awlád abu Ḥammad
4. Awlád Nowása
5. Awlád Ḥamayd
6. Awlád abu Ismá'íl
7. Awlád abu Um Gūd
   (*a*) Awlád Ma'ala
   (*b*) Awlád Ḥammūda
   (*c*) Awlád 'Alyán
8. Dár Zabali
9. Dár Ḥaybulla
10. Dár Binát
11. Raḥma
12. Faḍlía

The subdivisions of the Ḥumr Felaita are[1] :—

A. El Metanín

1. Awlád Ziáda
2. Shamía
3. Shabíb
4. 'Arafa
5. Aríf
6. El Zawayt

B. Awlád Surūr

1. Awlád abu Khamís
2. Awlád Gima'a
3. Awlád 'Alyán
4. Awlád Um Bokatr
5. Ga'afir
6. El Geriffín

[1] From material supplied by Capt. W. Lloyd.

C. El Gubarát

1. Awlád abu Hilál
2. Awlád Maḥámíd
3. Awlád Budrán
4. Abu Gikák

D. El Salamát

1. Awlád 'Ali
2. Awlád Sa'ada
3. Awlád abu Idrís
4. El Gebábara

It is said that both the Messiría and the Ḥumr are descended from 'Aṭía the general ancestor of the Baḳḳára, as appears in the table[1] on p. 147.

[1] This table was given by Mekki Ḥusayb "náẓir" of the Ḥumr Felaita. For comparison with it one should compare the tree given by Dr Helmolt, viz.:—

Mohammed el Hauri
|
'Abdalla el Dja'ânis, ancestor of the Djôheina

- Hammed el Afzer
- Hammed el Ajzem (ancestor of the group of El Djuzm)
  - Djunêd
    - Râschid, ancestor of the *Auldd Râshid* in Wadâï and Bornû
    - Heimat, ancestor of the *Heimat* (Heiyimat or Hêyimat); Ta'âïsha and Habanîya
    - Rakal, ancestor of the *Erêqât* ('Orêqât)
      - 'Atiâ
        - Messîr, ancestor of the *Messirîya*
          - Ta'aleb, ancestor of the Ta'âliba
        - Rizq, ancestor of the Rezêqât
          - Mahar, ancestor of the Mahârîya
          - Mahmud, ancestor of the Mahâmîd
            - Scheiq
            - Barik
              - Yâsîn, ancestor of the Auldd Yâsîn
          - Nâïb, ancestor of the Nawâïbe
- Shâkir
  - Dahmesh
    - Bedr, ancestor of the Bedrîya
- daughter (wife of one Turrudj) ancestress of the *Hamr* (Homr)

"Abdalla el Dja'ânis" is of course 'Abdulla el Guhani.

For the descendants of Ḥámid el Afzár see Chapter IX, on Dár Ḥámid.

"Ta'aleb, ancestor of the Ta'âliba" is interesting: cp. note 4, p. 148. It is possible that these Ta'âliba (i.e. Tha'áliba) may be only a section of Messiría descended from Tha'álib who is mentioned in both trees as a son of Messir; but on the other hand there is probably involved a reminiscence of the ancient Tha'áliba from whom the Messiría are said to be descended.

The insertion of "(Homr)" after Hamr explanatorily is probably a mistake. The Ḥamar are an entirely distinct tribe and not to be confused with the Ḥumr (Homr).

It may be convenient to add here the tree printed in the *Handbook of the Sudan*

It is added that the sons of 'Abdulla el Guhani emigrated to Fezzán from Arabia and that his great-grandson Ginayd died and was buried in Egypt. Of 'Abdulla's descendants who went to Fezzán it is said some stayed there and others pushed south to Borgu.

The story is that Agair the ancestor of the Ḥumr Agaira was left exposed as a child by his father Ḍai in the desert: Messir the cousin of Ḍai found Agair and handed him over to his son Muḥammad Felait to educate: the point of this story of course is that the Ḥumr Agaira are deeply indebted to the Felaita.

Before leaving the Ḥumr it is amusing to note that the "Dongola nisba" remarks of their origin, "They are descended from the master of the Ass, El Aswad, the Liar, the False Prophet who appeared in Yemen, of the tribe of 'Ans, whose name was Aihala[1]." The animosity here displayed is due to the

and based on the statements of Kubr 'Abd el Raḥmán sheikh of the Guberát section of Ta'áisha:—

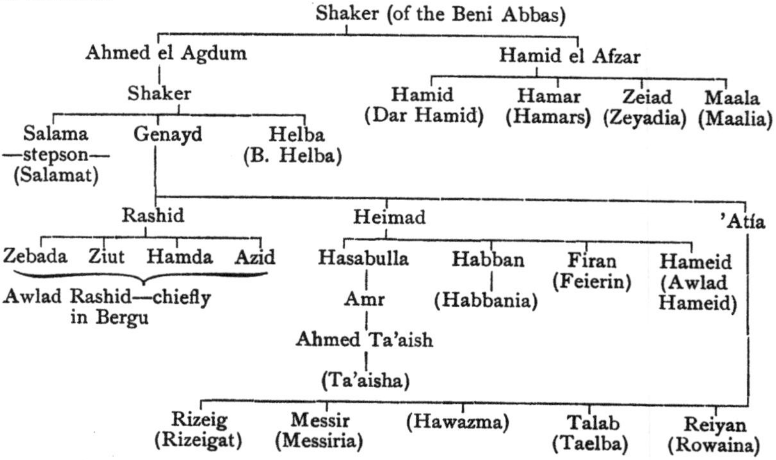

All these trees are of course partly faked, but this last one has an even more spurious air than the other two.

The "Dongola nisba" says, "The Salamát Arabs in the west are descended from Ḳuḍá'a" [one of the old Arabian tribes] "and blacks".... Ibn Duḳmáḳ mentions a tribe of the same name at the siege of Fostat by the Arabs (c. 640 A.D.): Barth (Vol. III, p. 455) mentions them as one of the chief tribes of Bagirmi.

[1] See Sale's *Ḳorán*, p. 139. A later gloss in the "Dongola nisba" says the Ḥumr are descended from the Arabs of El Ḥelb in Upper Egypt.

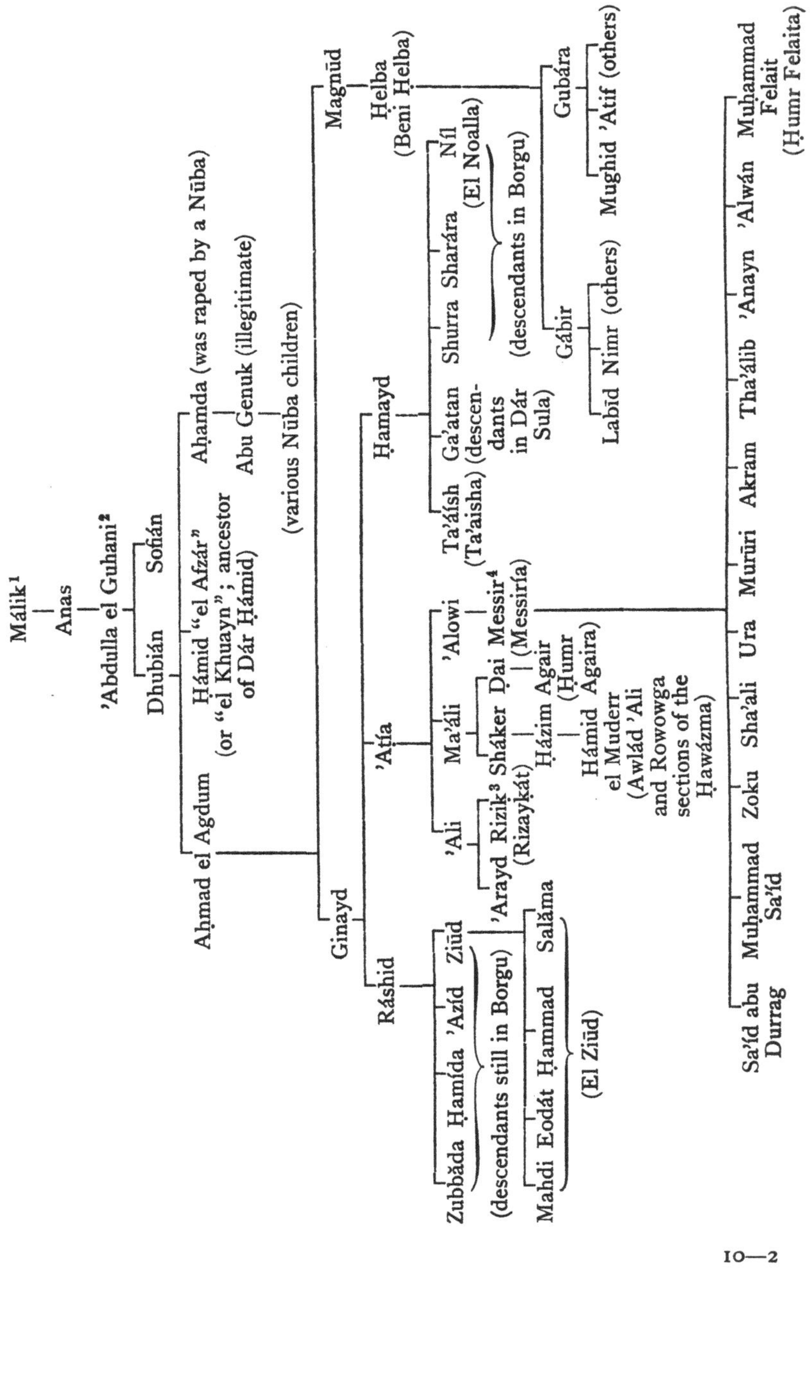

For notes see p. 148.

fact that the Ḥumr were particularly rabid Dervishes during the whole of the Khalífa's rule. The present "náẓir" of the Agaira, 'Ali Gula, was one of the Khalífa's "mulázimín[5]."

The tribe suffered very severely in the "Mahdía" from war and pestilence, but their country—a vast sandy plain north of Muglad and another great plain of black soil covered with thick bush and crossed by sandy belts to the south—is sufficiently spacious to admit of their eventually settling down and recuperating without the necessity of quarrelling with their neighbours on each side as the Messiría are almost compelled to do.

They cultivate chiefly round Muglad and Baraka, but in the dry season flock southwards to the Baḥr el Ḥumr, where raids and counter-raids with the Dinka occur yearly.

[1] He gave his name to the Máliki school of Islám. He is obviously out of place here and has only been dragged in as a suitable figurehead.

[2] See note 1, p. 145.

[3] The "Dongola nisba" says, "The Rizayḳát are descended from Rizayḳ el Thaḳífi and belong to the Beni Thaḳíf." The Beni Thaḳíf were a great Arabian tribe and are frequently mentioned in histories, etc. See also Sale's *Ḳorán*, pp. 14 and 83.

[4] The "Dongola nisba" states that the Messiría are descended from the tribe of Tha'áliba: "The Messería Arabs properly so called are the children of Messir son of Tha'áliba son of Nuṣr son of Sa'ad son of Nebhán, which [i.e. the tribe of Tha'áliba] is a section of the tribe of Ṭái." Ṭái was a great Ḳaḥṭánite Arab tribe in the old days. The tribe of Tha'áliba is mentioned by Maḳrízi as settling in Egypt at the time of the conquests of Saláḥ el Dín (Saladin). See Quatremère's *Mémoires*, p. 190. The Kenána also told me unprompted that the Messiría were originally an offshoot of Tha'áliba. See also note 1, p. 145.

[5] Ali Gula's pedigree is as follows:—

'Abd el Raḥmán Na'ala
- Ṣadíḳ
  - Gid
    - Muḥammad Gamar
      - Aḥmad
        - Um Gabír
      - 'Ali Gula
        - Muḥammad Nimr
        - 'Othmán
        - Aḥmad
        - Gamar
        - Khadíga
      - Maunis
        - Idrís

"'Ali Gula 'náẓir' of the Ḥumr Agaira, 1906."

PART II. THE ḤAWÁZMA.

The Ḥawázma are at present divided into three main divisions, each of them again subdivided as in the following table. Though known under the single name of Ḥawázma they are originally of very composite formation as will be shewn.

A. 'Abd el 'Áli
  1. Dár Gawád
    (*a*) Dár Bakhóti
    (*b*) Dár Shalango
  2. Awlád Ghabūsh
    (*a*) Dár Bat'ḥa
    (*b*) Awlád Ba'ashóm
    (*c*) Dár Debl
    (*d*) El Ma'anát
    (*e*) Awlád Gama'a
  3. Dár Bayti
    (*a*) Awlád abu Ádam
    (*b*) El Ḳura'án
    (*c*) (two other sections)
  4. Dár Na'ayli

B. Ḥalafa
  1. Dár 'Ali
  2. Dár Fay'at
  3. El Asirra
    (*a*) Um wad Gáza
    (*b*) Awlád Gómer
    (*c*) El Zurruḳ
    (*d*) Awlád Mesheri
    (*e*) Awlád Serár
    (*f*) Awlád Ma'ada
  4. Awlád Ghonaym
    (*a*) Dár Iga
    (*b*) Awlád Tadu
    (*c*) Dár Tangal
  5. El Tógía (there are four subsections)

C. Rowowga
  1. Dár Gamá'i
    (*a*) El Ṭowál
    (*b*) El Ḳuṣár

2. Awlád Nūba
   (*a*) Awlád Raḥma
   (*b*) Dár Bilál
   (*c*) El Foghra
3. Delamía
   (*a*) Awlád Tayna
   (*b*) Sulaymánía
   (*c*) Um Maginda
   (*d*) Dár 'Agūl
   (*e*) El Mūminín

To take these sections in turn:—

A. The *'Abd el 'Áli* claim to be descended as shewn in the following table[1], and thus consider themselves the true Ḥawázma, and the rest of the tribe as later accretions. As a matter of fact even they are of by no means pure descent:—Ḥammad Asósa their head sheikh, and many others, are by race rather Takárír than Arabs.

'Abdulla el Guhani
- Ginayd
  - 'Aṭía ("El 'Aṭowa" viz. Rizayḳát; Ḥumr; Messiría; Ḥawázma; Beni Ḥelba[2])
  - Ḥaymád (Ta'áísha and Habbánía)
- Magnūd
  - Agdum (Ḥamar 'Ásákir)
  - Afzár ("El Fezára" viz. Kabábísh; Dár Ḥámid; Beni Gerár; Ma'ália)
- Ráshid (Awlád Ráshid)

The "Ḥawázma" referred to in this table are the 'Abd el 'Áli section, whose descent is as follows:—

Abu el Hum
- (a son)
  - *Gawád
  - *Bayti
  - †Ghabūsh
- Na'ayl

* By one mother. † By another mother.

It is related that the three brothers Ginayd, Magnūd and Ráshid were settled in Dárfūr, whither they had come from

[1] This table and much of what follows was obtained from Sheikh Ghanowi of the Dár el Gawád section of the 'Abd el 'Áli Ḥawázma.

[2] The "Dongola nisba" says, "The Beni Ḥelba Arabs in the west belong to the Beni 'Ámir Arabs in the Ḥegáz."

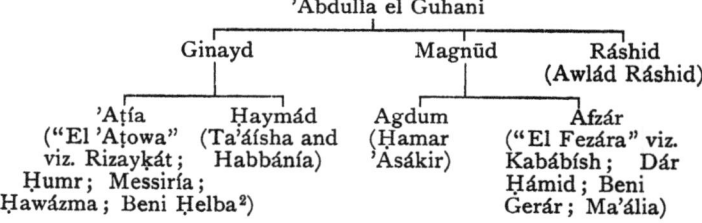

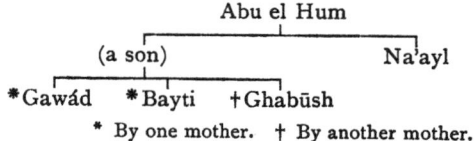

Plate X

"Ḥawázma sheikhs, 1906. Ḥammad Asósa on the right.'

Tunis. They and their sons owned a wonderful she-camel whose udder was like an ever-running waterspring: she used to roam the country at will with a pail tied under her, and the people used to drink therefrom. Now the tribe of Khuzám[1] stole this "náḳa," and a battle ensued: in this battle there perished so many of Khuzám that the wedding rings (worn by the young men for only a week after marriage) alone covered the haft of a long spear. After the defeat of Khuzám their conquerors became supreme and gradually worked their way eastwards to Kordofán with their camels. It was at this time that they first bought a bull and a cow from a Felláti pilgrim bound for Mecca. Those descendants of the three brothers who settled in South-west Kordofán bred cattle for the future and abandoned camel rearing as unsuited to the local conditions.

A different version of the story of the wonderful "náḳa[2]" relates that it belonged to 'Aṭía and Ḥaymád, the sons of Ginayd. Ḥaymád, the younger of the two, was under his brother 'Aṭía's rule but dared to seize the náḳa for himself and his people. The brothers and their respective adherents fought: 'Aṭía was victorious and his people spread into Kordofán and were the progenitors of the present Kordofán Baḳḳára, viz.: Messiría, Ḥumr, and Ḥawázma. Ḥaymád and his people stayed in the west and from them are descended the Rizayḳat, Ta'áísha, Habbánía and Beni Ḥelba[3].

B. *The Ḥalafa.* It is said[4] that the Ḥalafa are composed of six different tribes, none of them Ḥawázma by origin. About the middle of the eighteenth century, in the days of the Fung, certain heads of families from six tribes, finding themselves unable to stand alone, came to the Ḥawázma and asked for protection and agreed to join the Ḥawázma: their suggestion

[1] Settled in the Western Sudan. There was a very famous Arabian tribe of the name Khuzám. It is said by some that the Deḳáḳím section of the Ḥamar are an offshoot of this tribe.

[2] Told by Ḍai Ḥáshi a sheikh of the Dár Gawád Ḥawázma (Dár Bakhóti subsection).

[3] Which of the Baḳḳára are descended from 'Aṭía and which from Ḥaymád is always a vexed question.

[4] The following is sheikh Ghanowi's version.

was followed and the six heads of families swore a solemn oath (حلفوا) binding themselves to the Ḥawázma: hence they were called "Ḥalafa." The six tribes represented were as follows:—

Bedayría	Gawáma'a
Takárír[1]	Zenára[3]
Gellába[2]	Slaves

Among these strangers were scattered a few original Ḥawázma. The Asirra were a separate tribe in Kordofán until early in the nineteenth century and joined the Ḥawázma *en bloc*. It is likely that they are connected with the Bedayría. At first they were not subject as at present to the Ḥalafa, and the latter pretend that in Turkish days the Ḥalafa paid half the tribute of the Ḥawázma and the Asirra the other half:—the implication (a false one) being that the Awlád 'Abd el 'Áli and the Rowowga were subject to the Ḥalafa.

C. The *Rowowga* themselves seem very vague about their origin. Some say their descent is thus[4]:—

- 'Aṭía
  - Ráshid el Wullád
    - Abu el Hum
      - Ḥázim ('Abd el 'Áli[5] Ḥawázma)
      - Ḥamd el Muderr (Rowowga Ḥawázma)
    - a son (all the Bakkára except the Ḥawázma)

[1] All Fellάta and other tribes that come from the west and pass through Kordofán on their way to Mecca for the pilgrimage are included in the general term "Takárír."

[2] The Gellába Howára are meant. El Nūr Hanūa, head sheikh of the Ḥalafa, belongs to the Tógía section and is by race a Gellábi Howári.

[3] The Zenára are an obscure and debased people. Maḳrízí, Ibn Khaldūn and Mas'ūdi all mention Zenára as one of the Berber tribes who, like the Howára, settled in Egypt and in the deserts. See Chapter IV.

[4] Ḥámid el Likka of the Awlád Nūba section gave me this table but with some hesitancy. He went on the pilgrimage in 1907 and on returning declared he had there met Ḥawázma with tribal pedigrees similar to his own. I know of no mention of Ḥawázma as a tribe in Arabia at any time (though the Ḥawázin are very frequently mentioned). Doughty (*Wanderings in Arabia*, Vol. II, 135) mentions "Házim an ancient fendy of Harb." Maḳrízí mentions Awlád Ḥazm as a subsection of the Arabs of Senbes (a branch of Ṭái) settled in Egypt.

[5] The attribution of the name of Ḥázim to the ancestor of the 'Abd el 'Áli is evidence that the 'Abd el 'Áli, as said above, are considered original Ḥawázma.

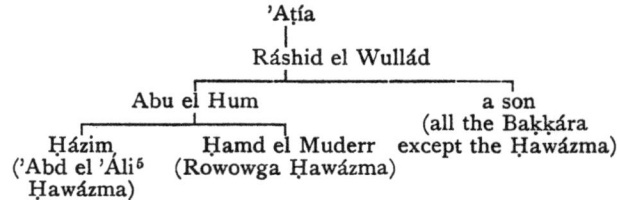

Others however[1] deny that the Rowowga are Ḥawázma by origin and say that they came from the east, and, as definite examples, state that the Sulaymánía section belong properly to the Beni Sulaym on the Nile, and that Sómi Towr himself, the head sheikh of the Rowowga, is by race a Kenáni. Probably many of the Rowowga are really Kenána.

Shortly before the Dervish revolt, in 1874, the Rowowga fought with the rest of the Ḥawázma; the quarrel being caused by the alleged unjust distribution of the tribute. Nawái was then head sheikh of the 'Abd el 'Áli and Ḥalafa, and Towr of the Rowowga. The Ḥawázma took part in the Dervish siege of El Obeid but when the Mahdi proposed transplanting them to Omdurman to assist in the attack on Khartoum, the bulk of the tribe retired to Gebel Goghub in the south and remained thereabouts till the reoccupation, fraternizing to a large extent with the Nūba of the mountains. A number of Messiría also joined them there.

The Ḥawázma sheikhs however were not all so fortunate. The Mahdi got hold of Nawái and Ibráhím Gaydūm of the Ḥalafa, Góṭía Ḥammád of the Dár Bayti, and Muḥammad el Tóm of the Awlád Ghabūsh, and proposed taking them to the river with him. Nawái and Ibráhím escaped later, but the latter was recaptured and put to death, and the former died of small-pox shortly after his escape. Góṭía died at Omdurman, and Muḥammad el Tóm, the last survivor, was killed at the battle of the Atbara.

The Ḥawázma are a good instance of the composite nature of most of the Sudan Arab tribes and their status is well summed up by the "Dongola nisba" which after stating that the Ḥawázma "are a subtribe of Bugīla and descended from Ḥázim," proceeds "but a number of Arab tribes and blacks attracted by the advantages of being with them, mixed with them, and the original stock and its accretions became indistinguishable"; and again, "The Ḥawázma include Bedouins from the Ḥegáz, and Bedayría, and Takárír, and many other tribes."

[1] E.g. sheikh Ghanowi.

PART III. THE HABBÁNÍA.

The Habbánía in Kordofán are merely an offshoot of the Habbánía Baḳḳára of Dárfūr, a tribe related closely to the Rizayḳát, Ta'áísha, Beni Ḥelba, etc., and claiming descent from Ḥaymád[1].

They migrated eastwards from Kalaka some four or five generations ago and made their home in the first instance at El Rahad by leave of the Gawáma'a. They were very shortly afterwards attacked by the Ḥawázma: the Gawáma'a succeeded in effecting peace between the two parties, but the Habbánía were compelled to move farther east, and finally settled round Sherkayla, though sending their cattle to graze into the surrounding country and especially southwards to the vicinity of Teḳali. Prout in 1876 mentioned them as being between El Rahad, Sherkayla, and Teḳali, and assessed their numbers roughly at 8000.

Being naturally a quarrelsome and restless people, and being also considered as outsiders, they have at various times been involved in hostilities with most of their neighbours. Very soon after their removal from El Rahad they had a fight with the "Mek" Naṣr of Teḳali, and again the Gawáma'a intervened and settled the quarrel.

With the Gima'a too they have several times come into conflict, the last occasion of importance being during the governorship of Ḥasan Pasha Ḥelmi, when a pitched battle was fought at 'Aḳayla.

In 1881 the tribute of the Kordofán Habbánía was reduced from £748 odd to £215 odd: the main tribe in Dárfūr were assessed at £2640[2].

The "amír" of the Kordofán section in the Dervish days and their "'omda" until his death in 1910 was El Tóm 'Owdūn. Their main subdivisions are as follows:—

[1] The "Dongola nisba" says, "The Habbánía are the children of Habbán son of El Ḳulūs son of 'Omar son of Ḳais, a subtribe of Báhila [which is] a tribe descended from Ḳais 'Ailán...." Ḳais 'Ailán was one of the chief tribes of Arabia.

[2] See Stewart.

A. El Ṭára

- El Shaybūn
- El Selmánia
- El Hilayát
- Awlád 'Áid
- Awlád Záid
- Awlád abu 'Ámir
- Awlád Gargar
- El Derábín
- Awlád Belo
- El Kamársa
- Awlád Rihayma
- Awlád Idrís, or Um Idrís
- El Kígama
- Awlád Ma'afin
- El Mahádi
- El Hadayli
- El Merírát

B. El Sóṭ

- El Shabūl
- El Rayáfa
- El Mesá'íd
- El Feraygát
- Awlád abu 'Ayád
- Awlád Um Sunṭa
- Awlád Borgáwi
- El Ghanáyát
- Awlád Sa'adán

CHAPTER XII

THE ḤAMAR

THE Ḥamar are a large but loosely connected tribe having closer affinities with the group containing Dár Ḥámid, the Ma'ália etc., than with the Baḳḳára or Gawáma'a—Bedayría group. As a tribe they are of comparatively recent origin, and until about five or six generations ago the name of Ḥamar was apparently unknown or at least not worthy of mention. They vaguely claim an ultimate descent from 'Abdulla el Guhani and a common parent in one Aḥmár from whom they derive their name[1]; but the first important name among them is that of El Ḥág Munaym, of the 'Asákir division of the tribe who lived so recently as the beginning of the last century. Until his time the Ḥamar had been an unimportant tribe living in Dárfūr round Um Shanga. Then quarrels arose between them and the Ma'ália and the bulk of the Ḥamar migrated eastwards to what is now Kordofán,—some, including El Ḥág Munaym's own family, settling in villages for part of the year, but the main body remaining permanently nomad and roaming from El Oḍaya to the open country north of Um Badr, and as far east as Abu Ḥaráz, Um Sumayma, Gebel abu Sinūn, Um Shidera [Shagera] and Gebel abu 'Asal. As was to be expected, they were not welcomed by the nomads of Kordofán: feuds sprang up between the Ḥamar on the one hand and the Kabábísh, Dár Ḥámid, and

[1] The Ḥamar Gharaysía say they came from Yemen in the Khalifate and settled in Dárfūr between Kebkebía and G. Marra. At a much later date, they say, they tried to migrate eastwards again, but perished from thirst in great numbers near G. el Serg and G. Audūn. See also pp. 150 and 151 (note 1).

" Sheikhs of Western Kordofán, 1906."

Zayádía, (who in addition were at feud with one another), on the other hand, and in the northern grazing grounds between Um Badr and Um Ṣonayṭa, far from all government authority, forays and counter-forays continually occurred to the very end of the Turkish *régime*.

The Ḥamar multiplied prolifically in Kordofán and not only did their herds of camels in the "Turkía" exceed those of most other nomad tribes on the west of the river, but their villages occupied extensive tracts between El Nahūd and Gebel abu Sinūn. The greatness to which the tribe attained in so short a space was almost entirely due to the enterprise of the family of El Ḥág Munaym, and it is therefore important to know who they were:—

- El Ḥág Munaym
  - Ismá'íl
    - Ibráhím
    - Muḥammad el Sheikh
      - Ismá'íl
        - Muḥammad el Sheikh
        - Aḥmad
        - Yasín
        - Yūsef
    - Gidía = El Melíḥ
      - Aḥmad
      - Ibráhím Bey
  - Mekki
    - El Melíḥ (= Gidía)
  - Mekín
    - El Bekri
      - Sálim

Ismá'íl succeeded his father El Ḥág Munaym, and after the conquest of Kordofán by the Turks was maintained as "náẓir" of the 'Asákir in Kordofán, while his brother Mekki, and later Mekki's son El Melíḥ, acted as head sheikh of the Ḥamar 'Asákir in Dárfūr (the boundary between the two countries at that time being Gebel Ba'ashóm[1]). Ismá'íl resided at Firsháḥa and proved the best and most powerful ruler the tribe ever had, a bold fighter, a just judge, and a capable and generous administrator[2]. He was for some time kept in prison by the Turks for refusing to furnish lists of the wealth in kind possessed by his tribe, but as the removal of his strong hand from the tribe caused more trouble than advantage, he was afterwards released and restored to power.

As being large camel owners the Ḥamar were frequently requisitioned by the Turks for transport purposes, and, in

[1] See p. 21, note 1.

[2] See Petherick, *Upper Egypt...*, Chap. XIX.

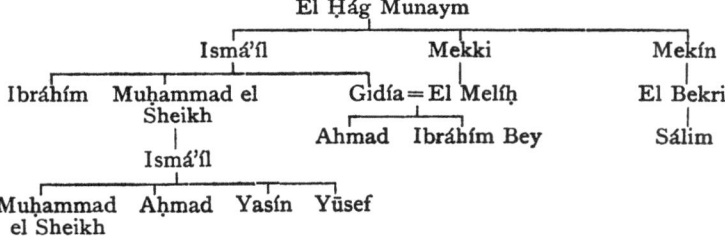

addition, to guard the Dárfūr frontier: in return they were given a free hand to raise their tribute by sending looting expeditions to Dárfūr, and were in fact encouraged and even assisted in these raids[1]. It was they too who late in the "Turkía" undertook the contract for the work involved in laying the telegraph line from El Obeid to El Fásher[2].

Petherick in 1847 estimated that the Ḥamar could mount 2000 men, most of them in mail shirts and helmets[3]. Pallme describes the Ḥamar as "one of the most amiable class of people in this province" and says "I never heard of their having ill-treated or robbed any stranger, much less of their having committed murder[4]." One can only remark that they have now degenerated into a dirty drunken community of thievish habits. In fact by 1876 Ensor had heard of them as "the most warlike and thievish of all the tribes in Dárfūr," and himself found them "an ill bred and surly lot of fellows." He also says of them "the Hamar are the richest of all the nomads in this part of Africa, far exceeding in number the nomad portion of the Kabbabbeesh, and almost equally [equalling?] the whole of that tribe including the settlers on the banks of the Nile." Most of their women were "of the semi- or full negro type, more or less pronounced. The Hamr keep their thoroughbred Arab wives at home in seclusion; they have not many of them, and they prize them accordingly...To be a Hamr wife is a lot envied by many of the women of other tribes[5]."

In 1874 the Turks annexed Dárfūr, and Ibráhím the son and successor of Ismá'íl now became "náẓir" of the 'Asákir in Kordofán and Dárfūr: the Deḳáḳim division, however, were not under his authority: they claim to have been independent of the 'Asákir since before the days of El Ḥág Munaym. The "náẓir" Ibráhím was succeeded by his nephew Aḥmad el Melíḥ, son of

[1] See Pallme, p. 143.

[2] See Ensor, p. 114.

[3] See Petherick, *Upper Egypt...*, Chap. XIX.

[4] See Pallme, p. 114.

[5] See Ensor, p. 86.

Ensor in 1876 found great numbers of Ḥamar at Um Badr. He mentions that just before the annexation of Dárfūr (1874) they attacked Munzinger Pasha and drove him from Um Badr (see Ensor, Chap. IX).

the old sheikh of the Ḥamar 'Asákir in Dárfūr before the conquest of that country; and Aḥmad was succeeded by his brother Ibráhím Bey el Melíḥ, who owed his title of Bey to the Turkish government.

In Ismá'íl Pasha 'Ayūb's time a further subdivision took place: 'Abd el Raḥím Bey abu Duḳl at the head of the Gharaysía section which had represented a third part of the Deḳáḳím separated himself from the control of the Deḳáḳím sheikh Ḥammad Bey Fatín and has remained independent. Thus at the outbreak of the "Mahdía" Ibráhím Bey was "náẓir" of the 'Asákir; Ḥammad Bey Fatín in the west ruled the Deḳáḳím, and Abu Duḳl the Gharaysía. All three became Dervish "amírs": the first named fell under the Khalífa's displeasure towards the end of the "Mahdía" and was thrown into prison: he died four or five years after the reoccupation of the country. Ḥammad Bey died about 1905. Abu Duḳl is still alive and "náẓir" of his people.

During the Dervish days the Ḥamar lost all their wealth and were more than decimated in numbers. To add to their woes, as soon as the power of the Khalífa was broken, their old foes the Kabábísh carried off most of the camels remaining to them, and as a result the camels of the Ḥamar at the present day are an almost negligible quantity. Their population has again increased but is practically all sedentary[1], and only concerned with cultivation, gum picking, drinking, and quarrelling.

They have large areas of cultivation and gum forests round Rihaywa (the birth-place of the present "náẓir" of the 'Asákir section, Ismá'íl Muḥammad el Sheikh, nephew of the Ibráhím wad Ismá'íl mentioned above), but most of them are further west round Nahūd and Fóga.

They cannot yet realize that "the glory is departed," and that the whole of the country over which they roamed as nomads in the palmy days of Ismá'íl wad el Ḥág Munaym and his son does not belong to them.

The Dár Ḥamar of the present is an almost waterless area of sandy steppes covered with bush. The water supply of the population, excepting a few isolated wells, e.g. at Nahūd, El

[1] The Gihaysát section who are reckoned Ḥamar are really by descent Shenábla. They are nomads and own many camels.

Oḍaya, and Um Bel, is from the baobab trees that they use as reservoirs. Their herds depend chiefly on wild melons. Unfortunately for them their decadence as a tribe has synchronized with a disappearance of their chief watering places:—Fóga once the site of many hundred good wells, and a large garrison town and "mudíría," is now dry in winter and summer; and Um Badr, where Ensor in March 1876 found 500 wells with 10,000 camels watering daily, and of which he said "just before the rains again begin to fall there is sometimes not more than sufficient water for a thousand camels to drink per day[1]," is now entirely dry in summer and winter, and in a bad year is not even flooded in the rainy season.

At present Ismá'íl Muḥammed el Sheikh is sheikh of the Ḥamar 'Asákir, Ḥammad Bey Fatín's son Abu Gelūf of the Deḳáḳim proper, and 'Abd el Raḥím Bey "Abu Duḳl" of the Gharaysía: the two latter are related as follows:—

Abu Ruba
|
Ḥámid
|
'Ísa
|
Yūnis
|
Náil
|
(1) a Ḥamar woman = Sálim abu Duḳl = (2) a Felláta woman

Ḥammad Bey = El Tóma (daughter of the Ḥamar woman) — Abu Gelūf (their son)

'Abd el Raḥím Bey "Abu Duḳl" (son of the Felláta woman)

[1] See Ensor, pp. 80 and 134.

In Northern Kordofán the alterations that are taking place in the underground water supply are remarkable (see notes on pp. 28 and 98). The general tendency is to a decrease in the water supply at the old watering places: at the same time fresh sites are now and then discovered (e.g. at El Gibaylát, see p. 100). This phenomenon throughout Kordofán is noticed by Escayrac de Lauture in his *Le Désert et Le Soudan*. He was convinced by the unanimous testimony of the people that in many places it was necessary of late years to dig three or four times as deep for water as it was in the time of previous generations. It is now over fifty years since Escayrac de Lauture wrote and yet the same phenomenon is still noticeable: e.g. it is an acknowledged fact that at Shershár the water level is very considerably lower than it was so recently as the days of the Mahdi.

De Lauture says (p. 67), "Je suppose, toutefois, que ces changements de niveau et de nature sont dus à l'action violente des courants souterrains se mouvant sur des

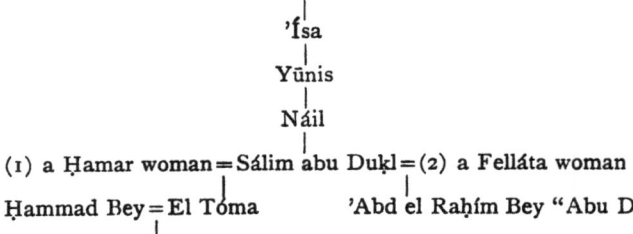

Plate XII

"(*back row, left to right*) 'náẓirs' of Ḥamar (Gharaysía, 'Asákir, and Deḳaḳím), and ''omda' of Megánín. (*front row*) 'náẓirs' of Kabábísh, Kága and Katūl, Kága el Surrūg, and Kawáhla, 1909."

"Abu Duḳl" was made a Bimbashi by Gordon Pásha and a Bey by 'Abd el Ḳádir Pásha. When the Sudan was abandoned he joined the Dervishes and was employed as an "amír" round Kassala. After the defeat of Aḥmad Faḍíl he surrendered and served against the Khalífa. The 'Asákir, Deḳáḳím and Gharaysía are mixed together to a great extent but, generally speaking, the 'Asákir own all the country lying west of a line drawn through Gebels Um Shirsh and El Ba'ashóm and continuing through Ghallabarra and Gareban, and also the districts of Shallóta, El Kul, and parts of Sheḳ el Dūd, El Sa'áta, Ḥuoi, and Firsháḥa. The Deḳaḳím and Gharaysía claim the country lying east of the line mentioned above as far as El Nahūd and El Oḍaya, and also Sheḳ el Ḥáfiẓa and parts of the districts of Shallóta etc. (excepting Firsháḥa).

The main subdivisions of the tribe are as follows:—

1. El 'Asákira
    - A. El Ghishímát
        - 1. Awlád Gamí'a
            - (*a*) Awlád Ma'ayz
            - (*b*) El Shenábír
            - (*c*) El Gharára
            - (*d*) El Merázíg
        - 2. El Sidayrát
        - 3. Awlád Ma'áli
        - 4. Awlád Ghási
        - 5. Awlád 'Ali
    - B. Beni Badr
        - 1. El Merámra[1]
            - (*a*) El Miláḥa
        - 2. El Sa'adát
            - (*a*) Awlád Ghanūm
            - (*b*) Maḥalḥil
            - (*c*) Nás Zaýd
            - (*d*) Nás el Ṣul
            - (*e*) Nás Maṭlūb

grandes pentes, altérant profondément les couches qu'ils traversent, et se frayant à chaque instant des routes nouvelles, en entamant surtout les dépôts salins, qui offrent à leur énergique action une moindre résistance."

[1] Dár Ḥámid in origin.

C. El Khamsát
  1. El Mayámín
    (a) Awlád Ṣubūḥ
    (b) El Bedránía
  2. El Menádír
  3. El Gihaysát[1]
    (a) Um Haysin
    (b) Awlád Ḍiáb
    (c) Abu Ḍán
    (d) Meraḥíl
    (e) Nás Muamar
  4. El Menána
  5. El Khayraysát

D. El Tarádát
  1. El Dáma'i
    (a) El Ṣubayḥát
      (1) Nás Sóderi
    (b) El Gelada
    (c) El Tayaysa
      (1) Awlád 'Ali
      (2) El Gawábra
      (3) El Nowara
      (4) El Abbásía
    (d) El Fawáḍil
    (e) El Ghanaymía[2]
      (1) Nás abu Gebel
      (2) Nás 'Ali
      (3) Nás Belál
      (4) Nás Gumū'a
    (f) El Noaygát
    (g) Awlád Khaḍra
    (h) El 'Abádía
      (1) Nás abu Guma'a
      (2) El Gerayni

2. El Deḳáḳím
  A. El Wáilía[3]
    1. Nás Házil
    2. Nás el Ḥurr
    3. Nás abu Ḥamaydán

[1] The Gihaysát were originally Shenábla of the 'Awámir section but split away from that tribe and joined the Ḥamar.

[2] Gawáma'a by origin.

[3] Alleged to be originally related to the Kawáhla.

4. Nás Ḥamír
5. Nás Ḥarūsh
6. Nás Raḥa
7. Nás abu 'Awín
8. Abu Gemanín

B. Nás abu Zayd

1. Nás Sári

(*a*) Nás Gabr
(*b*) Awlád Ṣubayḥ

2. Nás 'Abd el Salám
3. Nás Faraḳalla
4. Nás abu Tenu

C. El Sha'ibát

D. Awlád Shadwán

E. Awlád 'Ámir

F. Awlád Bur'ás

G. Awlád Siháia

1. Nás el Ṣód
2. Nás Feraywa
3. Nás Ribayḥ
4. Nás abu Na'amir
5. Nás Musellam
6. Nás Khala

H. El Gema'anía

J. El Gharaga

3. El Gharaysía

A. El Ḥadáḥda

1. Awlád Ḥammád
2. Awlád Um Buṭnayn
3. El Dubūba
4. Awlád Sheríf
5. Awlád Nimr
6. El Bará'ím

B. Awlád Shighán

1. Nás Ismá'íl
2. Um Kisayba
3. Nás Nuṣr
4. Nás abu Merákiḥ
5. Nás Muḥammad
6. El Ḥomrán

C. Awlád Guayd

1. Nás abu Ḥigaywa
2. Nás Turfa
3. Awlád 'Ádi
4. El Habábísh
5. Nás Murmi
6. El Sa'adía
7. Awlád Gábir
8. Nás Saḥáríf

D. El Ṣubaḥa[1]

[1] El Ṣubaḥa are not Ḥamar by race at all, but are subject to them.

CHAPTER XIII

THE MÍMA

THE Míma probably represent one of the old half Arab and half black tribes of the Western Sudan, and those in Kordofán are merely a branch of the main tribe.

Needless to say they claim an exalted Arab descent, and even speak of the third Khalífa of Islam as their progenitor.

So early as the eleventh century the state of Ghána was at war with a people called Míma, and three hundred years later Timbuktu was "peopled chiefly by natives of Míma[1]." These Míma were in all probability the ancestors of the tribe now bearing the same name.

In the reign of Muḥammad Faḍl, Sultan of Dárfūr, when Muḥammad el Tunísi visited that country, the Míma were still under a Sultan who paid tribute to Dárfūr but was semi-independent: the Zagháwa, Dágu, Tungur, etc. were in similar case.

The Míma have shewn themselves in later days a turbulent unsettled tribe. Soon after Gordon's appointment as Governor-General of the Sudan they and the Khawábír revolted, and though quelled remained disaffected[2]. Again in 1883, after the outbreak of the "Mahdía," they ejected their Sultan Da'ūd, appointed another, and with their old friends the Khawábír, broke into rebellion. 'Omar Darho was sent against them by Slatin Bey and defeated them, and posts were established at Fáfa and Wūda in their country; but before the year was out they had again rebelled and annihilated 'Omar Darho and his men at Wūda. Further efforts to subdue them proved abortive and for the rest of the "Mahdía" they were fervent Dervishes.

[1] See Cooley, p. 86.

[2] See Slatin, Chaps. 2, 7, and 9.

At present the bulk of the tribe is in Dárfūr, but there are a number of them scattered in Upper Egypt and Dongola[1]. In Kordofán some are to be found round El Rahad and Teḳali among the Ghodiát: others again are to be found settled rather farther north among the Dár Ḥámid tribes, the Awlád Murg Gawáma'a, the Baza'a, and the Zagháwa: the latter tribes have in each case granted the Míma land to cultivate on condition of the payment of small dues.

The Kordofán Míma say that the Míma in the west migrated thither from North Africa direct[2]—but that many other Míma came to Kordofán *via* the Nile under one called El Ḥág Mūsa, and were granted lands and wives by the Gawáma'a and Dár Ḥámid.

They also say that their tribe is a branch of the 'Amuía (singular 'Amáwi), and that they called themselves Míma after the letter *mím*, which by its shape typifies solidarity and cohesion.

[1] They also allege there are Míma in abundance at Mekka. The "Dongola nisba" connects them with the Beni Tha'áliba of the Ḥegáz.

[2] They may possibly have come with the Tungur.

CHAPTER XIV

THE KENÁNA

THE name of Kenána is familiar as that of one of the greatest and most famous tribes of Arabia, for not only were they a numerous and powerful community, but the tribe of Ḳuraysh itself was but a branch of them.

The tribe of Kenána probably came into being some 100 years after the beginning of the Christian Era, and took up its abode in the Ḥegáz round the site of Mekka and in Yemen.

In these early days its members were worshippers of 'Ozza. Little is known of their early history, but we hear of them as defeating the Ḥimyarites of Yemen between 270 and 272 A.D. In 580 A.D. began the internecine wars known as "El Figár" between the Kenána and cognate tribes on the one hand, and the Beni Ḥawázin on the other.

At the rise of Muḥammad, Islam received no support from Kenána and Ḳuraysh, and it was they who in 625 A.D. under Abu Sofián defeated the prophet at Ohod.

Five years later 'Ozza's image was broken down by Khálid ibn Wálid, and the Kenána submitted to Muḥammad after the capture of Mekka.

Their allegiance to Islam, tardy as it had been, was not strong, for they revolted during the Khalífate of Abu Bukr[1]. When Africa was invaded great numbers of the tribe migrated thither, while others stayed in Arabia, where their descendants

[1] See Caussin de Perceval, Vol. 1, pp. 193 to 241.

are still to be found scattered over the northern and central districts, and more especially in the Ḥegáz[1].

In 1249 the Kenána formed the garrison of Damietta and greatly distinguished themselves in defending that town against the attacks of Louis IX's crusaders[2].

A part of the Kenána in time pressed southwards through Egypt, and others westward as far as Morocco.

Maḳrízi (fl. 1400 A.D.) mentions many Kenána settled round Saḳia Kolta in his day and offshoots of them scattered elsewhere in Egypt. They were divided into three sections, viz. Leïth, Damra, and Feras[3].

As regards those who had moved westwards from Egypt, according to Leo Africanus they had by the beginning of the sixteenth century become subject to the kingdom of Fez[4].

Marmol, writing a little later, mentions that they could raise over 23,000 armed men in Morocco.

It was probably the Kenána settled in Egypt whose descendants are generally met with in the Sudan.

The tradition of the Kenána in Kordofán is to the effect that their ancestor was El Sayyid Aḥmad Zubbad el Baḥr, a "feḳír" of Mekka, descended from Ḥamza the youngest son of the prophet's grandfather 'Abd el Muṭṭalib. After his death one of his sons, Manṣūr, quarrelled with the other sons as to the succession and left Mekka for Egypt with his younger brother 'Abdulláhi. Hence he was nicknamed "El Ḥardán" (one who sulks and isolates himself).

From Egypt Manṣūr passed up the Nile to the Sudan. The Gamu'ía (of Ga'alíín extraction) and the Maḥass of Dongola each provided him with a wife and he begot six sons, Yasín, 'Ali abu el Fahra, Ḥammad Aṣla'a, Sowár, Idrís Serág, and 'Alwán. These were the forefathers of the sections of Kenána now in the Sudan, excepting the Da'ūdía, who are descended from 'Abdulláhi.

[1] E.g. see Palgrave, Vol. I, Ch. IX, p. 459. Note that Ibn Baṭūṭa (fl. 1353) when he crossed from Suákin to Yemen found a Kenáni Sultan at the port of Hali and Kenána and Beni Ḥarám inhabiting the neighbourhood. (Vol. II, pp. 162 et seq.)

[2] See Lane Poole, *History of Egypt*, p. 232.

[3] See Quatremère, Vol. II.

[4] See Leo, Bk I, p. 146.

The Serágáb section of the Kabábísh are also said to be descended from Idrís Serág[1], and indeed there are probably many other claimants to Kenána parentage scattered among the various tribes.

The earliest Kenána arrivals in the Sudan are said to have settled finally at Gebel Kurun, south of Teḳali, and subsequently to have come into conflict with a party of Kawáhla[2] settled in the neighbourhood, and to have driven them to the south.

According to the Kenána "nisba" Manṣūr lived 16 generations ago and 17 generations after 'Abd el Muṭṭalib. This total of 33 generations, if the generation be reckoned at 40 years, gives a total of 1320—i.e., approximately the number of years that have passed since the time of 'Abd el Muṭṭalib. The Kenána "nisba" therefore is not necessarily so incredible as the majority of those produced by other tribes. It may then be supposed that the truth is that some Kenána, following the example set by their kinsmen in previous centuries, emigrated from Arabia into Egypt about the beginning of the fourteenth century and pushed their way up the river as far as Dongola, and there temporarily settled and intermarried, and later split into various sections, of whom a party went south to Kurun, and a part eventually attached themselves to the Kabábísh.

The bulk of the tribe at present is on the east side of the White Nile, and it is not improbable that in addition to the influxes that occurred at various times from the north some Kenána have crossed to Africa by the straits of Báb el Mandeb, for the Arab forces that were mustered round Sennár under 'Abdulla el Kerináni and 'Amára Dunkas about 1500 A.D.[3], and that coalesced with the Fung and adopted to some extent their name, are said to have included Kenána and other tribes, who had fled from Arabia about 750 A.D., as a result of the struggle between the Beni Ommayya and the Beni 'Abbás, and gradually filtered through Abyssinia to the vicinity of Sennár[4]. Others may have crossed the Red Sea to Africa at various dates from very early to most recent times.

[1] See Chapter XV, on the Kabábísh.
[2] See Chapter XVI, on the Kawáhla.
[3] See Chapter I, and Appendix 2.
[4] See Na'ūm Bey Shuḳayr.

The main subdivisions of the Kenána in the Sudan, as known to those in Kordofán, are as follows:—

A. El Sowáráb[1]
  1. Awlád Yasín*[2]
  2. El Zoayda
  3. El Isayba'a*

B. El Serágía[3]
  1. Awlád Dáli[4]
  2. Um Belál
  3. Awlád Roaya
  4. El Zaydán
  5. El Námia*
  6. El Habaylía*
  7. Abu Riḥán*
  8. El Koatil*
  9. El Gilayráb*
  10. El Bayláb*

C. El Aṣála'a[5]
  1. Awlád Guberán*
  2. Awlád Ḥuzíl*
  3. El Su'ūdía*
  4. El 'Amaría*
  5. Awlád Rishayd*

D. El Da'ūdía* (including El Monáṣir, who again include Nás Ḥamdūk)

E. El Fahría*[6]

F. El 'Alowna*[7]

Those marked with an asterisk are mainly inhabitants of the Gezíra: the others and certain of the Asála'a are in Kordofán; but no hard and fast line can be drawn.

During the Turkish days, as now, part of the tribe appears to have been in Sennár and part near Abu Ḥaráz in Kordofán[8]. That the latter were not very numerous is shewn by the fact that

[1] I.e. descendants of Sowár ibn Manṣūr.

[2] I.e. descendants of Yasín ibn Manṣūr. There are a few Sowáráb at Teḳali in addition to those mentioned.

[3] I.e. descendants of Idrís Serág ibn Manṣūr.

[4] Some Awlád Dáli live at Teḳali; others are with the main body of Kenána in Kordofán.

[5] I.e. descendants of Ḥammad Aṣla'a.

[6] I.e. descendants of 'Ali abu el Fahra.

[7] I.e. descendants of 'Alwán.

[8] Sir C. Wilson speaks of Kenána having been in Sennár in 1821, and of Kenána 60 years later S.W. of Abu Ḥaráz.

previous to 1881 their nominal tribute was £293 odd, and that it was then reduced by £200[1].

Before the Mahdi had gained his first successes in open war, and while he was still at Abba Island in 1881, he was joined by many Kenána, and it was with a retinue of them that he set out for "Gebel Mása" (as he was pleased to call Gebel Gedír). Many more Kenána joined him there, and with their aid he defeated the force under Rashíd Bey[2].

In 1885 when the "amír" Mūsa wad Ḥelu met the British advance guard at Abu Ṭelayḥ ("Abu Klea"), the bulk of his force was composed of Kenána, Berbers, Ga'aliín, and Deghaym. The Kenána and Deghaym were almost annihilated in this battle[3]; but they have to some extent recuperated since, and those in Kordofán certainly own no inconsiderable herds of cattle between Dilling and Abu Ḥaráz. That the bulk of the tribe is to be found on the east side of the Nile has already been mentioned.

[1] See Stewart's Report.

[2] See Slatin, Bk I, Ch. IV.

[3] See Slatin, Bk II, Ch. X.

CHAPTER XV

THE KABÁBÍSH[1]

THE Kabábísh are not a homogeneous tribe in the sense that they are descended within comparatively modern times from any one single family and that there is any definite distinctive racial difference between them and all other tribes in the country—it will be made clear that such is not the case—but at the same time the several elements of which the tribe is compounded, if considered as a whole, will be found to be less contaminated with non-Arab blood than are those of any other Sudan-Arab tribe to which a single name is now applied[2]. The

[1] Part of the matter contained in this Chapter appeared as an article in Vol. XL of the Royal Anthrop. Instit. 1910.

[2] Mr Parkyns says, "the Kababish date their origin from the Howàra, a tribe of Upper Egypt said to be of Mógrebín extraction, and who fled from Tunis, being driven thence by Abou Zeyd-el-Hillaly." This tradition is reproduced by Petherick and Sir C. W. Wilson on the authority of Mr Parkyns. Now the Howára are a well-known Berber tribe whose prolonged struggles with the invading Arabs in the seventh and subsequent centuries are recounted by Arab historians, and there is no doubt that the present Howáwír represent these Howára (see chapter on the Howáwír).

The Howáwír, at present in Dongola, though neighbours of the Kabábísh, are now separate from them; but since in Mr Parkyns's time the Howáwír (whom Sir C. W. Wilson, by the way, speaks of as being "of pure Arab blood") were only counted a section of Kabábísh, though under a separate chief, it seems most probable that the tradition of the descent of the Kabábísh from the Howára either originated from one of these Howáwír who was anxious to glorify his own people in the eyes of Mr Parkyns, or at least referred exclusively to them. It is quite certain, at any rate, that any tradition which gives a single origin to the whole of the Kabábísh must necessarily be inaccurate.

The mention of Abu Zayd el Hiláli is of no weight, since with the Arabs of Kordofán almost any important event that occurred in the dim past is in some way

fact is sufficiently accounted for when one remembers that they are desert nomads as their fathers and their fathers' fathers were for generation after generation both since the Arab conquest of Northern Africa and in the centuries that preceded it, and the nomad has changed but little since the days when Jacob watered the flocks of Laban at Haran.

At present the following are the subdivisions of the Kabábísh in Kordofán[1]:—

A. El Nūráb

1. El Ribayḳát
   (a) El Ayáyíd
   (b) El Deraywáb
   (c) El Ferūḥáb
   (d) El Aḥaymeráb
   (e) El Báṭáb
   (f) Um Sirayḥ
2. Dár Kabír
3. Dár Um Bakhīt
4. Awlád el Kír
5. El Neḳáda
6. Dár Sa'íd

or other connected with the names of this wholly or half mythical and altogether extraordinary hero and his Hilála (see Chapter II, and Appendix 3).

Sir C. W. Wilson hazarded a guess that the Kabábísh were the ancient Zingáni (referred to by Leo Africanus) whose descendants in the desert of Goran (Bayūda desert) were constantly at war with the king of Nubia. "May not this reference," he says, "be to the Kabábísh not then arabicized. The view that the Kababish are not Arabs is supported by the fact that they say the Kawahleh, one of their clans, is not Kababish but was affiliated to them many years ago. Kawahleh is a name of Arab formation and Burckhardt......mentions them as a distinct tribe....... It seems not unlikely that the Kababish received Arab rulers, like the Ababdeh, after their arrival in the Sudan." Sir C. W. Wilson's theory cannot be supported: in the first place we have seen how confusion arose from the Berber affinities of the Howáwír and their supposed connection with the Kabábísh, and in the second it is admitted that the Kawáhla are not properly Kabábísh (see Chapter XVI, on the Kawáhla) but it is the Kawáhla who are more nearly related to the 'Abábda in spite of the Arab formation of their name: thus the racial difference between the Kabábísh and the Kawáhla lies not in the fact that the latter are pure Arabs and the former not so to the same extent, but in the converse proposition. That the Kabábísh probably contain Berber and Bíja elements is not denied; but the Arab predominates.

[1] The names bracketed together belong to sections that are either closely allied by race or subject to the section which in each case is placed at the head of the bracket. It is not always easy now to draw a hard and fast line between the bonds that have been formed by consanguinity on the one hand and by force of arms on the other.

7. El Kibbaysháb
    (*a*) Nás wad Yūsef
    (*b*) El Mesá'íd
    (*c*) Nás wad Shet·ḥán
    (*d*) Nás wad Duḳushayn
8. Awlád 'Awaḍ el Síd
9. El Howáráb
    (*a*) Awlád Dábo
    (*b*) Awlád 'Ali
    (*c*) El Rahūda
10. Awlád Núáí

B. Awlád Ḥowál
1. Dár Ḥámid
2. Dár Maḥmūd

C. Awlád 'Ón
1. El Labábís
2. El Berásha
3. El Ḳurūnáb
4. Dár el Ḥág
5. El Tamásíḥ
6. El Likayritáb

D. Awlád Ṭerayf
1. El Merayḳát
2. El Ísháb
3. El 'Alowna
4. El Gerámda

E. El Ghilayán

F. El Ṭowál

G. El 'Awáída
1. El 'Awáída el Zurruḳ
    (*a*) Nás Walad Raḥma
    (*b*) Nás Walad Maḳbūl
    (*c*) Nás Walad el Hiláli
    (*d*) Nás Walad Rábiḥ
    (*e*) Nás Walad el Bashír
    (*f*) Nás Walad el Ní'ama
2. El 'Awáída el Bayyiḍ
    (*a*) El Bisháráb
    (*b*) El 'Adlánáb
    (*c*) El Sunūnáb

H. El 'Aṭawía
1. El Fárisáb
2. El Baḳaráb

3. Dár 'Ali
    (*a*) Dár Sulaymán
4. El Manūfaláb
5. El Kufár
6. El Shigayáb

J. Awlád 'Uḳba

1. El Dariáb
2. Dár 'Ali
3. El Shilaywáb
4. El Ḥámdáb
5. Dár 'Omar
6. Dár abu Nisay'a
7. El Karásób
8. El Shenáshím
9. Dár Muḥammad
10. El Sa'aduláb, or Sa'adía

K. El Berára

1. Um Ghaybish
2. Nás Atayrinna
3. El 'Aṣayfír
4. Nás wad Maṭar
5. Dár 'Ali
6. El Zerágni

L. El Serágáb

1. Dar Sa'ad
2. El Ganádba
3. El Derimía
4. El Mahaláb
5. Nás wad el Fezári
6. El Ghegayría
7. El Shukhūnáb

M. El Ruwáḥla

1. Dár abu Ginna
2. Dár Gamí'a
3. El Nishába
4. El Mesáráb
5. El Gegádíl
6. El 'Awáídáb

N. El Ḥammádáb

1. El Rahūdáb
2. El Teraykát
3. El Bishára

O. Awlád Sulaymán
1. El Ghanáwáb
2. Dár Musa'ad
3. El Abbátín
4. Awlád Ḥamdulla
P. El Bashír

The following are the main subdivisions of the Kabábísh in Dongola:—

Um Matū[1]	El Aḥaymeráb
El Meraysáb	El Bilaylát
El Gungonáb	Dár Bashūt
El 'Awáída	El Deládím
El Bayūdáb	Dár Ḥámid

Now many changes in the composition of the tribe have befallen in the last two centuries:—sections or subsections have broken away from it or joined it, permanently or temporarily, and it is consequently difficult to give any exact or coherent account of the history of the tribe, and many confusions are apt to arise.

Two hundred years ago the very name "Kabábísh" may not yet have been assumed. The Kabábísh themselves if asked will often say they had an ancestor called Kabsh: this person occasionally appears in "nisbas," generally as son of Afzár son of Dhubián son of 'Abdulla el Guhani. More frequently Kabsh does not appear in the "nisbas" at all. He has no doubt been simply invented as a convenient ancestral figure-head with a view to proving the racial unity of the tribe. Nothing further is ever related of him, nor is insistence laid upon his having ever existed. There is little doubt I think that (as Mr Parkyns says) "Kabábísh" is simply derived from "Kabsh," i.e. "a male sheep": the tribe was once perhaps a weak and poor community and owned no great herds of camels as they do at present, and may have been given their name slightingly at first[2].

[1] The Um Matū are said to be closely related to the Serágáb. They are the paramount section in Dongola. The other Dongola-Kabábísh tribes are said to be considerably mixed in blood with the various ancient riverain tribes.

[2] Little importance need be given to Müller's statement in his edition of *Claudius Ptolemaeus* that the Gapachi mentioned as living beyond Meroe are the present Kabábísh.

The nomenclature of one or two Arabian tribes may be adduced perhaps as supplementary evidence of the derivation of "Kabábísh" from Kabsh if such be needed: e.g. the name Ma'áza would seem to be derived on similar lines from ma'az (goats), and 'Aneza is suggestive of 'anz, another word for a goat.

Tribes that even a few years ago fell under the denomination of Kabábísh are now either separate or included in other tribes, and groups of families and individuals that were once reckoned part of other tribes are now to be found calling themselves Kabábísh[1].

As an instance of this, in the list of the subdivisions of the tribe given in 1850 by Mr Parkyns, there appear among others the names of the following:—

Aḥámda ("Lahamdy"), Guhayna ("Jeheyna"), Kawáhla ("Koahly"), Baṭáḥín, Shenábla, Geriát, and Ghazáya: of these the Aḥámda, the Geriát, the Kawáhla, the Baṭáḥín, and the Shenábla have now for years been entirely independent tribes, and it was no more than a portion of them that ever joined the Kabábísh. The Guhayna rejoined the independent Guhayna on the east of the Nile in 1909 and 1910, and the Ghazáya are counted a section of Kawáhla.

The looseness of the ties connecting this complex conglomeration—the Kabábísh—became most apparent in the Dervish days. The tribes that had long been living together as Kabábísh mostly remained firm and loyal with Ṣáliḥ Bey Faḍlulla. Those later adventitious recruits who had only attached themselves for the sake of protection and the advantage accruing from a participation in the rights and privileges of the Kabábísh as a rule broke away and joined the revolt. After its suppression, some of them—e.g. the Guhayna and Berára—returned to the ranks of the Kabábísh, and others, being strong enough to stand alone, remained permanently separate—e.g. the Kawáhla and Shenábla.

But on the other hand it must not be supposed that the numerous tribes alluded to above as distinct from one another differ radically in their composition: they do not. The fact of importance is that the numerous points of connection between these communities of different names, and also the points in which they differ from one another, equally forbid one

[1] Escayrac de Lauture gives the following as the subdivisions of the Kabábísh:— Nūráb, Ghilayán, 'Aṭawía, Kibbaysháb, Berára, "Gheiat," Amer, Awlád 'Uḳba, Um Matū, Serágáb, Shenábla, "Fazala" [Fezára?], Ruwáḥla, Sawálma, Ghazáya, "Hedouza," "Refaia," "Debaïna," Awlád Abu Róf [i.e. Rufá'a under the Abu Róf family], Howáráb.

to deal with the past history of the Kabábísh as though the Kabábísh formed an entirely distinct racial entity. In consequence it is advisable to commence by treating of certain sections separately.

Kordofán traditions unanimously point to the Awlád 'Uḳba as being the original Kabábísh or the foundation upon which the present tribal structure has been built. I will try then to explain first the origin of the Awlád 'Uḳba so far as possible.

Investigation has been somewhat obscured by the fact that there were several *Aṣḥáb* of the name of 'Uḳba, e.g. 'Uḳba ibn 'Ámir, 'Uḳba ibn 'Othmán, and 'Uḳba ibn Wahháb; and in consequence it has generally been considered polite to say that the Awlád 'Uḳba are descended from one of the above—preferably the first mentioned, who was a Guhani and became governor of Egypt in A.D. 665. Often they are said to be descended from an "'Uḳba ibn Yásir, governor of Egypt and *Ṣáḥib* of the Prophet"; but in whatever form the story may appear there is little to support it.

Whether their ancestor was governor of Egypt or not it is practically certain that the Awlád 'Uḳba did reside for some time in Northern Africa.

All accounts to-day unite in saying that of the Awlád 'Uḳba who crossed into Egypt from Arabia a large portion passed through Tripoli and eventually drifted into the ranks of the Felláta in West Africa; this branch of the Awlád 'Uḳba are said to be known nowadays as "Nás el Sheikh 'Omar el Fúṭa" and "Nás el Sheikh 'Othmán ibn Fóḍia[1]." Others of the tribe are said to have stayed in Egypt and to be known there as "Awlád 'Ali[2]"; while a third portion settled in the Syrian desert near 'Aḳaba. This, I think, is quite sufficient to identify the Awlád 'Uḳba now in Kordofán as being connected with those Beni 'Uḳba whom Dr Wallin met near 'Aḳaba in 1848.

Dr Wallin says of these people that they claimed to have

[1] See note 3, p. 106.

[2] There is a powerful camel-owning tribe of nomad Arabs called Awlád 'Ali between Cairo and the Siwah oasis. They revolted in the first half of last century and were suppressed. See Junker, p. 33. At the present day the Awlád 'Ali are the chief tribe in the Libyan desert. Their subdivisions are given by Klippel (q.v. p. 10).

"Kabábísh (Awlád 'Uḳba) sheikhs at Um Inderába, 1911."

once been a very large tribe owning the country between the Syrian desert and Dámá, and that they still held the important seaport of Muweilaḥ, and were accustomed to escort pilgrims bound for the holy cities as far as their border at Ẓoba They also told Dr Wallin that they had early in the history of Islam been divided into Musálima and Beni 'Amr and that these two sections quarrelled and the former expelled the latter from Muweilaḥ and forced them to join the Hegáyá, with whom they still resided near Ṭafíla. They added that numbers of their tribe had passed over into N. Africa and that others had mixed with the Egyptian Felláḥín.

Probing further into the descent of these Beni 'Uḳba, Dr Wallin quotes numerous Arabic authorities whose evidence further strengthens the assumption of connection between the two tribes whom it is my object to identify: the author of *al 'Ibar* corroborates the author of *al Mesáliku-l-Abṣár* in saying that the Beni 'Uḳba are bound to secure the road between Egypt and Medína, and adds "In Afríkía in the West there are some of them as well as in the neighbourhood of Ṭerábulūs" (Tripoli). The same authors both mention "the Beni Wáṣil whose abodes are in Egypt as being a branch of the Beni 'Uḳba son of Moghraba, son of Gudhám of the Ḳaḥṭanía," and Dr Wallin also quotes El Ḳalḳashendi in support of the descent of the Beni 'Uḳba from Gudhám the Ḳaḥṭáni.

A word must be said here as to this Gudhám:—He and Lakhm are said by Abu el Fidá to have been the sons of 'Adí son of 'Amr son of 'Abd Shams Sabá son of Yashḥub son of Ya'arib son of Ḳaḥṭán the brother of Fáligh. Now Fáligh is of course the ancestor of the prophet Ibráhím and through him of Ismá'íl and thus of all the Must'arib Arabs including 'Adnán and the Prophet himself. Ḳaḥṭán, on the other hand, is known as the ancestor of the true "'Arab el 'Ariba." These latter lived at first in Southern Arabia but at some very early period many of their tribes (notably Ṭái) migrated north to the parts round Gebel Shómer, where they mixed with the Nejed tribes, and to a great extent became nomads.

The Ḳaḥṭánites of S. Arabia have a large amount of African blood in their veins from intermarriage with Abyssinians, Galla and other tribes on the African mainland; and probably the early Kaḥṭánites who, as we saw, displaced the Must'arib Arabs in the north had even more.

The Beni 'Uḳba then may roughly be said to be descendants of the Kaḥṭánite Arabs who came north and became fused with the impure Syro-Egyptian Must'arib stock (personified by Ismá'íl) who, in their turn, no doubt already contained a plenteous leaven of Kurds, Copts, Turcomans, Phoenicians, Armenians, etc., in their ranks. At what time the Beni 'Uḳba crossed into Egypt, and how long they have taken to reach their present home is difficult to say.

Marmol (c. 1520) calls the "Oulád Okba" a branch of Beni Hilál and estimates their military forces at 11,500 men in Algeria. They were also previously mentioned by Leo Africanus (c. 1495–1552) under the name "Hucben" as a branch of the same tribe and as being in the pay of the king of Tunis—"a rude and wilde people and in very deade estranged from al humanitie[1]."

So much for the Awlád 'Uḳba at present.

Now the Guhayna, as has been noted, do not now contribute at all to the composition of the Kabábísh, but since the Laḥáwiín section of Guhayna were reckoned Kabábísh till 1910 and their history illustrates well the general process that has been in force, they will be dealt with next.

There is no doubt of the identity of the Guhayna with the great western Arabian tribe of Guhayna. These Guhayna are also Kaḥṭánites, being a section of Ḳuḍa'a.

They are still a large tribe in the Ḥegáz mountains, and Burton says that they extend from the plains north of Yanbu' (which were granted them by the Prophet in 624) into the Sinaitic peninsula, and are a noble race and good fighters.

Mr C. M. Doughty also mentions them among the "strong free tribes" near Tayma, and speaks of a village about forty miles east of Khaybar where intermarriage with Guhayna and Ḥetaym had made the villagers lighter in colour of late years.

Guhayna were well represented among the tribes which flocked into Egypt, and Maḳrízi, early in the fifteenth century,

[1] See John Pory's translation of Leo, Brown's edition, Bk I, pp. 144 et seq.

mentions them among the six most numerous and potent tribes of Upper Egypt. They were established at this time at Manfalūt and El Siūt.

They are mentioned too by El Nuayri as taking part with the Fezára and others in the expedition of 647 A.D., and by Ibn Sa'íd as settled in great numbers between Syene (Assuwán) and Abyssinia. Again, it was Guhayna and Rabí'a who in 869 formed the main body of the Arab horde that invaded the Beja country and settled there and intermarried with the Beja and within a century were supplying their clans with sheikhs[1].

Great numbers of them are still living east of the Nile and many of these have immigrated within the last few years. Others are to be found in Bornu and Dárfūr. In this connection too one may call to mind the claim that is so extremely common, to be descended from "'Abdulla el Guhani[2]."

Until the last century the Guhayna formed no part of the Kabábísh, and they have never been more than temporary adherents. A sign of this fact is their branding their camels on the left side, whereas every one who reckons himself a true Kabbáshi by birth brands upon the right.

With regard to the 'Aṭawía (i.e. Beni 'Aṭía) I do not know of any direct evidence that they are connected with the Beni 'Aṭía of Arabia, but it seems very probable, since Beni 'Aṭía have long been a great tribe and are frequently mentioned together with Guhayna and the other tribes whose names recur again and again among or alongside of the Kabábísh[3].

The Beni 'Aṭía, like the Fezára, joined the invasion of N. Africa by the Beni Hilál, being at that time counted a branch of the great Hilála tribe of Athbeg. Ibn Khaldūn says they resided in the province of Constantine but became enfeebled and few in numbers. In spite of this, however, we

[1] E.g. the case of the 'Abábda. See Chapter XVI, on the Kawáhla.

[2] See Introduction.

[3] Klippel (p. 5) mentions 'Aṭawány (elsewhere called 'Aṭíát—both of which words are essentially the same as 'Aṭawía or Beni 'Aṭía) as a nomad tribe occupying the banks of the Nile near Thebes at present. Among others mention is at the same time made of Beni Wáṣil, Awlád Sulaymán, Awlád 'Óna, Guhayna, Shenábla, and Fezára, as represented among the nomads of Egypt. As all these names are found also in connection with the Kabábísh in this chapter, it is the clearer that many of the Kabábísh split away from Arab tribes of Egypt.

have the authority of M. Carette, the Algerian explorer, that in the middle of the last century there were some 3000 of them in Constantine among the Arab and Berber tribes and 500 or so in the Sahara.

Palgrave computed their numbers in Gebel Shomer at about 6000, and says they and Ḥarb infest the pilgrim road to Medína.

Mr Doughty mentions them also as subject to the "amír" of Hayil and living with Guhayna near Tayma and on the western borders of the Hayil dominions. Dr Wallin too found 'Aṭía in the plains of Al Ḥisma east of Muweilaḥ, and they claimed large territories round Tebúk (where Guhayna also lived in the times of the Arab historians).

The 'Aṭawía in Kordofán are always counted as closely related to the Kawáḥla, one of the largest tribes in the Sudan. Of the latter, who claim descent from Zubayr ibn el 'Awám el Ḳurayshi (the famous butcher cousin-german of the Prophet), the greater part were subject to the Kabábísh until the outbreak of the "Mahdía."

It may be noted that the Kabábísh 'Aṭawía have kinsfolk of the same name among the Rizayḳát Arabs of Dárfūr. These Rizayḳát are Baḳḳára and of the same descent as the majority of the Kordofán Baḳḳára. It may be a mere coincidence that the Kordofán Baḳḳára unanimously name as their common ancestor 'Aṭía, whom, if pressed, they somewhat perfunctorily connect with the inevitable 'Abdulla el Guhani; but in the course of years and in their movements from North Africa through the western kingdoms, they have forgotten all details of their history and origin, and merely remember a few names.

Perhaps it would be fantastic for no other reason than this to assume that they are connected with the Arabian Beni 'Aṭía: it is just possible however that the Beni 'Aṭía, after entering Egypt, divided their forces, some going on west through Tripoli and finally moving south till they became Baḳḳára in Kordofán and Dárfūr, and others staying awhile in Egypt and gradually drifting up the Nile till they joined the conglomeration of tribes that is now called Kabábísh.

Another well-known Arabian tribe that has certainly contributed largely to the formation of the Kabábísh, as of most of the camel-owning nomads of the Sudan, is Fezára.

Fezára are said by Arab historians to be among the descendants of that Dhubián (of the Ismá'ílitic tribe of Ḳays 'Aylán) who though in reality son of Baghídh of the tribe of Ghaṭafán, is quoted in the "nisbas" of the present as son of 'Abdulla el Guhani and therefore ancestor of so many Kordofán tribes.

In was in 627 A.D. that Fezára, Guhayna, and other tribes marched against Medína, and gave continuous trouble to the Prophet till their final subjugation. They mixed extensively with the Ḳaḥṭánites and colonized the eastern coast of Arabia when driven from Nejed.

Now the Fezára were in the eighteenth and nineteenth centuries one of the best-known tribes in Northern Kordofán, as travellers have testified, and until very recently the term Fezára was used by the Baḳḳára Arabs to denote any camel-owning nomads.

Whether the mentions of Fezára in books of travel of the last century referred to any separate tribe as they appear to do, or whether they are merely due to a misunderstanding, is not clear; nor is it very important to know. The latter view is more probable[1].

Mentions of the Fezára are by no means lacking in the Arab writers:—From El Nuayri we know that some of them took part in the expedition of 'Abdulla Ibn Sa'ad westwards from Egypt in 647 A.D. Ibn Khaldūn tells us that a number of them were with the Beni Hilál in their great invasion of the eleventh century; and Idrísi (c. 1154) speaks of the territories of old Ptolemais as inhabited by Zenáta and Fezára, whom he calls Berber tribes arabicized. Ibn Sa'íd and Maḳrízí mention a colony of them near Barka from the thirteenth century till the fifteenth. In 1853 there were still some of them in the province of Constantine according to M. Carette.

[1] El Tunísí speaks of camel-owning nomads called Fezára comprising the Maḥámíd, Megánín, Beni Gerár, Beni 'Amrán, and Blue Messiría; and the map appended to Perron's edition also includes most of these under the general denomination of Beni Fezára.

Other sections of the Kabábísh are again of varied origin. The earliest recruits to the ranks of the original community are said to have been the Ruwáḥla and the Awlád 'Ón. Not long afterwards the Serágáb, Ḥowál, and Nūráb, unwilling to relinquish the nomad life and settle permanently on the river, sought safety in numbers and attached themselves to the Awlád 'Uḳba, Ruwáḥla, and Awlád 'Ón.

Since the Nūráb are the ruling clan they will be dealt with first.

By race the Nūráb claim to be Rikábía, as shewn in the following tree:—

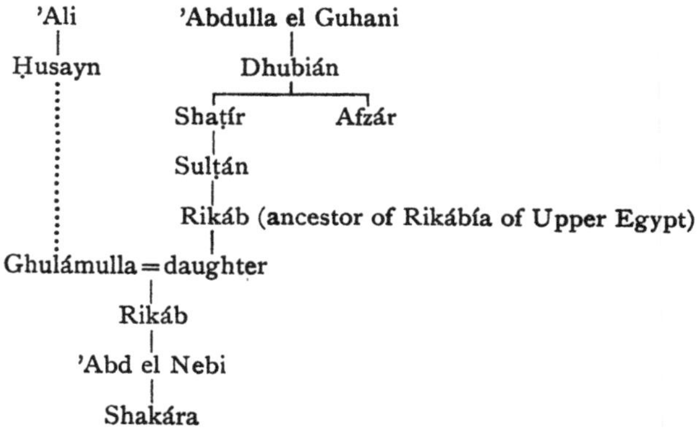

This Shakára is called by the "Dongola nisba" ancestor of the "Nūráb who live at El 'Afáṭ in Dongola, some of whom joined the Kabábísh and multiplied with them and became nomads."

We may then assume that the Kabábísh (even if they did not at that time possess the name) after reaching Dongola in their southward movement were joined by some Rikábía calling themselves Nūráb[1].

Were it known whether the Nūráb at once assumed the chieftainship of the tribe or not, it would be comparatively easy to fix roughly the date of their adhesion, since the present Sheikh 'Ali Walad el Tóm, nephew of the great Ṣáliḥ Bey

[1] It may be noted here that this affixing -áb to denote a patronymic is not so used among any of the Kordofán tribes or sections which have not come from the north-east; e.g., it is unknown among the Baḳḳára proper.

Faḍlulla, represents the ninth generation from Kurbán. This Kurbán was of the Ribayḳát section and the first of that family to hold the chieftainship. Before his death he surrendered it to his sister's son Kerádim (of the Nūráb) from whom it has since been handed down from father to son.

It is said that Kurbán had attained his position by purchasing the headship of the tribe from one 'Abūda of the Awlád 'Uḳba for twenty young she-camels each with its foal and each pure white, twenty cows each uniformly red in colour, twenty pure white sheep, and a horse with its henchman; and to have parted with it on account of the fewness of his adherents as compared with those of his kinsmen the Nūráb.

Another very large and scattered section of the Kabábísh is the Serágáb. The Kenána of Kordofán who are Arabs of what is comparatively speaking pure descent from the noble Kenána of Arabia, of whom Ḳuraysh themselves were but an offshoot, say that their tribal "feki" traces his descent to 'Abd el Muṭṭalib through a certain Idrís Serág who lived fifteen generations ago—i.e. about 1300 A.D. This Idrís Serág the Kenána declare to be the ancestor not only of the Serágía (one of the main divisions of the Kenána in Kordofán) but of the Serágáb who are incorporated with the Kabábísh: additional proof of this is afforded by the fact that the Serágáb in the Dervish revolt split away from the Nūráb and joined the Kenána with whom they claimed kinship. This is the more worthy of note since the Kenána are better informed than is usual as to their past history; and the fact of the identity of the ancestor of the Serágáb Kabábísh (or their nucleus at any rate) with Idrís Serág, if established, gives us some idea of the time and circumstances of the migration of these particular Arabs to Africa[1].

This Serág lived, according to the "nisba," fifteen generations ago and eighteen generations after 'Abd el Muṭṭalib: this total of thirty-three generations, if the generation be reckoned at the allowance of forty years, gives a total of 1320—i.e. approximately the number of years that have passed since the time of 'Abd el Muṭṭalib. The Kenána "nisba" therefore is

[1] See Chapter XIV, on the Kenána.

not necessarily so incredible as the majority of those produced by other tribes. So, if it be allowed that the Kenána Serágía and the Kabábísh Serágáb are identical in origin, it may be supposed that some Kenána emigrated from Arabia into Egypt about the beginning of the fourteenth century and pushed their way up the river as far as Dongola, and there temporarily settled and intermarried, and later split into various sections, of whom a part went south with their kinsmen and a part eventually attached themselves to the Kabábísh. In fact they probably had many ties of kinship with some sections of the Kabábísh already, since the Kenána are of Nejedean origin and have long been settled on the east coast of Arabia among the Ḳaḥṭánite tribes and Fezára[1].

To take another section of the Kabábísh:—the 'Awáída are so called because their founder's name was 'Áid. This 'Aid was a famous sheikh who lived, as tradition says, at Aden, and it is related of him that some unbelieving "Turks" doubting his powers asked for a sign. He promptly declared he would do anything that was suggested. The "Turks" said, "Draw milk from the air": 'Áid did so. The still incredulous "Turks" then demanded blood from the air: this also was miraculously performed. The "Turks" not yet convinced said that they would not believe in 'Áid's powers until he brought the dead to life: 'Áid at once took a sword, cut off the heads of seven of the bystanders and then gathering up the heads off the ground replaced them on the necks of their owners, who had suffered no harm at all from the performance and shewed no signs of doing so in the future. The "Turks" were perforce convinced at last and 'Áid was deservedly known thenceforward as 'Áid el Ruūs ('Áid of the Heads).

An investigation of the names and origins of the subsections of these 'Awáída however clearly shews that all of them are not of the same race. They are divided first into two divisions—'Awáída Bayyiḍ and 'Awáída Zurruḳ. These distinctions of colour refer not to the men of the tribe but to their camels. The Zurruḳ when they joined the tribe brought with them a

[1] It is not suggested that there were no Kenána to speak of in Africa before the fourteenth century. We know that there were.

very dark breed of camel and received their nickname in consequence. The fact, mentioned by Mr C. M. Doughty, that these dark camels are peculiar to the southern and middle tribes of Arabia, such as Ḥarb, Metayr, and Atáybán may possibly afford a clue to the direction whence the 'Awáída Zurruḳ came to Africa. Another and more direct clue as to their antecedents is furnished by Bruce, who noted in his Journals, "The camels of the Refaa [i.e. Rufá'a], near Haseeb, on the Rahad and Dender, are black; those of Atbara are white."

Not only are there numerous 'Awáída in the vicinity of the Rahad and the Dinder and the Atbara still; but Rufá'a and Guhayna are, as Bruce[1] also remarks, closely connected. It is not unlikely therefore that the 'Awáída are an offshoot of the Rufá'a who joined the Kabábísh in the same manner as did a section of the Guhayna.

The Bayyiḍ include some Bisháriín of Beja origin from the eastern desert, and some of the Awlád Kanz who lived round Assuwán. A third division is for the sake of euphony called "'Adnáláb"; the name is written however "'Adlánáb," and the presumption is that its bearers are of Fung or Sháíḳía origin, since the name 'Adlán was common in those tribes[2].

Living among the Kabábísh also is a small offshoot of another famous tribe—viz. the Awlád Sulaymán. These Awlád Sulaymán had originally settled between the great Syrtes and Fezzán, but owing to dissensions with the ruler of Tripoli they migrated in large numbers to Egypt. About 1811 they returned to Fezzán but were almost annihilated four years later. When they had sufficiently recovered their strength they began moving southwards upon Borgu and Kánem and again became the terror of the country. However in 1850 they had so seriously provoked the Tuwarek Berbers that the latter attacked them in force and almost annihilated them for the second time. After this they apparently remained in Bornu and recouped their energies until they were again sufficiently strong to terrorize

[1] Vol. VI, Appendix XLVI, pp. 411 and 413.

[2] The name 'Adlánáb was held by the most powerful of the Sháíḳía sections in Burckhardt's time.

every tribe with whom they came into contact. Some of them are said to have been employed as mercenaries by the "Turks" in the nineteenth century.

Another of the Kabábísh sections which is clearly distinguished from the rest of the tribe is the Berára. These people are Ga'aliín, who have joined the Kabábísh comparatively recently and become subject to them: a sure indication of this is the fact that they, like Guhayna, brand their camels on the left side.

Now we have seen that roughly speaking the Kabábísh of the present may be said to represent a congeries of various tribes of more or less pure Arabs, leavened with remnants of the old Nilotic population of Dongola, and that in the course of several centuries they have gradually penetrated southwards, generally following the course of the Nile.

The ancestors of that portion of the tribe which in past generations as in the present has formed its constant backbone and includes such sections as the Nūráb, Awlád 'Uḳba, and Ruwáhla were a century ago in occupation of much the same country as that they now inhabit; but the possession of the grazing grounds was continually and fiercely contested among Kabábísh, Beni Gerár, Dár Ḥámid and Zayádía. The main result of a century of vicissitudes has been to leave the Kabábísh virtually supreme.

The Beni Gerár have been pushed southwards and largely become sedentary: Dár Ḥámid have built villages in their own country to the south and only send a small proportion of their population to the grazing grounds of the north and west: and the Zayádía nomads confine their activities to Dárfūr. The Howáwír are on amicable terms with the Kabábísh and graze where they will with them.

In the days when the Fung power was at its zenith and when Dongola and Kordofán were tributary states of the kingdom of Sennár, the Kabábísh were reckoned subject to it and in theory paid tribute through Muḥammad wad 'Agíb, the "hereditary prince of the Arabs[1]."

[1] See Bruce.

As a matter of fact their dependance was but nominal: little tribute but what was seized by force was ever collected, and Kabábísh, Beni Gerár, etc., not only in the days of the Fung power but for half a century after its wane, were little more than wild raiders ready to intercept any caravan that tried to cross the Bayūda desert or to journey from Shendi or El Siūt to Dárfūr: and in like manner they infested the locality of Bír Naṭrūn[1] far to the north-west.

Though well mounted they appear to have never at any time owned many firearms[2]. They are said to have assisted Háshim the Musaba'áwi in his wars against Tiráb the Sultan of Dárfūr[3].

When the "Turks" conquered the Sudan in the first quarter of the nineteenth century the Kabábísh pretended to submit, "mais un fois rentrés dans leurs déserts ils avaient sans doute oublié qu'ils devaient payer un tribut en chameaux, car ce tribut n'arrivait point[4]."

However after a generation or so despite their wildness and inherent tendency to raid they affected certain more peaceable pursuits. They had already tried their hand at exporting salt from Northern Kordofán[5], and as the value of the gum forests of Kordofán became appreciated, it was to the Kabábísh and their immense herds of camels that the transport was largely entrusted. To what extent they were swindled and maltreated by the rapacious Turks has been already mentioned[6].

At the same time their inability to protect their herds in the summer when drought compelled them to move to the river or well-known watering places rendered it comparatively easy for the government to collect tribute in kind from them.

Mr Parkyns's paper on the Kabábísh read before the Royal Geographical Society in 1850 divides the Kabábísh into three rough divisions, viz.:—

1. Sections that remain all the year "in the desert" and only occasionally send to the cultivated country for supplies of

[1] Also known as "Bír el Melh" and "Bír el Sulṭán." See Bruce, Burckhardt, and Browne.

[2] See Browne, p. 205.

[3] See El Tunísí.

[4] Cailliaud.

[5] See Cailliaud.

[6] See Chapter I.

corn. It is said they were ordered by the government thus to remain in the desert in order to prevent incursions of raiders, especially Beni Gerár, on to the caravan routes: of the loot taken a quarter was supposed to be handed to the government and three quarters to be retained. These sections were El Howáráb, Dár Sa'íd, and El Aḥámda.

2. Sections that reside during the dry season on the river or other cultivated parts, passing only the rainy season in the desert. These were fifteen in number, and included El Nūráb, El 'Awáída, Awlád 'Ón, Awlád Ḥowál, El Ruwáḥla, El Serágáb, El 'Aṭawía, El Ghilayán, and El Ḥammádáb. The remaining sections mentioned are here omitted as they are not now included in the Kabábísh.

3. Sedentary sections inhabiting villages and cultivating the land. These were fourteen in number and the names included among others the Howáwír, Um Matu, El Gungonáb, El Meraysáb and Dár Ḥámid (i.e. most of the Kabábísh now subject to Dongola and not now under the hereditary "náẓir" of the main body of Kabábísh), and also Awlád Sulaymán, Awlád 'Uḳba, El Berára, El Aḥaymeráb, and Awlád Ṭerayf.

Now it would appear that in Mr Parkyns's time the Kabábísh were considerably more sedentary than they are at present. In the first place, parts that Mr Parkyns includes in the term desert, e.g. El Ṣáfia, Baḳḳaría, Abu Sabíb, and G. Abu Ḥadíd, where only his purely nomad portion of the tribe remained in the dry season, are, with the possible exception of Baḳḳaría, not to be reckoned as at all far afield to any of the Kabábísh of the present. There are large numbers of the Kabábísh at these places in the dry season, but they are not at all the most nomadic portion of the tribe.

Were Mr Parkyns writing now he would put the great majority of the Kabábísh under his first heading and even so use the word desert for less hospitable tracts than he actually does.

Again reference is made to the Kabábísh villages, e.g. those of the Nūráb, Kawáhla, and others round Sheḳayḳ, of the 'Awáída at Kagmár, of the Awlád 'Ón and Awlád Ḥowál at Gabra el Sheikh, of the Serágáb at Um Ḳanáṭír, of 'Aṭawía and Ghilayán at Kerreri, of Shenábla at Shatt and Zerayḳa, of the present Dongola Kabábísh in the Wádi el Kab, of Awlád Sulaymán near Shendi, of Awlád 'Uḳba, Berára, etc., at the northern Gabra and near Kerreri, and of Awlád Ṭerayf at Abu Haggár. It is true that the Kawáhla and Shenábla (now no longer Kabábísh) still have considerable cultivation at Sheḳayḳ and Shatt respectively, but even so the main body of both (and more especially of the Kawáhla) is purely nomad. The Nūráb have a few dependants who cultivate at Gabra el Sheikh, Abu Sebíb, and El Magerr, but are themselves entirely nomad. The 'Awáída are purely nomad; and no Kabbáshi cultivates at Kagmár. There are still Awlád 'Ón at Gabra el Sheikh in the dry season but they have practically no cultivation. The Awlád Ḥowál remain as a rule far north-west and never cultivate. The Serágáb have quitted Um Ḳanáṭír and live as nomads to the north round Um Ṣonayṭa[1] and 'Id el Merakh: near the latter they generally plant a few acres of corn. The bulk of the 'Aṭawía and Berára remain permanently on the Wádi el Melik and do not cultivate; nor do the Awlád Ṭerayf. The Dongola Kabábísh though owning crops on the river send large herds westward and most of the men and women are nomads pure and simple. Among the Kordofán Kabábísh it is only the poorest of the poor, and they are very few, and the dependants of the nomads, also not numerous, who remain behind when the rains fall to plant corn. The tribe as a whole migrates far afield and sends caravans at intervals to purchase corn for themselves and their horses from the sedentary tribes of Central Kordofán. At present the most entirely nomadic sections in the rains penetrate a week's journey or more north and west of the Wádi el Melik, and in the dry season come but little east of it:—such are the Awlád Ḥowál, 'Aṭawía, Berára, Howáráb, and others.

In the rains the great majority of the remaining sections, e.g. Nūráb, Awlád Ṭerayf, 'Awáída, Serágáb, Awlád Sulaymán, etc., send large herds and most of their families with the previously mentioned sections to the north-west until the "gizzu"

[1] The dependants of various Kabábísh cultivate a few acres here as a rule, but not every year.

grass[1] is finished; and in the dry season shift their camps from place to place round Um Ṣonayṭa, Kága, 'Id el Merakh, Gebel Um Dam, Gebel Abu Ḥadíd, El Ṣáfia, Wádi el Muḳaddam, Gebel el Ḥaráza, and Kagmár—all of which localities, except Kagmár, were counted "desert" by Mr Parkyns.

The Awlád 'Uḳba and Awlád 'Ón are chiefly sheep owners, and though a number of them go far north-west in the rains with the rest of the tribe, many of them spend the year between Abu Tubr, Um Inderába and Um Sidr, and round Gabra el Sheikh respectively.

The only portion of the tribe that can be really reckoned sedentary are some few scattered poor individuals in the east near Ḥelba and Um Gurfa, and some of the Dongola Kabábísh.

Thus it would be a mistake to expect the Kabábísh to become at all sedentary in the near future: that certain tribes are more settled now than in the Turkish days is chiefly due to the loss of all their wealth in kind under the Dervish *régime*, and some of them as their herds increase may again become nomad.

It is only in the desert and during the rains or in the winter while water is still on the surface that the Arab is really happy. The whole desert is his to roam and he sees his animals fattening on lush grass. He is not bothered by the petty thefts of villagers and he is far beyond all control. He feels a free man and an Arab, and this frame of mind is reflected in his behaviour to a stranger: he greets him joyfully and with full ceremonial,

[1] "Gizzu" is a generic name for three or four kinds of grass that grow in the winter in the far distant deserts north and west of Gebel Mídób. The Arabs "go to the gizzu" generally about October or November, i.e. the time when the rain-water has mostly dried up and those who have no taste for hardship are being compelled to move south-eastwards to the wells. The main herds of camels and of sheep are sent to the "gizzu" with sufficient men to look after them and the animals subsist entirely on this grass and are not watered at all until they return to the south about February. Horses cannot be taken because of the lack of water. Donkeys can only be taken to such parts as bear the little wild melon known as "khandal." Life on the "gizzu" is a hard one: the cold is comparatively intense, clothing is scanty, corn and water to drink has to be fetched on camel back from distances two to eight days away, there is practically no fuel and no cover, and camel's milk is the staple support of life. The advantage far outweighing all disadvantages is the complacent pleasure of seeing the animals put on flesh!

"A Kabábísh camel with ''uṭfa' ready to transport the daughter of the wife of a sheikh from one camping ground to another. (Note the leather work and cowrie shells.)"

"The same—Nearer view."

whereas had he been camped near some frequented wells in the country of the sedentary villagers he would have been listless, suspicious, and inclined to take no more trouble than he need. In the desert in the rains his primitive instincts derived from far-off ancestors, and never killed, assert themselves, and to meet him is to return to the patriarchal days. Exultingly I have heard it exclaimed, "Strong is the sheikh of the Arabs in the season of the rains."

To return to Mr Parkyns:—he speaks of the Nūráb as being the most wealthy of the sections and the best armed. He adds that the Kabábísh under the "náẓir" Faḍlulla wad Sálim (i.e. the whole tribe except a negligibly small portion living in Dongola) were "taxed 2000 camels, which impost is now changed into the carriage of 4000 loads of gum from Al Obeid to Dongola. Last year, besides these, they voluntarily carried 3000 loads for wages. The government pays for each load delivered 80 piastres (16*s.*)....Besides this the people of Fadl Allah have to pay 100 horses, and 2000 dollars of 15 pt. each, not taken in money (which would be a great relief to the poor Arabs), but principally in 'umless' or choice camels for his highness, Ibrahim Pasha, which are valued by the government at 8 dollars each, while they are worth perhaps 30 to the Arabs. This year alone 100 were taken. The remainder of the tribute is made up in sheep....Besides these they pay 50 slaves, or rather their value, reckoned at 30 dollars each."

Mr Parkyns then gives an account of the migration of the nomads to the north-west over the Wádi el Melik at the beginning of the rainy season, of their habits and customs, and of their warfare with the Beni Gerár[1].

One point may be noticed:—Mr Parkyns speaks of certain localities as though they were invariably the yearly resort of certain sections. This is to some extent misleading: many of the sections which he mentions as frequenting certain places no longer frequent them. Increase or decrease in cattle and flocks accounts for this. In the dry season the various sections

[1] The "Màhamíd Wald al Sany" referred to as killed by the Beni Gerár was Muḥammad wad Sáni the first cousin of Faḍlulla Sálim. See genealogical tree on p. 195.

part their ways and go in different directions in different years. The years are only known to them by the name of the place in which they spent the hottest season just before the rains[1]; and it will generally be found that they have been, for instance, one year at one place, three at another, one at a third, and two at a fourth. Certain sections however almost always go to the same place because of their owning wells there; e.g. Awlád 'Uḳba to Um Inderába and Um Sidr, and Awlád 'Ón to Gabra. The Nūráb in the dry season are always to be found between Kága and Kagmár, which is however a distance of some eighty miles. The "náẓir" owns land at Gabra el Sheikh.

The chief summer watering places of the Kabábísh are Baḳḳaría, El Kulga, and Abu Za'íma on the Wádi el Melik[2]; Um Ṣonayṭa, 'Id el Merakh, El Ḥabísa, El Ṣáfia, Gabra el Sheikh, Abu Umayra, Um Inderába, Um Sidr, various wells in the Wádi el Muḳaddam, and El Magerr.

They also have watering rights at Kága Sóderi and Kagmár, but do not own the country there.

At numerous other places wells are dug in various years, but the supply of water at these is precarious and often fails in the first few months of the year.

To return now to the history of the Kabábísh.

In the Turkish days we have seen that the sheikhship of the tribe was vested in the Nūráb to whom it passed in the time of Kerádim. On the opposite page is the genealogy of the family of Kerádim, whose family still holds the sheikhship.

Accounts of the succession previous to Sálim Faḍlulla vary, but El Sáni, Faḍlulla Muḥammad, Abu Saybir, and El Kír all appear to have held the sheikhship at one time or another.

It was Sálim Faḍlulla whom Muḥammad 'Ali in 1838–9 summoned to Khartoum and conciliated by concessions as has been narrated[3]. In the same years a number of Kabábísh migrated to Dárfūr in disgust at their treatment, but they

[1] To settle down into the hot weather camp is called "damara" and the place is "damíra."

To migrate northwards in the rains is "nashaḳa" and the migration is "nushūḳ."

[2] El Kulga and Abu Za'íma wells do not always last till the rains.

[3] See Chapter I, page 26.

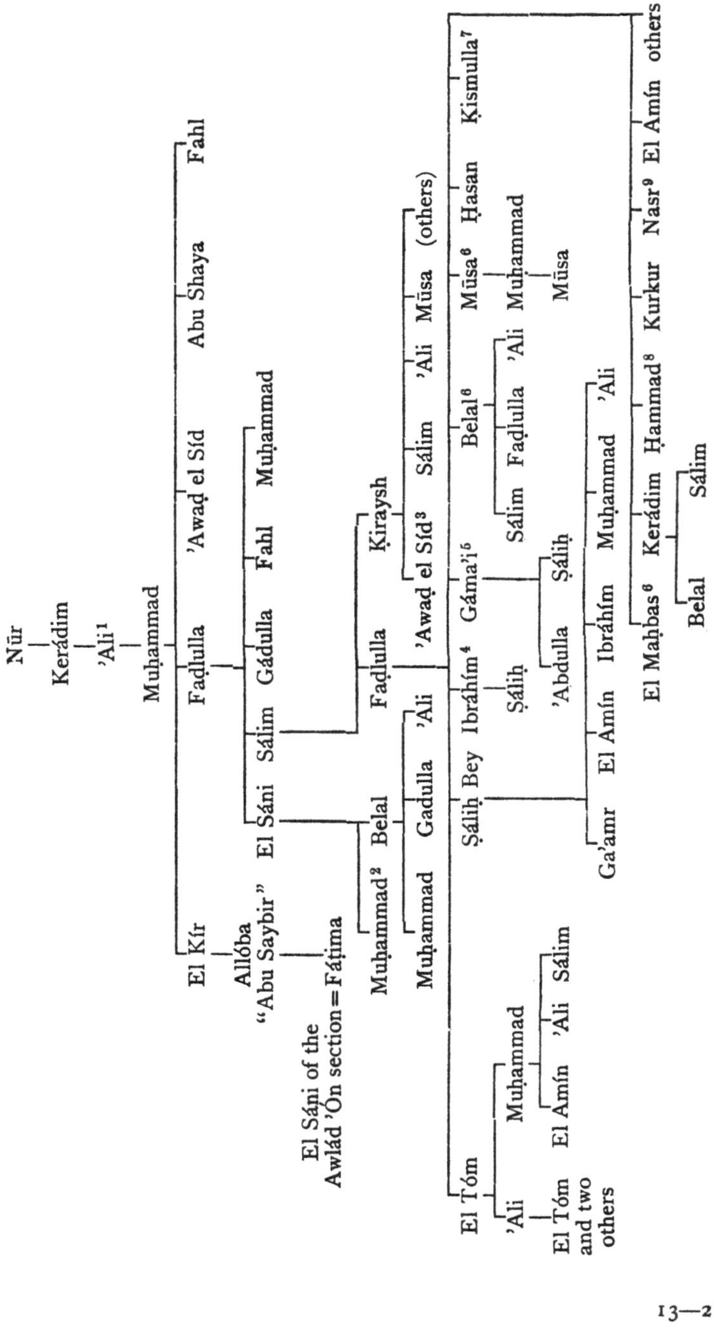

For notes see p. 196.

were hunted back by the Sultan after he had seized their camels.

Sálim was succeeded by his son Faḍlulla. In his day according to Petherick the tribe paid annually to Egypt a tribute of 5000 camels. He ruled for 40 years. Escayrac de Lauture in 1853 reckoned Faḍlulla's own camels alone at the lowest estimate to be 5000 males and 5000 females, in addition to a like number of sheep and some 300 horses. He was the richest Arab chieftain in the Sudan. The Kabábísh at this time were at deadly feud with the Ḥamar, who by now had taken to disputing the ownership of the western grazing grounds[10].

At the time of Faḍlulla's death the tribe was probably at the zenith of its power. Their tribute in 1880 was £8482 odd and the amount was not reduced in 1881.

Faḍlulla was succeeded with General Gordon's sanction by El Tóm his eldest son; but Eliás Pasha wad Um Berír while governor of El Obeid deposed him and appointed in his place his brother Ṣálih Bey Faḍlulla. Gordon on his return from Dárfūr rescinded this action and reappointed El Tóm, who was thus the official "náẓir" at the outbreak of the revolt.

The Mahdi after the capture of El Obeid seized El Tóm and beheaded him[11]. The greatest confusion now arose among the Kabábísh: most of the sections joined the Dervishes, but the Nūráb and their subtribes, with some exceptions, defied the Mahdi and Khalífa alike, and retiring into the desert carried on desultory hostilities and raids, now suffering a reverse and now effecting a coup. The career of Ṣálih Bey between 1885

[1] The Kabábísh say that in the days of 'Ali, his sons, and grandsons they were largely occupied in extirpating the "Nūba" from the smaller hills in Northern Kordofán. See Chapter VI, on the northern hills.

[2] See note on p. 193.

[3] "Amír" in Omdurman in the Khalífa's day.

[4] Known as Ibráhím Gunkūl Gehennum. He was executed by the Mahdi at El Obeid.

[5] Killed by Dervishes at Um Badr.

[6] Belal, Mūsa, and El Maḥbas all died of smallpox.

[7] Executed at Gabra el Sheikh.

[8] Killed with Ṣáliḥ Bey.

[9] Killed by the Nūba of Um Durrag.

[10] See Petherick and Ensor, and Chapter XII, on the Ḥamar.

[11] See Ohrwalder, pp. 62 and 73.

"'Ali Wad el Tóm, 'náẓir' of the Kabábísh, 1911."

and May 1887 has already been sketched[1]:—An expedition at the Khalífa's directions was sent by 'Othmán Ádam from Kordofán and pursued Ṣáliḥ Bey from Um Badr to Gebel el 'Ain in the far north and there killed him and many of his family. The victors were chiefly Dár Ḥámid Arabs: on their way back to El Obeid they found a number of Kabábísh round Gabra el Sheikh. These latter were driven to El Obeid and there executed. It is alleged that four wells were filled with their dead bodies and the rest were left to rot outside[2].

After the death of Ṣáliḥ Bey the Kabábísh seemed to have ended their existence as a tribe: some of the Nūráb remained outlaws and others joined the sections that had become Dervishes and were sent to Omdurman. Here 'Awaḍ el Síd Ḳiraysh was appointed "amír" of the Kabábísh by the Khalífa, and the family of Ṣáliḥ Bey and El Tóm were kept in confinement.

At the reoccupation 'Awaḍ el Síd was killed in battle, and the Kabábísh decamped to their beloved deserts and amused themselves by cutting off small parties of flying Dervishes, and raiding Ḥamar and Zayádía camels. The Ribayḳat, Serágáb, and 'Aṭawía were particularly successful at this time.

El Tóm's son 'Ali[3] was appointed "náẓir" of the tribe, and as the country became settled most of the scattered sections of the Kabábísh rallied to him.

The era of intertribal raiding among the Arabs is now past, although from time to time wild Dárfūr tribes, such as Bedayát and Ḳura'án from the north-west carry off a few score of Kabábísh camels before the latter have returned from the grazing grounds of the rainy season, and retaliation ensues.

The Kabábísh country is bounded to the south by an imaginary line drawn from north of Um Badr, between Gebels El Ṣenáḳir and Abu Fás to Kága Sóderi, and thence over Katūl and close to the north of Shershár to Kagmár, and from Kagmár north of Um Siála and El Faḍlía to Sheḳayḳ close to the river.

[1] See page 46.

[2] See Ohrwalder, pp. 250–253. The camels and sheep of the tribe were confiscated and mostly killed for meat.

[3] 'Ali el Tóm is now aged 37 (i.e. in 1911). He is of dark complexion but Arab featured. He is a fine type of the highbred enlightened Arab, and is regarded with the greatest awe by his people.

The Kawáhla and Shenábla remain south of this line unless permitted by the Kabábísh to cross it; but Ḥamar, Dár Ḥámid, Howáwír, and all the lesser tribes roam at will where they please on either side of the boundary, subject only to certain restrictions as to where they may dig wells.

The western boundary of the tribe is the Dárfūr border, its eastern the land of the riverain tribes, its northern the desert wastes only.

Plate XVII

"Kawáhla, 1911."

CHAPTER XVI

THE KAWÁHLA

THE Kawáhla do not properly belong to Kordofán or Dárfūr at all, and only later accretions to the tribe claim relationship to any of the tribes inhabiting either country[1].

Their real home is on the east side of the Nile and their connection is with the eastern tribes.

It is a relief to find they do not even claim 'Abdulla el Guhani as their forbear, but invariably trace their descent to Zubayr ibn el 'Awám, the cousin of the Prophet. Their name has been known for some hundreds of years on the east of the Nile, and it is among the 'Ababda and kindred tribes, with whom they are still mixed, that one must look for their origin.

There is an interesting notice of the Kawáhla or "Beni Káhil"—the first so far as I am aware—in Ibn Baṭūṭa's works[2]. That traveller, who flourished about 1353 A.D., sailed from Jedda to Rás Dowáír, between 'Aidáb and Suákin, and visited the Beja tribes there living on the coasts: among these Beja he found a camp of Awlád Káhil speaking the Beja language[3]; and again at Suákin he found the Sultan's troops included Beja, Awlád Káhil, and Arabs of Guhayna[4].

[1] The 'Aṭawía section of the Kabábísh and the Wáilía section of the Ḥamar are said to be Kawáhla by origin, and the insignificant Tuaymát section of the Awlád Bíka Gawáma'a claim that their ancestor Tuaym was grandson of the Kahli Budrán.

The large section of Kawáhla, Dár Ḥámid, are said to be closely related to the Megánín (see p. 130).

[2] See Defrémery and Sanguinetti's translation, Vol. II, pp. 161–2.

[3] "اولاد كاهل....مختلطين بالبجاه عارفين بلسانهم."

[4] "ومعه عسكر من البجاه واولاد كاهل وعرب جُهينه."

The Kawáhla at present claim the 'Abábda and the Bisháriín of the east among their numbers: the Bisháriín likewise claim Káhil as the ancestor of themselves and the 'Abábda[1]. The fact is that as these eastern tribes became subject to the Arab invaders after the conquest of Egypt, they intermarried with them to a large extent and a certain number of the resultant medley formed themselves into a tribe which came to be known as Beni (Awlád) Káhil (Kahel; Kahl) or Kawáhla. The majority of these Kawáhla remained on the east of the Nile, on the banks of the Rahad and the Dinder[2], but a part crossed the river and joined the nomad Kabábísh. Burckhardt and Cailliaud both mention that the Shukría and Kawáhla[3] living in the neighbourhood of the Atbara were at deadly feud with the Ga'aliín about 1814–19: at this time the nomad Arabs owned little allegiance to any government and the collection of tribute from them was no easy matter; but, on the other hand, Bruce[4] speaks of "Arabs Cohala" [Kawáhla] on the Rahad as a stationary tribe tributary to the "mek" of Sennár and regular and obedient taxpayers.

For some generations previous to the "Mahdía" a great number of the Kawáhla lived with the Kabábísh and were reckoned as a section of that tribe. Many others remained independent on the Rahad and the Dinder[5].

[1] See *Handbook of the Sudan*, p. 91, where the Bisháriín are said to claim descent thus:

Kahl
Bishar — 'Abad — Amar.

Sir G. Wilkinson (p. 386) speaks of the 'Abábda as apparently aborigines and Arabs only in habits: among their chief divisions he mentions the Gowaléëh (i.e. Kawáhla).

[2] See e.g. Cailliaud..."La partie est du Dinder, et delà vers le Rahad, est habitée par des tribus d'Arabes Kaouâhlehs." He also mentions some others near El 'Atshán on the White Nile.

[3] Burckhardt (*Nubia*...) gives the Arabic as قواحل instead of كواهله. Cailliaud says, "Les tribus Arabes du voisinage [S.E. of Shendi] sont toutes indépendantes. Les Choukryehs et les Kaouâhlehs vivent dans une continuelle inimitié avec les Dja'leyns [Ga'aliín], qui sont la tribu la plus nombreuse."

[4] Vol. IV, p. 416.

[5] See Stewart's Report. He also mentions that the nominal tribute of the independent Kawáhla under the Turkish *régime* previous to 1881 was about £2759, but that it was then reduced to £1300½.

"Aḥmad 'Abd el Ḳádir el Á'aiser, 'náẓir' of the Kawáhla, 1911."

On the outbreak of the "Mahdía" the Kawáhla among the Kabábísh broke away from that tribe and joined the insurgents[1], and therein lies the root of the ever latent hostility between the two tribes. The Kawáhla would claim to have grazing and watering rights over the Kabábísh country because for many years they exercised such rights: the Kabábísh, of course, contend that they did so by virtue of their being Kabábísh at that time, but that now, having become independent, they have surrendered their privileges. Hence in the dry season of the year (i.e. from December till June) the Kawáhla in Kordofán camp in the vicinity of the villages and especially in the Khayrán, where wells are plentiful; but so soon as the rains fall they and their herds with one accord move north-westwards to the Wádi el Melik and the neighbourhood of Um Badr: there they remain till the water supply again gives out: then they move south-eastwards again, for they are "strangers in a strange land" and those few places in the north-west where wells can be dug belong to other tribes who guard jealously their privileges[2].

The Kawáhla are very rich in flocks and herds and pay a tribute of £1225, but they own no cultivation at all in Kordofán[3].

The principal subdivisions of the tribe in Kordofán are the following:—

A. Dár Ḥámid
   1. Hashŭna
   2. Awlád Gerays
   3. Awlád Shinaytír[4]
   4. Awlád Zayd

B. El Berákna

C. El Ḥaláyifa
   1. Nás wad el Maṭayriḳ
   2. Nás wad el Azraḳ

[1] Their chief "amírs" were Gádulla Balilu of the 'Abábda section and Aḥmad 'Abd el Ḳádir of the Dár Ḥámid section. At the reoccupation 'Abdulla the son of the former was chosen as "náẓir." In 1910 he was deposed and Aḥmad 'Abd el Ḳádir appointed in his place.

[2] Concessions to strangers to graze or water from wells dug by the owners of the land are extremely common, but concessions to dig wells are rare unless the parties are on very intimate terms.

[3] They have cultivation at Sheḳayḳ on the border of the White Nile province with Kordofán.

[4] Shinaytír is the diminutive of Shinátir, which is the Himyaritic word for earrings.

D. El Bedáriín

1. Awlád Raḥal
2. Awlád 'Arabi

E. El 'Abábda

1. Nás wad el Misayk
2. Nás Báb
3. Um Rádi
4. Nafar

F. Um 'Amár

G. Dár Baḥr

1. Awlád el Sheikh
2. Awlád el Dibayd

H. El Beḳayráb

1. Awlád Sulaymán
2. Awlád Ádam
3. Kurun

J. El Gihaymáb

K. El Ghazáya

1. El 'Omarát
2. Awlád Ṭerayf

L. El Nifaydía

1. El Utiáb
2. El Mulkáb
3. El Kuára

Many other subdivisions of Kawáhla live in the Gezíra and on the Blue Nile, but these are more sedentary. It is generally said that Káhil the ancestor of the tribe had thirteen sons, but the names of these thirteen vary in different accounts. In the following pages are two pedigrees of the Kawáhla[1].

From what has been said, and especially from the pedigrees given, it may be clearly seen how closely the Kawáhla consider themselves connected with the semi-Arab or non-Arab tribes of the Eastern Sudan between the river and the Red Sea.

It is curious to find that there is a colony of debased Kawáhla settled among the primitive Nūba in the southern mountains of

[1] These two pedigrees were found among the papers of the ex-"náẓir" 'Abdulla Gádulla: several names of subtribes were illegible and are omitted.

I.

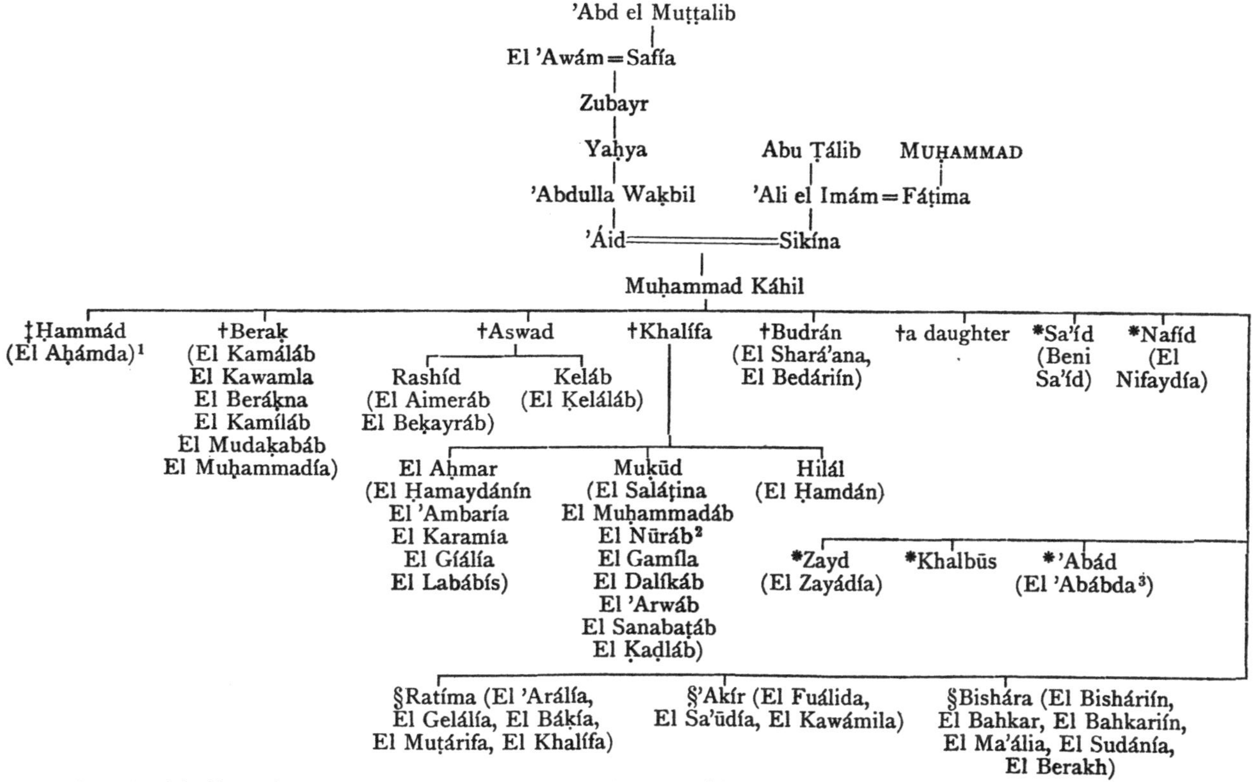

‡by Khadria (?) †by the daughter of Affán son of the Imám 'Othmán *by a concubine §by El Fungáwía

For notes see p. 205.

II.

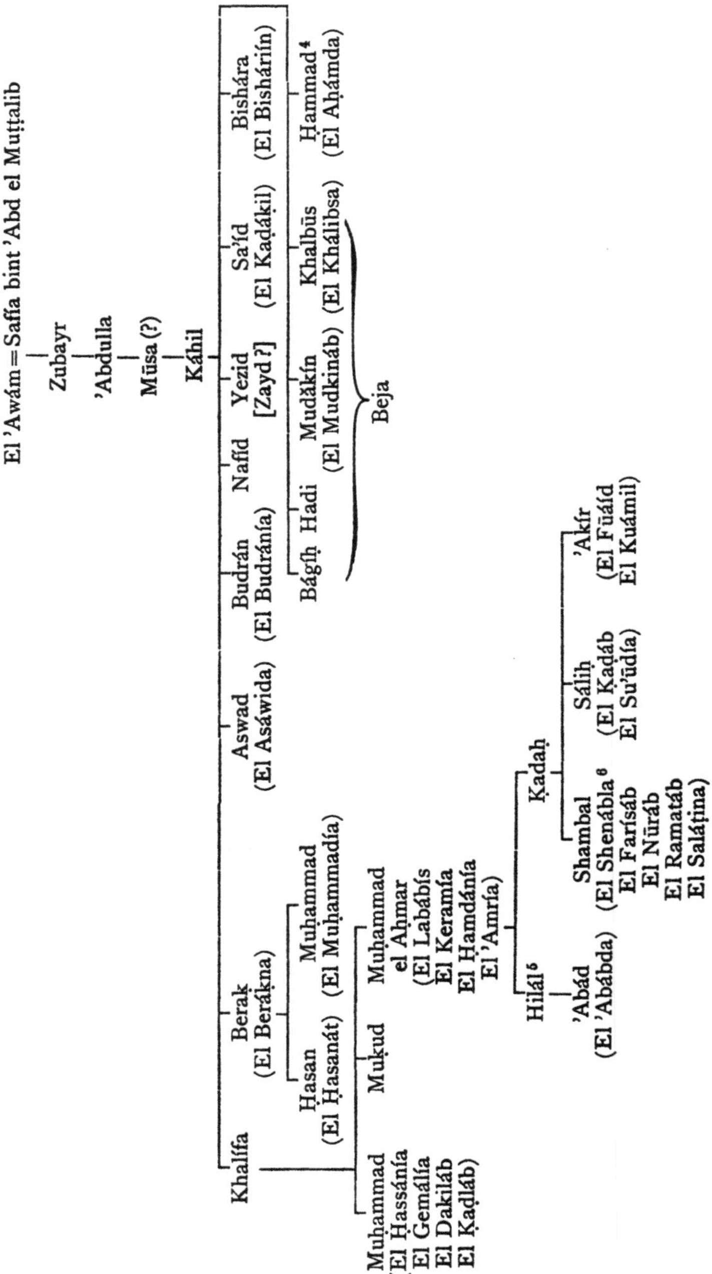

For notes see p. 205.

Kordofán at Werna and the vicinity[7]. How many of the Kawáhla have at various times split away from the parent stock and joined other tribes or become independent communities is difficult to say, but the number must be large.

[1] El Aḥámda. A tribe of this name is mentioned by Burton (*Pilgrimage to Mecca*...) as a section of the B. Ḥarb in the Ḥegáz. Parkyns met them ("Lahamdy") among the Kabábísh. Stewart mentions them as a separate tribe. There are many of them on the Blue Nile and in the Gezíra now.

[2] The Nūráb are the ruling section of the Kabábísh and probably have no connection with the Kawáhla. Their name is only inserted from vanity.

[3] See page 200, note 1. Descriptions of the 'Abábda of Eastern and Upper Egypt may be found in Burckhardt, Klunzïger, Wilkinson (p. 386) and Sir C. W. Wilson, and numerous other travellers. They are said to represent the ancient Troglodytes and are in a great measure of Beja blood. They were of course in Africa long before the Arab invasion of 'Amr ibn el 'Áṣi. The singular of 'Abábda is 'Abádi, and of Bishárín Bishári. "'Abádi" was also the word used to denote a Christian Arab, and "Bishára" means gospel or annunciation. Whether this is mere coincidence I do not know, but it is curious when one remembers that there was a Christian Kingdom at Dongola till about the fourteenth century. The present 'Abábda section of the Kordofán Kawáhla is a large and rich one and after the Kawáhla split away from the Kabábísh and until 1910 it was a member of the 'Abábda that acted as chief of the whole tribe.

[4] Ḥammad is sometimes spoken of as "El Nuaykir."

[5] The ascription of Hilál as father of 'Abád reminds one of Burckhardt's remark that the 'Abábda pretend to be descended from " Selmán an Arab of the Beni Hilal."

[6] The Shenábla are probably not connected originally with the Kawáhla: they were however a section of the Kabábísh at the same time as the Kawáhla and split away at the same time.

[7] They are said to be descended from the Budrán mentioned in the pedigrees. Ohrwalder (p. 8) says those of them living at G. Gedír "are possessors of a very celebrated and holy stone, on which there is a tradition that the prophet Mohammed sat and prayed."

CHAPTER XVII

THE SHENÁBLA

THE Shenábla as a tribe are of no great antiquity, and their name does not occur before the nineteenth century[1].

The tribe said to be most closely related to them in the Sudan is Dár Ḥámid[2]. Some time in the eighteenth century when all the Northern Kordofán tribes were nomad camel-owners the Shenábla severed their connection with Dár Ḥámid: part migrated to the east banks of the White Nile and settled near Shatt and Zerayḳa: others joined the Kabábísh in the north. Of the former colony again some afterwards joined the Mesallamía, and some, namely the Gihaysát, attached themselves to the Ḥamar 'Asákir in the west[3].

The party who joined the Kabábísh remained nomads with that tribe until the "Mahdía." They then espoused the Dervish cause and threw in their lot with their kinsfolk on the river. Their chief "amír" at Omdurman was 'Ísa Bakhayit el Ḥumráni. He died before the reoccupation and was succeeded by Munhal Khayrulla. The latter was appointed "náẓir" of the tribe at the reoccupation.

The bulk of the tribe are still nomad camel-owners, but they also own land near the White Nile. In the rains they roam

[1] Burton mentions (see *Unexplored Syria*, Vol. I, p. 148) that Burckhardt in 1810 found some "Esshenabele" close S.E. of Damascus, partly subject to the Druses: they were notorious robbers and had been so since the time of Herod son of Antipater. Since at the present day there are Shenábla living east of the Nile valley in Egypt (see Klippel, p. 8), there is a fair presumption of some connection between the Shenábla of Kordofán and the afore-mentioned tribes.

[2] See the tables of descent given in Chapter IX, on Dár Ḥámid.

[3] See Chapter XII, on the Ḥamar.

with the Kawáhla in North-west Kordofán and return *via* Kága el Ḥufra, Girgil, and Dár Ḥámid about October and November. During the winter and summer they remain round Bára, Um Bósha, El Taiára, and Sherkayla.

They own no land except near Shatt and Zerayḳa, and the conditions there are unsuitable for their herds: they are therefore in the same position as the Kawáhla with regard to watering and grazing facilities.

In 1911 it was found necessary definitely to divide the tribe into two: the nomads with 'Ali Mukhammas as "'omda" were placed under Kordofán province, which provides them with their grazing grounds, and the sedentary members of the tribe were left subject to the White Nile province.

The subdivisions of the tribe are as follows:—

A. Um Braysh
  1. El Ámira
  2. El Ga'aba[1]

B. Um 'Abdulla
  1. El Góara
  2. Nás Guma'a
  3. Nás Um Gád el Kerím[2]

C. Awlád Náṣir
  1. Nás Muḳábil
  2. Nás Nukmusha

D. Awlád Dáni

E. Nás Hadád
  1. Nás Sallas
  2. Nás Ḥadád[3]
  3. Nás Fenayḥa

F. El Awámira
  1. Awlád Fáḍil Zowráb
  2. Nás wad 'Abdulla
  3. Nás wad el Nūr
  4. El Shuwayḥát

G. Awlád Ḥowál
  1. Nás Merra'i
  2. Nás Ma'ak

[1] The section of Munhal Khayrulla.
[2] The section of 'Ali Mukhammas.
[3] The original sheikhship of the tribe was vested in this section.

H. El Ḥamdía[1]

J. El Ṣubayḥát

1. Awlád Amíra
2. El Khamísáb
3. El Náfa'áb
4. El Kuwiáb
5. Nás Um Laóta

K. Abu 'Imayr

1. El Nagágír
2. El Taibát
3. Nás wad Zayn

L. Awlád Hashūn

1. Nás Na'ím
2. Abu Ruḍḍi
3. El Menán
4. Nás Gharayra

[1] Originally a subsection of Abu 'Imayr.

CHAPTER XVIII

THE BAZA'A AND BENI GERÁR

PART I.

THE Baza'a are a small tribe scattered over Central Kordofán. There is a colony of them in the waterless tracts lying in the south-east part of Um Dam district, another with the Beni Gerár at Kadmūl near Bára, a third owning a considerable number of gum gardens round Um Shiḥayṭa and Um Gózayn, south of Gebel Um Shidera, and a fourth near Abu Zubbad to the west. A number of the last-mentioned colony are nomad throughout the year. There are also a few of them at Tisóma in E. Dárfūr.

In race they are closely connected with the Beni Gerár and both tribes trace descent to one Sálim el Ḥamám. This Sálim is usually reckoned a descendant of Ḥámid el Afzár, and it is probable that both Baza'a and Beni Gerár are offshoots of the great tribe of Fezára[1].

The name Baza'a is explained as being derived from Abza'a the son of Sálim el Ḥamám.

It is said that their original settlement in Kordofán was at the site they still occupy in Um Dam district and that they displaced certain Kenána there.

[1] For the Fezára see Chapter XV, on the Kabábísh, and the account of the Beni Gerár that follows in this chapter. There is no warrant of which I am aware for connecting the Baza'a with the Báza whom Barth speaks of as a powerful independent tribe with a dialect of their own and living in the east of Bornu, nor with the Bazah of whom Maḳrízi speaks as living in the Eastern Sudan between the Beja and the people of Aloa on the Blue Nile (see Quatremère, Vol. II, pp. 17 et seq.) and in later days described by Werne in his *African Wanderings*. It must surely be pure coincidence that the Baza'a trace descent to Sálim *el Ḥamám* and that it was from the country of the Bazah came the birds called "pigeons bazin" (see Quatremère, *loc. cit.*). For Sálim el Ḥamám's alleged descent see Chapter IX, on Dár Ḥámid.

There appear to be none of them to the east of the Nile nor to the north of Kordofán.

They have intermarried to a great extent with the Beni Gerár and to some extent with the Ḥamar.

The following are the subdivisions of the tribe:—

A. El Maḥmūdía[1]
   1. El Ḥamdilla
   2. Awlád Náṣir
   3. Awlád el Aḥaymer
   4. El Sa'īda
   5. Awlád 'Abd el Maḥmūd

B. El Shafa'ía

C. El 'Aiádía (or Abu 'Aiád)

D. El Ga'adía[2]
   1. Awlád Ḥasan
   2. Awlád Ḥusayn

E. El Nowágía, or, Nowágát
   1. El Fárisía
   2. El Ṣubayḥát
   3. Awlád 'Abd el Raḥmán
   4. Awlád el Bashír

F. El Ḥuṣana

G. Awlád Ḍán

H. El Keraymát

J. El Razaḳa

K. Um Tímán

L. El Fuayta

PART II.

The Beni Gerár more than any other tribe probably represent the old Fezára Arabs who are frequently mentioned in the eighteenth and nineteenth centuries as roaming Northern Kordofán and Dárfūr[3].

They appear to have extended over a considerable extent of country towards the end of the eighteenth century. Bruce

[1] The Maḥmūdía are descended from 'Abd el Gibár Maḥmūd who married Wadída bint Ḥowál of the Awlád Ḥowál section of Kabábísh. Their son was Ḥammad and Wadída is consequently spoken of as Um Ḥammad.

[2] The Ga'adía are the nomad section of the tribe. The remainder are sedentary.

[3] For remarks on the Fezára see Chapter XV on the Kabábísh.

travelling on the east of the Nile from 1768 to 1773 speaks of the crossing of the Bayūda desert, between Gebel Kerreri and Korti, as being unsafe owing to the truculency of Beni Fezára, Beni Gerár and Kabábísh, "which come from the westward near Kordofan from fear of the black horse[1] there"; and at the same time speaks of these three tribes having "lately...expelled the ancient Arabs of Bahiouda" [Bayūda] and being nominally tributary to the kingdom of Sennár through Muḥammad wad 'Agíb "hereditary prince of the Arabs." He also has an entry in his Journals dated August 1st, 1772, to the effect that news had been received that as the people of Dárfūr were marching to attack Abu Lekaylak in Kordofán "the caravan, which was bringing all the valuable effects from Kordofan, was plundered at the Bahar el Aice [i.e. *the White Nile*], or near it, by the Beni-Gerár, a tribe of the Beni-Faisara." In like manner we hear from Burckhardt that about 1814 these three tribes were still dangerous raiders in Northern and North-eastern Kordofán. At the same time the Beni Gerár and the Beni Fezára are mentioned by Browne among the Arab tribes of Dárfūr[2] in the years 1792–1798, and by Muḥammad el Tunísí in similar terms in 1803.

At this time and for some years to come the Beni Gerár probably paid little allegiance to any power and were entirely occupied in raiding and in grazing their herds in the Northern deserts.

We hear of them again in 1850 from Mansfield Parkyns who spent some time among the nomads. He says "the Beni Jerar, ancient enemies of the Kubbabísh, and former co-inhabitants of the desert between Dongola and Kordofan, are now scattered to the westward, on the frontiers of Darfur. The oldest traditions assert them to have been from all antiquity the sworn foes of the Kubbabísh, though sometimes a treaty between them allowed them both a short time for peaceful occupations." He proceeds to narrate a raid committed by the Beni Gerár on the

[1] The black horse may refer to the black cavalry of the Fung who were at this time nominal rulers of Kordofán. It might however refer to the cavalry of the Musaba'át who were then coming into power.

[2] See Browne, p. 325.

Kabábísh "one rain season while the Mamelukes were governors at Dongola," and revenged by the Kabábísh in the following year.

A continual bone of contention between these two tribes in the old days before the Turkish occupation appears to have been the great watering place of Kagmár. The Beni Gerár still regard it as being theoretically theirs by right, although they were ousted from it probably almost a century ago[1].

At some time probably in the first half of the nineteenth century a number of the Beni Gerár became sedentary and built their villages on the west bank of the White Nile and farther inland, especially at El Busáṭa. A number of them also settled in Central Kordofán with the Baza'a at Kadmūl. In 1876 Prout estimated the number of them in Kordofán, east of Khorsi and round Gebel el Tiūs, at 2500; but the figure is probably greatly underestimated.

The tribute of the Beni Gerár previous to 1881 was fixed at £1134 odd, and though in 1881 a number of reductions were made in tribute, that of the Beni Gerár was left unaltered.

In the time of the Dervishes the chief "amír" of the tribe was Muḥammad Nubáwi. He was killed by the Kabábísh near Gebel el Ḥaráza in the time of the Khalífa and succeeded by his son Ḥammad Nubáwi: the latter gave place to his brother Muḥammad Aḥmad temporarily and then again succeeded to the sheikhship.

The name Beni Gerár is said to be derived from جَرّ "to draw," and is due to the fact that their ancestor was a notorious freebooter who spent much of his time "drawing" along the ground by the leg the sheep he had stolen in order to take them to a place of safety[2].

The main subdivisions of the tribe are as follows:—

A. El Maḥabíb

B. Awlád Rabí'u

1. Nás el Aḥaymer
2. Nás el Sha'iba
3. Nás Khaláfa

[1] It is sometimes recorded that the Beni Gerár were, like the Kawáhla and Shenábla, subject to the Kabábísh previous to the "Mahdía." This is an error.

[2] This is the story given proudly by the Beni Gerár.

C. El Gubárát

1. Nás Abu'a
2. Nás Guayd
3. El Sinūt
4. Um Simayra
5. Nás Sálim
6. Awlád Giūt

D. Awlád Ḥayla

1. Nás Mūsa
2. El Bilaylát

E. Abu Hagūd

F. Awlád Barakát

The nomad portion of the tribe wander north-west with the Kawáhla in the rainy season, and return south-east to the Khayrán and the vicinity of Kadmūl in the winter and dry summer months.

CHAPTER XIX

THE HOWÁWÍR AND GELLÁBA HOWÁRA

IN the north of Kordofán and in the deserts west of Dongola roam the nomad camel-owning tribe of Howáwír.

In Central Kordofán near El Obeid are settled a colony of people known as Gellába Howára. The latter are by origin an offshoot of the former though now debased by admixture of black blood and completely cut off from the nomad Howáwír of the north. Reference will be made later to the connection between these two peoples, but first some account of the antecedents of the Howáwír must be attempted.

They are the remnants of the great Berber tribe of Howára. The history of North Africa for many years after the Arab invasions of the seventh century A.D. is mainly a record of wars between the Berber tribes and the Arabs.

To what stock the Berber are ultimately attributable is uncertain and need not detain us here. Suffice it to say that ancient traditions generally held that the Berber were a Hamitic race from Syria and connected with the Philistines[1], and it was held by a majority of writers that certain of the Berber tribes were once Yemenite settlers round Márib.

Ibn Khaldūn gives a long account of the various theories as to the origin of the Berber, and quotes El Bekri as saying that the tribes of Ketáma and Ṣanhága were Yemenite as opposed to the Himyaritic Howára, Lamta, and Luáta[2]. He

[1] E.g. see Mas'ūdi, Vol. III, pp. 240 et seq.; and Ibn 'Abd el Ḥakam quoted by Gelál el Dín el Siūti, etc., etc.

[2] Ed. de Slane, Bk I, pp. 167 et seq.

himself is disposed to admit the Arabian origin of Ketáma and Ṣanhága, but dismisses as unreliable all traditions that deny that the remaining bulk of the Berber were descended from Canaan son of Ham and related to the Philistines. It is however interesting to note that so early as the time of the great Arab historians the Berber were inclined, like the Howáwír have been for centuries and are now, to claim an Arabian descent.

In later days Rinn has claimed an Indian origin for the Berber and finds linguistic affinities between them and the pre-Aryan races of the third millenium B.C. and even more so between the Berber and the Aryans, "Et il sera facile de montrer que la langue Berbère a eu longtemps des origines communes avec celles qui parlaient les premiers Aryas, avant leur entrée dans l'Inde." The resemblance between Berber tribal names and Vedic names is certainly very marked.

This theory in no way clashes with that of the old Arabic writers for Rinn would claim an Indian origin equally for Canaan, and indeed does explain "Canaan" as meaning "the peoples of Enn" (the great Turanian deity).

The actual word Howára ("Haouara") is said by Rinn to be found on the inscription of Behistoun in Assyria—a Turanian country—as a proper name[1].

Others have held that the Berber were the stock that inhabited Spain, France, and the British Isles prior to the Celtic invasion, and that they retreated through North Africa and settled there.

Whatever the origin of the Berber, the Arabs found them in possession of North Africa in the seventh century.

M. Carette in 1853 contributed a paper on the origin and migrations of the chief tribes of North Africa. As regards the Howára, he quotes El Bekri and Idrísi as mentioning "Awlád Haouár" in the province of Oran in Algeria, and many writers for their presence in large numbers with the Zenáta in the province of Constantine (Algeria). The greatest number of the tribe would appear, however, to have lived till the fourteenth century at least in Tripoli and the Fezzán. In

[1] Rinn, p. 342.

Tunis only one town of Howára is mentioned by the Arab writers, and none in Algiers itself at all: the few Howára now in Algiers are said to be mixed with the Arabs there and forgetful of all Berber descent. It is only Idrísi that mentions a village of them in his days in Morocco, and he speaks of them as "naturalized Berbers by cause of their nearness to and relations with the indigenous population." M. Carette comments on this, "one must conclude from this that the Haouára were strangers in the country." He lays stress on the fact that the same tribes which to the east in Tripoli are regarded as Berber arabicized are in the west in Morocco spoken of as Arabs berberized, the reason for this being that the original home of the Berber was to the east where their true race was well known to be Berber, and that they settled at a later date in the west and were able there to pose as Arabs. He accounts for the scanty mention of Howára and Zenáta in Morocco, where they abounded later, by supposing that between the death of Ibn Khaldūn in 1406 and the Portuguese conquests in the middle of the same century there was an extensive migration of Berber from east to west, and holds that the present "Chaouia" represent the old Howára and Zenáta.

The prolonged struggles between the Arabs and the Berber in North Africa have been recorded with great detail, and we are only concerned here with one tribe of the Berber.

The Howára took a prominent part in these wars and as usual not only fought but intermarried with the Arabs and very soon shewed a tendency to join them as allies. Thus, though the bulk of the tribe remained unsubdued and implacable, a number of Howára accompanied the Arab forces that invaded Spain, and others at a later date assisted in the conquest of Sicily[1].

Their power was great from 640 A.D. and earlier till the time of the Fáṭimite dynasty (908–1171 A.D.), but then received a series of reverses from which it never entirely recovered[2].

[1] See Ibn Khaldūn, Bk I, pp. 273 et seq.

[2] Their chief revolts were in 741–2 and 772; but they were on each occasion crushed temporarily (see Fournel and Ibn Khaldūn). In 811 they took Tripoli but were subsequently defeated (see Ibn Khaldūn, Bk I, pp. 273 et seq.).

In 1049 the Fáṭimite Khalíf El Mustanṣir summoned the great Arab tribes of Beni Hilál and Sulaym from the Sa'íd to crush Moizz the rebellious chief of the Ṣanhága at Ḳairuán. The Zenáta and others assisted Moizz, but most of his natural allies abandoned him to his fate and the Arabs laid waste the country and utterly crippled the strength of the Berber[1].

The Almohades ("El Muwaḥḥidín"), who were chiefly Masmūda Berber, in the following century destroyed the Ṣanhága kingdom of the Almoravides ("El Merábitín") in Morocco. The Howára, who had already adopted the Arabic tongue, now followed the example of the Almohades and adopted Arabic manners and customs, paid tribute to the Almohades and assisted them in their wars against Ibn Ghania, the last of the Almoravides in Africa.

Fourteen years after the death of Ibn Ghania when Abu Zakáría of the Hafsite dynasty was in power, they refused to pay their taxes and committed a number of acts of brigandage. Enraged at this, Abu Zakáría slaughtered a vast number of them in cold blood and so temporarily at least broke their power in the north-west of Africa.

Leo Africanus (1495 [or 1496]—1552), however, mentions the Howára and Zenáta and Ṣanhága as still inhabiting Temseena (Tlemsen) in N.W. Algeria[2] and the modern Tafíla[3] in Morocco, and being so powerful in Morocco that they could put 6000 horsemen in the field and owned 200 castles.

According to Marmol Caravajal[4] (1520) the Howára were subject to the Zenáta.

But while many of the Howára appear to have moved westwards through the northern provinces of Africa, others went to the east. Thus Ibn Khaldūn mentions a colony of them in his day near Alexandria[5]; but the majority of those who moved eastwards were either forced or voluntarily migrated

[1] Ibn Khaldūn (Bk I, p. 197) speaks of the Howára as subject to the Arabs of Sulaym.

[2] See Leo, Vol. I, p. 131 and Vol. II, p. 396.

[3] See Leo, Vol. II, p. 780.

[4] See Bk I, Vol. I, p. 69; but the authority is an unreliable one.

[5] See Bk I, pp. 9–11.

further southwards, and a large colony of them about 1382 A.D. were settled in Upper Egypt by the Sultan Barḳūḳ[1]. Here they abode and set about cultivating tracts previously desert, and at the same time established their power to a considerable extent; and we learn from Maḳrízi that before the end of the century some of them, in league with the Aḥmadi and Awlád Kanz Arabs, attacked and pillaged Assuwán[2].

In 1412 A.D. (Muharrem 815 A.H.), when Egypt was distracted by internal disturbances and Assuwán no longer subject to her, the Howára attacked the town, then in the hands of the Awlád Kanz, and destroyed it[3].

After Maḳrízi's time the Howára remained in Upper Egypt for several centuries. Burckhardt (c. 1814) found them still settled in villages on either side of the Nile from El Siūt to Farshiūt on the west and to near Keneh on the east, and still remembering their Moghrabi descent.

They were extremely powerful during the Mamlūk *régime* in Egypt, and the Hammám, their principal section, in the eighteenth century had assumed the whole government of Upper Egypt and the Northern Sudan south of El Siūt as far as Maḥass, and the Mamlūks had been obliged to cede this great territory to them by treaty[4].

They appear to have used their power reasonably well, but were given to oppressing and enslaving the Copts: they were also in a practically permanent state of rebellion against Egypt and of war with the Beduins of the surrounding districts. In the latter Mamlūk days when 'Ali Bey was in power, he attacked the Hammám and defeated them in several battles[5].

The power of the Howára was not finally broken however till the time of Muḥammad 'Ali. That ruler spent several years reducing the Howára, and it was his son Ibráhím who in 1813 slew over 2000 of them and finally subdued them.

[1] See Maḳrízi in Quatremère's *Mémoires*.

[2] Maḳrízi mentions the Berber origin of these Howára, their claim to have come originally from Yemen, and their previous settlements from Sort to Tripoli.

[3] See Maḳrízi (*El Khetát*); Quatremère; and Burckhardt (*Nubia*).

[4] See Burckhardt (*Nubia*).

[5] Hamilton (1801–2) speaks of these Howára as Arabs and of "Hamam" as a sheikh, not a section of the tribe.

Burckhardt, and Hamilton (1801–2), both mention the richness of the tribe in horses, and the latter records that at the time of the defeat of Hammám by the Mamlūks they are said to have had 36,000 horsemen in the field.

Again, Sir G. Wilkinson writing in 1843 comments on the fame of the Howára as breeders and trainers of horses[1], and mentions that the large rough wire-haired sheep-dogs of Upper Egypt were a Howári breed.

That the Howáwír (sing. Howári) of the Northern Sudan are a remnant of the powerful tribe of which some account has been given above is attested to not only by the identity of names but by the fixity of the tradition still current that the Howáwír were originally not Arabs but Berbers descended from Ham: they have also manners and ways that are non-Arab but approximate more nearly to those of the Danagla and Berber of the Northern Sudan. Singing and dancing, so dear to the Arab, have little attraction for them; and they are to a notable degree more "feki"-ridden than the nomad Arabs such as the Kabábísh with whom they now roam the desert for most of the year. It may be noted too that Sir C. Wilson (1887), while speaking of the Howáwír as nomads of pure Arab blood roaming over the Bayūda desert, mentions at the same time that they claim to be related to the "Huweir" [Howára] of Egypt, who, as we have seen, were certainly more Berber than Arab.

The Howáwír at present are almost entirely nomad, though a few of them are settled on the river in Dongola at much the same places as those occupied by their more powerful ancestors in Mamlūk days.

The nomad Howáwír and their herds in the season of the rains move westward with the Kabábísh from the Wádi el Kab to the borders of Dárfūr, and in the dry weather they return eastward, either to the river or at least as far as the Kabábísh wells of El Ṣáfia and El Ḥabísa, etc. Only a few scatterlings remain west of El Ṣáfia.

[1] See Wilkinson, Vol. II, p. 114. He says the name Howári means properly a horseman and is applied to native horse-breakers in Egypt. This is probably an inversion of the facts. It would be the fame of the Howára that caused the appellation of Howári to be given to a skilled horseman.

Their main divisions are:—

Ḥarárín	Ḥobázáb	Gótáb
Muálka	Hamásín	Fezáráb
Rūbáb (or Um Rūba)	Sálḥáb	Tamásíḥ

The Gellába Howára who were mentioned previously as residing near El Obeid, viz. round Khummi and Um Delayka and elsewhere, give the following account of themselves:—

They say they are an offshoot of the same tribe as the Howáwír and that their ancestors lived in Upper Egypt ("El Ríf") and were almost white in colour. The first of them to come south to Kordofán proper was one El Ḥág 'Ísa wad Muḥammad wad Manṣūr, a pedlar from Manfalūt (near El Siūt): he was followed by other Howára pedlars, and hence it happened that the immigrants were called Gellába Howára ("Pedlar Howára").

They obtained a grant of land from the Gawáma'a at Khummi and settled there; but the first generation after El Ḥág 'Ísa, finding themselves oppressed by the rulers of Kordofán started to return to Egypt under El Ḥág 'Ísa's son El Ḥág Muḥammad abu Menána: they did not get far however, for when they reached Dóm el Khatráb near Sheraym, after a single short day's journey, the people there persuaded El Ḥág Muḥammad to stop and be their "feki." He died and was buried there and his people returned to Khummi and remained there. A few years ago one of their headmen received an invitation from the Howáwír of Dongola to pay them a visit since it was held a pity that the old ties of relationship should be neglected, but the project was found impracticable.

The sections of Gellába Howára in Kordofán differ from those of the Howáwír and are:—

Kawamna (including the descendants of El Ḥág Muḥammad abu Menána—at Khummi, and a few near Gebel Kón).

Adawía (at Um Delayka, and a few at Um Ruába).

El Dikayráb (at El Obeid).

Awlád Kaysán (near Abu Ḥaráz).

But since the present is said to be the eighth generation from El Ḥág 'Ísa these divisions may well have been formed since the time when the Gellába Howára left the main tribe.

The Gellába Howára of the present are a dark and dirty people of indifferent morals and shew obvious traces of plentiful admixture of black blood.

The Howáwír on the other hand, being nomads and less brought into contact with the baser races of the south are comparatively light complexioned, with lank black hair.

APPENDIX I

THE WORD "KORDOFÁN"

THERE are four theories regarding the origin of the word Kordofán.

1. That it is identical in origin with the name of the district of Goran (or Gorhan or Gorham) referred to by Leo Africanus and others. An advocate of this theory is Cooley, who says "Gorhan can be no other spot than Kordofán. This name might easily by negligent writing become Korhan, or, as Leo, uniformly writing Kej with a g and omitting the aspirates, would represent it, Goran." Dr Brown in his edition of Leo quotes Cooley, apparently with approval.

Now there is sufficient evidence that the district of Goran in part represented the northern portion of what is now loosely called Kordofán, but it is a hard proposition to say that the two names Goran and Kordofán are connected from the philologist's point of view; and it is surely doubtful whether the theory will hold water: for the following reasons—

(*a*) Goran is certainly a corruption of Ḳura'án—the name of the heathen tribe of Tibbu origin, who probably represent the ancient Garamantes. But though "Kordofán" and "Ḳura'án" may be superficially alike to the European ear, they are very different in reality: in Arabic one is كردفان and the other قرعان: a difference by no means negligible.

(*b*) Every one in Kordofán knows the Ḳura'án—at least by name; and yet neither does anyone now suggest any connection between the words, nor did they do so to Petherick and Rüppell who made enquiries as to the origin of the name Kordofán in the last century.

(*c*) There is no doubt whatever that the name Kordofán as applied to the province is derived from the hill of that name south of El Obeid where it is unlikely that the Ḳura'án ever penetrated: the name Kordofán was never applied to the deserts and open country north of latitude 14° 30′, and to this day the Arabs north of that latitude speak of "going to Kordofán," and it is nothing to them that for administrative purposes under the Turks and the present government the whole country from Dongola to the Baḥr el Arab has been officially styled "Kordofán." To the Arab Kordofán is only the low-lying country between the southern Gebels (Dáir, Teḳali, etc.) and the northern Gebels (Kága, Abu Ḥadíd, etc.). It was not so much to this comparatively fertile tract that the term "desert of Goran" was applied by old geographers as to the wild country north of it, where the Ḳura'án roamed, and to which the term "desert" is applicable. Were Kordofán connected with Goran it were natural to suppose that the country where the Ḳura'án lived would have longest kept the name derived from them.

2. Petherick (p. 262) says: "The province [i.e. Kordofán] takes its name from a...mountain...to the south-east of El Obeid, and perhaps 10 miles distant from it. The name Kordofán is evidently of Nuba derivation: the meaning of the last syllable, 'fan,' is country, but the signification of the two preceding syllables I was unable to learn." Petherick is a dubious authority who plagiarizes from Pallme, and I have my doubts about "fan" meaning country. The Zagháwa of Dárfūr and many of the Arabs pronounce the word Kordofál; and Major Denham quoted from a letter from a sheikh in the Western Sudan (in 1824): "...the Turks who are in Kordafal or Kordofal...." The use of the form Kordofál for Kordofán may be a corruption only or it may represent the older form of the word: if the latter then it also provides a further argument against identifying قرعان and كردفان.

3. Now curiously enough, while Petherick thought he knew the meaning of one syllable—viz. "fan," and not of the others,

Rüppell, after corroborating the fact that the country was named after the "gebel," says Kordu means "man," and the meaning of "fan" is unknown.

In support of Rüppell's statement is the fact that the word for "man" in the Dilling group of hills is "Kortando."

4. The Ghodiát of Southern Kordofán, an old people chiefly Fung by origin, but mixed with Nūba and debased Arab blood, who were probably, as they say, the first to invade the country and wrest the land round Gebel Kordofán from the Nūba, allege that "Kordofán" is a corruption of Kuldu fár meaning "Kuldu is boiling-wroth." Kuldu they say was the name of the last king of the Nūba who ruled from G. Kordofán, to which he gave his name. The weak point in this theory is the fact that "fár" is apparently connected with the Arabic فار (to boil). However the name Kuldu may be genuine; or it may possibly be connected with Kordu or Kortando.

Of these four theories that of Rüppell seems to have the least against it. If Petherick too is to be trusted, "Kordofán" *in toto* may mean "the land of men," i.e. "the inhabited country" or "the cultivable country." The Ghodiát story may have some foundation or be only the work of ingenious invention.

It is at least most probable and natural that a Nūba origin should be attributed to the word Kordofán, considering that the Nūba ruled the land from round G. Kordofán and that the country takes its name from the Gebel.

APPENDIX II

THE FUNG

CONSIDERABLE confusion has existed at times with regard to the question of who the Fung are. The chief cause of this confusion has been that two peoples have been spoken of under this name, viz.: (1) the original and comparatively pure Fung, (2) the mixture of these Fung with Arabs formed at and after the time of 'Amára Dunkas (1493 or thereabouts).

To deal with the second first:—Some of their own accounts naturally pretend that they are Arabs on the strength of the Arab blood that was certainly in them. As Gleichen (*Handbook...*) says, they represented themselves as orthodox Muslims connected with the most venerated Arab tribes, and forged pedigrees for themselves tracing back their descent to the relatives of the Prophet:—"They were a mixed race forced into an Arab mould and in varying degrees modified by Arab blood."

Na'ūm Bey Shuḳayr (*History of the Sudan*) says, "Their traditions and claims are that they are of the Beni Ommayya, and they say that the 'Abbásía after conquering the Ommayya in Syria and wresting the power from them in A.H. 132 captured many of the Ommayya, while those who escaped spread all over the world: some went to Spain and established the kingdom of Andalūsia and some went to the Sudan and settled in Sennár": the manner of this settlement in Sennár was, he says, as follows:—The Ommayya first went to Abyssinia, but on the 'Abbásía protesting against their being harboured there, the king of Abyssinia turned them out and settled them in the Sennár mountains "whose inhabitants were blacks, including the Fung."

The Ommayya then intermarried with and subdued these black Fung and gradually themselves got darker in colour and called themselves "Fung." Traditions of the present day generally corroborate this account.

Bruce (Vol. VI, App. XLVI, p. 417) also records, though incredulously, that the "mek" of Sennár claimed descent from the Beni Ommayya.

So much for the Arab strain in the later Fung; but we are still no nearer knowing who were those black tribes in the Sennár mountains, also called Fung.

Now Bruce who was in Sennár in 1772 heard more about the descent of these Fung on the negro side and not so much about their Arab descent. He says, "The royal family were originally negroes and remain so still when their mothers have been black like themselves, but when the king has happened to marry an Arab woman, as he often does, the black colour of the father cedes to the white of the mother and the child is white." Not only so but "An Arab who is white, marrying a black woman slave, has infallibly white children." King Ismá'íl was "white in colour as an Arab[1]," but his father and grandfather were blacks.

Poncet nearly a century earlier had remarked that the king of Sennár in his day though black in complexion was well shaped, "not having thick lips, nor flat nose, like the rest of his subjects," and later (p. 70) again speaks of the people of Sennár as "flat-nos'd, thick-lip'd, with very black faces."

Of the general population of Sennár Bruce gives rather a confused account, if one consult not only the text of his work as published but also his Journals and MSS. The following quotations may be taken from the latter.

I. (Vol. VI, App. XLVI, p. 416.)

"The king of Sennaar commands both sides of the Nile, all the way up to near Agow-midre. There are Shangalla, and thence comes the gold...and they are governed by Shekhs

[1] If, as appears, Bruce means by "the mek of Sennaar" the king of Sennár he is guilty of a contradiction for he speaks of the "mek" as having "woolly hair and black flat features" in his manuscript notes (Vol. VI, p. 417), though in the text he twice calls him white.

appointed by the king of Sennaar, or rather the vizir. These are Shangalla, or natives of the place, relations of the king and great men at court; and are, as they are called, Funge, that is, Shangalla converted to Islamism, of the country whence those Shangalla came who drove out the Arabs under Wad Ageeb [i.e. *about* 1493–1504]. Of these the government is composed. The common Shilook, or troops of the king, are mostly pagans even yet, and have their priests. They worship a tree, etc., as God. Between the Nile, or Azergue, and the Abiad, or Bahar el Aice, is another sort of Nuba, and this is Nuba Proper and the Gold country. Also, beyond the Bahar el Aice, in the same parallel, are likewise gold, ivory, etc., and the inhabitants are also Nuba, Pagans, and their language is a distinct one." That the terms "Shangalla" and "Nuba" are used very vaguely is seen from a remark later (p. 419)—"South of Darfoor are the Shankala, or Nuba, of Darfirteet."

2. (Vol. VI, App. XLVI, p. 420.)

"The people of Sennaar have all the mixed features of all the negroes. The Shilook, or Funge, seem to have the head longer and broader at the base; the cranium tending to conical, high raised; the nose long and pointed downwards...the lips not in any way remarkably thick...the southern Hamidge have the head large and well shaped...the nose flat at the end, and turning rather upwards; the nostrils large and open; the nose broken in the middle, which feature their children born at Sennaar immediately lose; the lips thick and blubber....They are much stronger made than any of the blacks; longer lived, and better inclined; and these qualities all increase as they go farther south, so that the best of all are those between Guba and Agow-midre...."

3. (Ditto, pp. 420–421.)

"The Nuba [are] bounded on the east by the river El Aice; on the west by Darfoor, or the desert between that and Kordofan; on the south by the high chain of mountains, Dyre and Tegla; and on the north by Harraza....The Funge occupy the river El Aice, and extend themselves up it to the mountainous tract south, which is but a continuation of the mountains of Fazuclo and Kuara, where they end. The Hamidge are those to the west of Kuara, bounded on the south by Agow; and by the river Yabous on the south, on the other, or western side of the Nile; all then is Fazuclo to Dyre and Tegla, confining with the Nuba."

4. (Vol. VI, App. XLVIII, p. 471.)

"The Abyssinians call all the black nations which surround them on the north, west, and south-west 'Shankala'; a generic name, which they apply even to the people in the provinces belonging to Sennaar. The Nuba, Funge, Shilook, Dinga, people called Fertit, the Doba, and Dobena, and, in short, all perfect blacks, go by this appellation. These nations form a race of men distinct from the Arabs and Galla, and seem to be the aborigines of Africa." (N.B.—The actual words quoted in this last extract appear to be not Bruce's own but his editor's.)

In his text Bruce says that the Fung pretend to be Muhammadan but so far from attempting to convert their Nūba slaves, pay pagan priests in every village. The Shilluk, he was told, invaded Sennár in 1504 in canoes from the west of the White Nile ("about latitude 13°") and founded the capital: they were pagans and only nominally adopted Islam for the sake of trade: they then took the name of "Funge," which means "Lords" or "Free Citizens."

As regards the more difficult question of the race to which these blacks, the original and true Fung, belonged:—Na'ūm Bey Shuḳayr also mentions the tradition that they were a branch of the Shilluk, and Cust (*Modern Languages*..., Vol. I, p. 142) includes in the Nūba-Fūla group the Nūba, Kungára, Fung, Hameg, NiamNiam, and Monbutto.

But the fullest accounts giving a theory of their origin from earliest times is given by Cailliaud in his *Voyage à Méroé*, in 1819; and by Trémaux in his *Voyage en Ethiopie*..., in 1863.

Cailliaud says: "La tradition rapporte que le royaume de Sennár était l'antique Macrobe, au temps de Cambyse; qu'après lui régnèrent douze reines et dix rois; qu'ensuite vinrent les Foungies, qui donnèrent leur nom à un partie du royaume dans le Bouroum nommé aussi Djébel Foungi, où habitent les soldats du mek....Les Foungis, dit-on, venus du Soudan, traversèrent le fleuve Blanc et arrivèrent à Arbaguy: là fut livré un grand combat dans lequel ils furent vainqueurs et qui les rendit maîtres du pays."

Trémaux says: "Dans les temps anciens, la race nègre devait donc occuper le Sennar, et les Foun ou Fout qui habitèrent plus tard ce pays, devaient encore être dans les régions sahariennes; car une stèle d'Osortasen nous les montre vers l'an 2000 environ avant notre ère, resistant encore vers le Sud à l'Egypte, qui voulait les chasser au loin." He adds: "A l'époque de Cambyse des peuples de race sémitique, déjà noircis par l'action climatérique...étaient établis non seulement dans le royaume éthiopien dont la capitale était Napata, mais encore dans l'île de Méroé, où ils étaient distingués sous le nom d'Ethiopiens-Macrobiens: et la ville de Méroé devait être leur capitale, puisque, toujours d'après Hérodote, cette cité était la capitale 'du reste des Ethiopiens.'...le degré de civilization et des coutumes égyptiennes que trouvèrent chez les Macrobiens les envoyés de Cambyse ne permettent pas de les classer dans la race nègre." His theory is that as they cannot be negroes and yet were distinguished by name from the rest of the Ethiopians, they may be the Fung. He also says: "Ces Fout, repoussés d'Egypte depuis Osortasen et anterieurement, et que nous retrouvons aujourd'hui dans plusieurs régions du Sudan, étaient venus en partie s'emparer des régions voisines du fleuve Bleu, d'où ils auraient repoussé les nègres vers le Sud, ainsi que nous verrons plus loin, par le retour qu'ils firent au Nord pour revenir au Sennar sous le nom de Foun, qu'ils se donnaient eux-mêmes. Comme appartenant à la race sémitique, ils devaient être, sinon réunis, au moins alliés, au besoin, à l'empire des Ethiopiens pour mieux maîtriser la race nègre." He adds that these Fung at first preserved many Egyptian customs (e.g. in their coiffure, and that their king, as Bruce also relates, always owned and sowed a patch of land himself), but that they lost these customs when they went south, and on returning amalgamated with the Arabs and adopted a nominal form of Islam. This "return from the south" spoken of by Trémaux would correspond to the invasion of 'Amára Dunkas, and explain more or less the extremely widely differing accounts of the Fung, according as the original race or the later mixed stock is being spoken of.

Now as regards the Macrobian Ethiopians alluded to above:—They are described by Herodotus as tall handsome men with customs differing from those of the other nations, and inhabiting "that part of Libya which lies upon the South Sea" (Bk III, 17).

Cambyses of Persia about 525 B.C., while Nastasenen was ruling most of the Sudan, quarrelled with Amasis II and Psammetichus III of Egypt and tried to invade the Sudan, and attacked the Macrobian Ethiopians. He failed however to effect anything definite[1].

Bruce (Vol. II, p. 562) identifies these Macrobians with the western section of Shangalla living on either side of the Nile north of Fazuglo.

Professor Budge considers that the black tribes of Sennár are no doubt the representatives of those "Automoloi" described by Herodotus as follows:—"Between Elephantine [Assuwán] and Meroe one reaches the country of the Automoloi whose origin dates from the time of Psammetichus. In his day there was a garrison at Elephantine against the Ethiopians. These garrison troops, numbering 240,000, were not relieved for three years. They therefore revolted and joined the Ethiopian king, who gave them the land of some of his own rebellious subjects to the south. These Automoloi taught the Ethiopians the manners of Egypt and helped to civilize them." (See Herodotus, Bk II; also see Strabo, Bk XVI, p. 770: the latter calls the Automoloi "Sembritae" and says they were ruled by the queen of Meroe. See also Diodorus Siculus, Bk I, p. 77.)

Whether however the Fung in their origin are to be connected with Automoloi or Macrobians or with both or with neither can hardly be successfully decided: Professor Keane in his article on the Sudan in the *Encyclopædia Britannica* speaks of the Fung as "a very mixed negroid race"—and the matter must be left at that for the present.

[1] See Budge. Exaggerated accounts of Cambyses's successes are given by Strabo and Diodorus.

APPENDIX III

STORIES TOLD OF ABU ZAYD EL HILÁLI

1. ABU ZAYD came from the East through Kassala with a great host, and each of the places where he camped in his march is known as Muḥaṭṭa abu Zayd. He crossed the White Nile near the present site of Kosti (see page 58, note 2) and continued westwards. Many of his adherents and many of his slaves fell away from the host on the march and settled among the Baḳḳára tribes, with whom they intermarried. [From Guma'a Bakhít—Tomámi—Alloba, Nov. 3, 1908.]

2. Abu Zayd of the great Arabian tribe of El Hilála came to Dárfūr from the East. He had a brother named Aḥmad, and the latter tried to seduce Abu Zayd's wife: the infuriated Abu Zayd bade his slaves attack Aḥmad, and they did so and wounded him in the leg: hence Aḥmad is known as "El Ma'aḳūr." Abu Zayd, dissatisfied with Dárfūr, now marched northwards to Tunis, leaving Aḥmad behind. The latter married the daughter of the Tungur Sultan and in time succeeded to the throne of Dárfūr. [From "El Sultán" Ḥámid Gabr el Dár, Musaba'áwi. El Obeid, 1907.]

3. Abu Zayd el Hiláli marched through Kassala, and crossed the White Nile at Muḥaṭṭa abu Zayd, on his way to Tunis el Khaḍra: with him was his relative Aḥmad, subsequently known as "El Ma'aḳūr" because of a wound he received from the relatives of a woman who had acted the part of Potiphar's wife towards him.

On reaching Tunis Abu Zayd warred with the Moors ("Moghrabín") and subdued them: during these wars his nephew fell in love with a Moorish princess, and the two conducted their intrigue without the knowledge of Abu Zayd as follows:—They caused to be hollowed out a great cavity in the earth, well lined, and built over it a dome: the cavity was kept full of milk, and the whole passed for a dairy, nor did there seem to be any room in it for aught but milk: in this milk Abu Zayd's wily nephew placed a couch raised on high legs, and upon the couch he conducted his amours unsuspected. [From the Kenána. El Gefowa, Oct. 1908.]

4. In the days of the Beni Ommayya Abu Zayd lived in North Africa and fought with the Himyaritic Zenáta: he subjugated them, but again they revolted under one named Khalífa (see page 58, note 1). Abu Zayd marched against them and drove them southwards before him till he reached El Ádayk, about 40 miles north of Bára in Kordofán. It was close to here, at a rock since known as El Zináti, that Abu Zayd finally slew Khalífa and completed the rout of the Zenáta. [From Misr Muḥammad, a Feraháni (Dár Ḥámid). Serág, Sept. 11, 1908.]

5. Abu Zayd el Hiláli, an Arab sheikh, lived in a bare wild desert in Arabia or Syria, and it was with difficulty that he and his people could find sufficient pasture for their herds. The camels in consequence became lean and weak—all but one young foal that used to return to the camp with distended belly, fat and healthy. This greatly puzzled Abu Zayd, and none knew where the foal could have found the rich fodder upon which it had fed, and he determined to discover the mystery. Accordingly he lay awake all night near the place where the camels lay and pretended to be asleep. In the middle of the night the foal got up and after pausing to see that it was not observed, set off at full speed westwards. Abu Zayd leapt upon his fastest camel and gave chase. After a long pursuit in the tracks of the foal he suddenly came upon a fair rich oasis, green with all manner of grass and trees. This was known to later generations as Tunis el Khaḍra. Abu Zayd retraced his steps

marvelling and told his tribe of the wonderful land he had discovered. They at once determined to migrate there; packed their belongings and set forth. They marched through Kassala, Gedáref, Sherkayla, and El Rahad to El Fásher in Dárfūr; and it was as they passed through Dárfūr that Aḥmad the grandson of Abu Zayd seduced his grandmother, the mother of Abu Zayd. To prevent this occurring again Aḥmad's father cut his son's tendon Achilles with a sword and mounted him on a camel for the rest of the journey. One night Aḥmad, faint and weary, fell off the camel and lay stunned. When he recovered his wits he crawled for refuge under a bush and was there found by the heathen blacks. He was tended by them and eventually taught them to read the Ḳorán and speak Arabic and converted them to Islam: finally he became king over them and founder of a great dynasty.

In the meanwhile Abu Zayd, unheeding, had passed on with his tribe to Tunis and settled there. He was a valiant hero and a mirror of chivalry. In an encampment near his own there dwelt one summer a fair maiden, and Abu Zayd beckoned to her to come to him and be his wife. The maiden replied, "Wait for me under this tree near the encampment of the Arabs and I will come to you." Abu Zayd, trusting her, sat under the tree and waited, but the maid did not appear. Then the rains fell and the Arabs all moved to fresh pastures and passed away from Abu Zayd; but he remained patiently at the trysting place. A full year passed and still Abu Zayd waited: then at the return of summer the Arabs came back and with them the beautiful maiden, and halted near by their old camp. To the astonishment of the people who had given up Abu Zayd for lost they beheld him, wasted and worn, still under the tree where they had left him, but those who knew Abu Zayd better had throughout maintained that he would do what he had declared his intention of doing.

The maiden, gratified by this example of true love and heroic patience, promised to wed Abu Zayd, but some of her kinsfolk said there was no use in a man who had fasted under a tree for a year. Abu Zayd, however, confounded his detractors: he lived on meat and milk for fifteen days, and at the end of that period reappeared in full strength and vigour and married his lady-love. [From Sheikh Ghanowi of the Dár Gawád Ḥawázma (Baḳḳára). Sungukai, Oct. 13, 1908.]

6. Abu Zayd and his host set out for Tunis from the East and passed through Kassala, Sherkayla and El Rahad: when he reached Dár Ḥumr he was dispirited by the attacks of the tsetse fly upon his camels and the difficulty of making his way with camels over the cotton-soil. He therefore left his brother Ḥámid (*sic*) el Ma'akūr there, and returning with his people led them to Dárfūr by the Arba'ín road that runs from the Nile across the North of Kordofán. [From Mekki Ḥusayb, sheikh of Ḥumr Felaita, Oct. 21, 1908.]

7. (For an anecdote of a meeting between Abu Zayd and Ḥámid el Khuayn see Chapter IX on Dár Ḥámid.)

APPENDIX IV

ḲURA'ÁN AND GARAMANTES

PERIODICALLY the Ḳura'án, a black race of heathen, sally forth from their country north of Wadái and Dárfūr, and raid the Arabs to the south and south-east for booty. A certain number of Ḳura'án too immigrated to Northern Kordofán about the same time as did the Zagháwa now at Kagmár. These immigrants have a few villages in Kordofán near Um Dam[1] and call themselves Muḥammadans, but they are regarded as of very low class and inferior to the Zagháwa.

It may be as well to preface the following remarks by saying that there do not seem to be sufficient grounds for supposing any connection to exist between the names "Kordofán" and Ḳura'án as has been suggested[2]; and that Barth was no doubt right when he stated in speaking of the Tibbu that the Arabs generally add to the name Tibbu (who include the Zagháwa) the term Ḳura'án "which I think myself justified in referring to the district Goran so often referred to by Leo Africanus[3]." Barth speaks of the Zagháwa and Ḳura'án as "two of the great divisions of the Tebu [Tibbu] or Tedá inhabiting the desert to the north of Wadai, who are very rich in flocks[4]."

[1] There are also a few of them mixed up with the Tarádát section of the Ḥamar 'Asákir.

[2] See Appendix I.

[3] See Barth, Vol. III, Appendix, p. 499.

[4] Vol. III, *Ethnographical account of Wadai.* Barth inserts the Ḳura'án among the black tribes who are indigenous and the immigrant negro tribes.

The word Ḳura'án as a matter of fact is often used vaguely for any pagan blacks. El Ḥamdáni includes Nūba, Ḳura'án, Zang and Zagháwa and other negroes among the descendants of Canaan son of Ham. See Cameron.

I note that Wallin (p. 302) includes "Ḳor'ân" among the Ḥuwayṭát clans in Wádi Azlam and round El Wegh in Northern Arabia.

To turn to Leo Africanus[1]:—El Ḥasan ibn Muḥammad al Wezáz al Fási, known as Leo Africanus, was a Moor and born in 1495 or 1496. He visited Central Africa in 1513–15. In speaking of the fifteen kingdoms of the negroes which he visited he says they have "many other kingdoms bordering on the south frontiers of them: to wit, Biro, Temiam, Dauma, Medra, and Gorham...[2]." He also says: "Nubia...is enclosed on the southern side with the desert of Goran...the king of Nubia maintaineth continuall warre partly against the people of Goran (who being descended of the people called Zingani, inhabite the deserts and speake a kinde of language that no other nation vnderstandeth, and partly against certain other people" (sc. the Bugiha or Beja to the east). The Zingani are presumably the Zang, a generic name for blacks in the Arab writers. Marmol in his account of Africa, chiefly purloined from Leo, says that Nubia has to its south the desert of Gorhan. The capital (i.e. of Nubia) is "Dangala." "...Le prince (i.e. of Dongola) a guerre ordinairement, tantost contre ceux de Gorhan, qui est une espece d'Egyptiens qui courent par les deserts, et parlent un langage particulier, tantost contre les peuples qui demeurent au Levant du Nil dans le desert[3]."

Pory too notes that Nubia borders to the south "vpon the desert of Goran[4]."

The latest editor quotes from Richard Blome's *Geographical Description of the Four Parts of the World* (1670) to the following effect: "Gorham is on the Nile and on the coast of the isle Gueguere. Sanutus makes a kingdom, a desert, and a people of this name, and extends them almost the length of the isle Gueguere: not making any mention of the city of this name, nor John Leon of Affrica, nor the Arab of Nubia [Idrísi], nor Vincent Blanck, who saith he has been in these quarters, and speaks only of the desert of Gorham. Other authors make mention of this city and describe it on the Nile. Sanutus saith that there are emeralds in these mountains, which bounds Gorham on the south." Dr Brown adds "'Gorham' or 'Gorhan'

[1] I follow the edition by Dr R. Brown of John Pory's translation (1600).
[2] Page 128.
[3] See Vol. III of Perrot's translation (1667).
[4] Page 28.

is clearly Kordofán[1]," and cites Cooley's evidence to the same effect[2]. He also remarks that Gueguere or Guengare is Meroe [i.e. the so-called "Island of Meroe"].

Refer now to a passage which was written in 1614 by El Doctor Bernardo Aldrete (Canon of Cordova) in a work entitled *Varias Antiguedades de Espãna Africa y otras provincias.* He says (p. 425): "Por estar la Assyria junto a los Arabes Scenitas, es la duda si son dellos los Garamaeos, que dize Tolemeo, i juntamente si son los mismos que los Goramenos, de los quales dixo Stephano, 'Gorama regio Scenitarum Arabum, accolae Gorameni[3].' Siendo tan poca la diferencia que ai, i si en esta Garamorum regio de qua San Epiphanio habla? a esta duda se llega otra, si destos Garamaeos, o Goramenos tomaron su nombre los Garamantes, i si son todos vna misma gente que vino de Arabia, i poblaron en Africa? No hallo luz con que poder mi determinar i affi quedara dudosa la causa a que otro la decida[4]."

The "Scenitae" or nomads of Africa are similarly coupled with the "Goranites" by Leo, who repeats gossip of a huge lake (which had not really any existence as Dr Brown points out) between Fez and Alcair (Cairo), "vpon the bankes whereof the Sinites and the Goranites doe inhabite[5]."

[1] Page 28. At the same time there is an editor's note identifying "the desert of Goran" as the "Libyan desert."

[2] See p. 128 of Dr Brown's edition of Leo, and pp. 129–30 of Cooley. Cooley's identification of the words Kordofán and Goran is dealt with in Appendix I. Leo is also quoted by Sir C. W. Wilson, with reference to this question, in his paper on the *Tribes of the Nile Valley*....

[3] See Stephano's *Dictionarium Historicum Geographicum Poeticum* (1670): Gorama is there described as "reg. Arabum Scenitarum"; and Arabes Scenitae as nomad Arabs of Arabia Petraea dwelling in tents: of course the term Arabes Scenitae is equally applicable to the nomads of Africa.

[4] I.e. "The fact of Assyria being joined to the Arabes Scenitae [nomad Arabs] raises the question as to whether the latter are the Garamaei, spoken of by Tolemeus [Ptolemy], and accordingly whether they are the same as the Gorameni that are alluded to by Stephanus, 'Gorama regio... etc.'; and whether, the difference being very small, it is that Garamorum regio of which San Epiphanio speaks. Upon the heels of this question arises another, viz. as to whether these Garamaei or Gorameni took the name of Garamantes, and whether they are all one and the same race that came from Arabia and settled in Africa. I have no means of determining these questions and so the matter must remain in doubt until decided by another."

[5] Page 173.

We must now consult the classical authors for what they say of the habitat of the Garamantes.

I. Herodotus speaks firstly of an unwarlike tribe of Garamantes near the Mediterranean coast, to the north of the Psylli and Nasamones; secondly, inland in the desert he speaks of (1) the Ammonians, (2) Augila, whence the Nasamones fetch dates, (3) the Garamantes who hunt the Troglodytes of Egypt in chariots and live 30 days from the land of the Lotophagi. Herodotus says all these people in the interior are nomads[1].

II. Claudius Ptolemaeus discussing the interior of Libya says: "*καὶ μέγιστα μὲν ἔθνη κατανέμεται τὴν Λιβύην τό τε τῶν Γαραμάντων διῆκον ἀπὸ τῶν τοῦ Βαγράδα ποταμοῦ πηγῶν μέχρι τῆς Νούβα λίμνης...καὶ τὸ τῶν Μελανογαιτούλων...*[2]."

III. Pomponius Mela says: "Super ea quae Libyco mari abluuntur, Libyes Aegyptii sunt, et Leucoaethiopes, et natio frequens multiplexque Getuli. Deinde late vacat regio perpetuo tractu inhabitabilis. Tum primos ab oriente Garamantas, post Augilas et Troglodytas, et ultimos ad occasum Atlantas audimus. Intra (si credere libet) vix iam homines, magisque semiferi Aegipanes, et Blemmyae...sine tectis passim ac sedibus vagi, habent potius terras quam habitent[3]."

IV. Pliny speaks of "Clarissimumque oppidum Garama, caput Garamantium," and says "ad Garamantas iter inexplicabile...[4]"

[1] See Herodotus, Bk IV, pp. 168 et seq.

[2] See Müller's edition, Bk IV, p. 743. Translated the passage runs: "and very large tribes dwell in Libya, both that of the Garamantes stretching from the sources of the river Bagrada as far as the Nubian lake...and that of the Melanogaitulae."

[3] "Above those (tracts) which are washed by the Libyan sea are the Egyptian Libyans, and the Leuco-Ethiopians, and the numerous and complex nation of the Getuli. Then one comes to a great empty tract, uninhabited from one end to the other. The most easternly people beyond it are said to be the Garamantes; next to them the Augilae and Troglodytae; and furthest west the Atlantae. Inland [i.e. southwards], if one may believe it, are Aegipanes and Blemmyae [Beja], who are scarcely men, but half beasts,...they are nomadic and have no houses or fixed abodes, and hold rather than inhabit the country." (*De Situ Orbis*, Chap. IV.)

[4] I.e. "and the most famous town of Garama, capital of the Garamantes"..."To the (country of) the Garamantes there is no access." (*Naturalis Historia*, Bk V, Chap. V.)

The general impression deducible from these quotations is that the Garamantes were a nomad race covering a very large stretch of country from Fezzán (and even north of it) as far as Upper Egypt: they may have extended even further south, for to the historian writing in the north, the wide spaces of the south would naturally be foreshortened. So then, if we make all allowances for the vagueness of the old geographists it will appear that, on the west, the country at present inhabited by the Ḳura'án; on the south-east, the "desert of Goran"; and, on the north, the southern part of the country of the ancient Garamantes, may be said jointly to include those inhospitable tracts over which the Eastern Tuwarek (part descendants of the old nomad Berbers) and Tibbu still roam. The south-easternly boundary of this area on a modern map would be the Bayūda desert and Northern Kordofán: westwards it would extend to the deserts north of Kánem and Wadái, and northwards to the oases of Libya.

Thus in support of the suggestion that the Ḳura'án may represent the ancient Garamantes we have in the first place seen that both probably inhabited the area of which rough boundaries have been given: a second point can now be made:—

We know that the Ḳura'án are of Tibbu stock, and Barth definitely identifies the ancient Garamantes with the Tibbu, whom we know used to reside in Fezzán till they were forced southwards by the migrations of the Berber[1]. There is too an obvious similarity between the names of Pliny's "Garama, caput Garamantium," and the Goran (or Gorhan or Gorham) which is again connected with "Ḳura'án."

[1] Müller in his edition of *Claudius Ptolemaeus* also accepts the identification of the Garamantes and Tibbu and refers to Barth and to Hartmann's *Die Nigritier*, Vol. I, p. 74. On the other hand we have Mr E. T. Hamy identifying the Tibbu with the Troglodytes rather than with their oppressors (see *L'Anthropologie*, Vol. II, 1891); and Dr Schurtz (see *History of the World*, p. 532) saying "They [the Teda] are certainly not to be identified with the Garamantes, who had a kingdom in Fezzan....It is much more likely that they are to be connected with the Troglodytic races south of the Fezzan, which Herodotus places among the Ethiopians." Why? I see too that Sir H. Johnston in his *The Nile Quest* (p. 20) says that the Romans had friendly relations with "the Tawareq people of Garama" near Fezzán. Now it is at least acknowledged that the Tuwarek are very largely mixed with Tibbu.

These facts point to the identification of the Garamantes not only with the Tibbu in general but with the Ḳura'án in particular, and lead one to think that the two words must be connected: the corruption of course would lie not so much in the word Ḳura'án as in the classical word Garamantes.

Now it will be remembered that Sanutus was quoted above as saying that Gorham was "a kingdom, a desert, and a people," and extended "almost the length of the isle Gueguere" (i.e. Meroe). I believe that the city of Garama is generally supposed to represent the modern Gadames: if so Sanutus, supposing him to have meant Garama as the "kingdom," Gorham (i.e. the Bayūda and westwards) as the "desert," and the Garamantes (i.e. the Ḳura'án) as the "people," probably did not realize the distance from the Bayūda desert to Gadames: that however is not surprising nor unique: the point is that he had the connection between all these names before his mind's eye.

I think that the arguments advanced above may incidentally lend further validity to the remark made, in writing of the Northern Hills, that the country round G. el Ḥaráza was once inhabited by "roaming tribes probably connected on the one hand with the ancient Garamantes and on the other with the Tibbu and Eastern Tuwarek,—part descendants of the old nomad Berbers." (p. 89.)

Two additional points may also be mentioned: firstly, that a matrilinear system prevails among the Tuwarek nomads as well as among the Beja tribes of the eastern desert, and the corresponding system traceable in the Northern Hills is as likely to have been borrowed from the former as from the latter.

Secondly, it may be remembered that there are ancient iron-works, long disused, at G. el Ḥaráza. Now Mr H. R. Palmer happened lately to mention to me the existence of an iron-working caste in Kánem called Ḳura'an [Guraan], and it is at least possible that these people may provide yet another link in the chain of evidence connecting El Ḥaráza with the Ḳura'án and Garamantes.

I may add, however, that I think it would be unjustifiable also to connect the name "Abu Ḳona'án" (see pp. 88, 89) with "Ḳura'án": if the two words had a common origin the people of the Northern Hills, who know both words well, would be the first to connect them. I incline to think that "Abu Ḳona'án" is a perversion of "Kana'án," i.e. Canaan, the son of Ham, whom Arab historians and writers of "nisbas" take as typical ancestor of the old pagan tribes (cf. p. 235, note 4).

APPENDIX V

OBJECTS FOUND AT FARAGÁB IN MIDDENS

THE objects depicted on the accompanying plate were unearthed at Faragáb, a Gawáma'a village some 22 miles east of Bara. I happened to be delayed here for a few days, and the natives mentioned that close by were the refuse heaps (" tanádil ") of an old settlement—of what race was not known. These middens I found to be of considerable size and to surround the ancient site of the village. I got a cutting made into one of them to a depth of a few feet and found the articles here portrayed and a number of fragments of rough thick pottery, generally ornamented with the common Sudanese trellis-work designs or roughly pitted with some pointed instrument.

Most of these fragments apparently belonged to shallow dishes with an ear at each end, each ear being perforated by a number of ornamental holes. Pots of precisely similar design have been found on many mediaeval sites in Dongola province. Other fragments had been broken from common " burmas " (the familiar large jar of the country).

In addition there were many roughly shaped lumps of granite about four inches long and two thick, that were probably held in the fist and used as hammers or pestles. Some of these were grooved as if some pointed instrument had been sharpened upon them. Similar stones are often found near Gebel Geili east of the Blue Nile. There were also numerous lumps of granite rather larger than golf balls and very roughly rounded. These

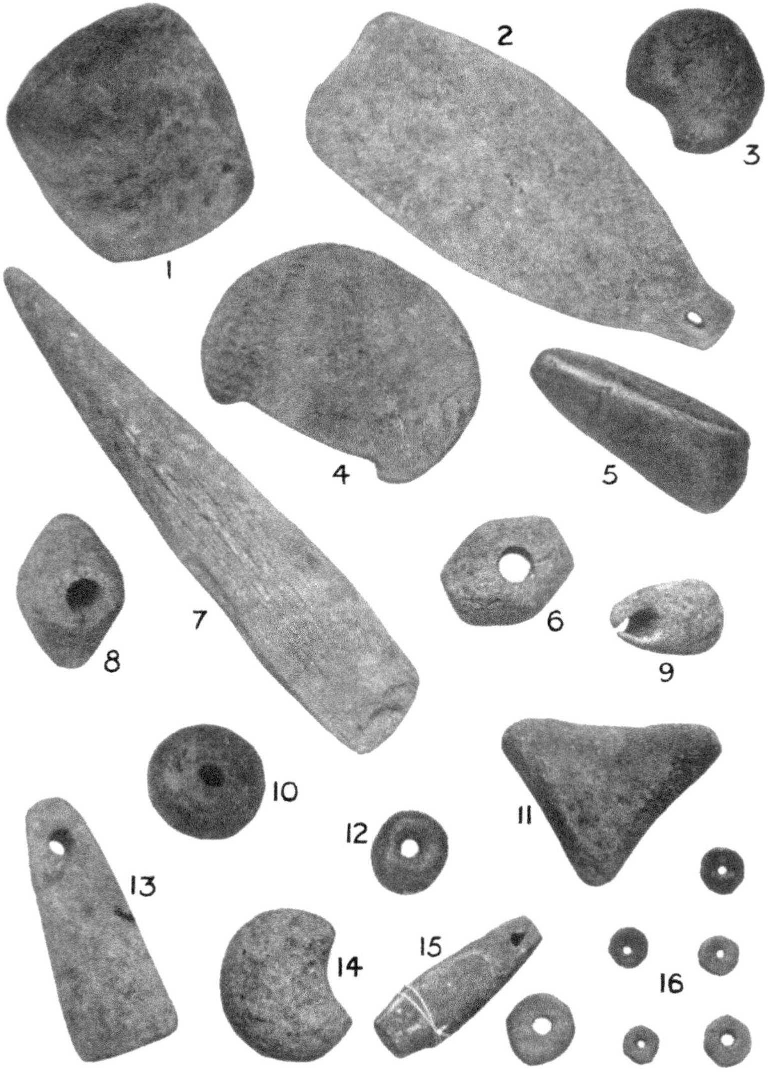

"Ornaments from Faragáb middens."

1. Porphyrite. 2, 6, 7, 8, 9, 13, 15. Probably bone. 3, 11, and 14. Sandstone. 4. Pottery. 5. Flint. 10. Fused glass? 12. Chalcedony. 16. Disc beads (black and white) made of egg-shell (ostrich?).

(*Illustrations two-thirds of actual size.*)

and certain small rounded stones the size of marbles must have been brought to Faragáb for some specific purpose, as no natural stone at all is to be found at less than a day's journey from the site. Few iron objects were to be seen, but there was a plain rough iron ring, an inch in diameter, and two iron pins with dangling rings as shewn in the accompanying illustration.

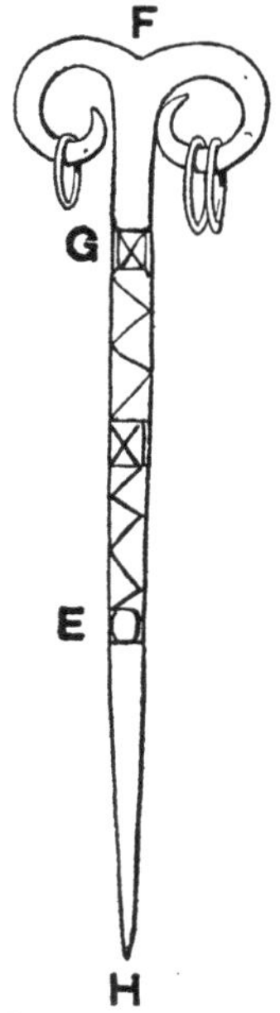

Total length 9½ inches. G to E is cut square (sides less than ¼ inch), F to G and E to H rounded.

These may have been used as hairpins or for applying "kohl" to the eyelids.

There was little iron otherwise, save a few indeterminate scraps that had evidently been parts of the blades of spears or hoes. Iron is procurable in the immediate vicinity and used to be worked so late as the middle of the nineteenth century.

The fragments of bone found apparently belonged to domestic animals: they had as a rule been cracked for the purpose of extracting the marrow.

Nowhere did I find any of the large stone rings such as those that have been discovered at El Ḥaráza and Um Durrag.

As regards the objects illustrated on the accompanying plate, they may be said, like the stones found in the northern hills, to shew a marked connection with northern influences. In particular this is true of the very numerous disc beads [see Fig. 16] that are to be found in the Faragáb middens. Some of them are yellowish white, some grey, some a pale reddish brown, and some nearly black. They appear to be of ostrich-egg shell; and, curiously enough, they bear a most marked resemblance to the ostrich-egg beads found in the so-called "pangraves" of Egypt which are now generally regarded as belonging to the Libyans. For drawing my attention to this fact I have to thank Professor William Ridgeway[1].

[1] The following particulars I owe to the courtesy of Drs F. A. Bather and C. W. Andrews and Mr W. Campbell Smith, of the British Museum.

The density of the whitish beads is 2·55. They appear to consist of carbonate of lime.

The density of the blackish beads is 2·52. The material effervesces with dilute HNO_3 but leaves a black insoluble residue: it appeared at first to be calcareous slate or hardened shale; but when sections of both the whitish and the blackish beads were prepared they were found to agree closely, and it is therefore probable that both are egg-shell.

Figure 7 on the accompanying plate has a density of 1·7 and was found to be very brittle and porous. Qualitative tests shewed the presence of calcium in large quantity and of phosphate. There is no trace of organic substance now and the object is probably made of a portion of a long bone of some mammal.

INDEX

1. Names of unimportant tribal sections and subsections and of persons mentioned only in genealogical trees are omitted from the index in cases where no explanatory remarks concerning them are made.

2. The following abbreviations are used:—

G. Gebel; i.e. mountain or hill.
R. River.
S.T. Section, or subsection, of tribe.
T. Tribe, or people.
V. Village, town, or small district.
W. Wells, or watering place.

3. When the page reference in the index is to a note, the number of the page is printed in italics.

4. It should be remembered in looking out words in the index that the Arabic ق, which is pronounced like a hard *G* in Kordofán, is throughout the text and notes transliterated *Ḳ* and not *G*.

CAMBRIDGE: PRINTED BY JOHN CLAY, M.A. AT THE UNIVERSITY PRESS.

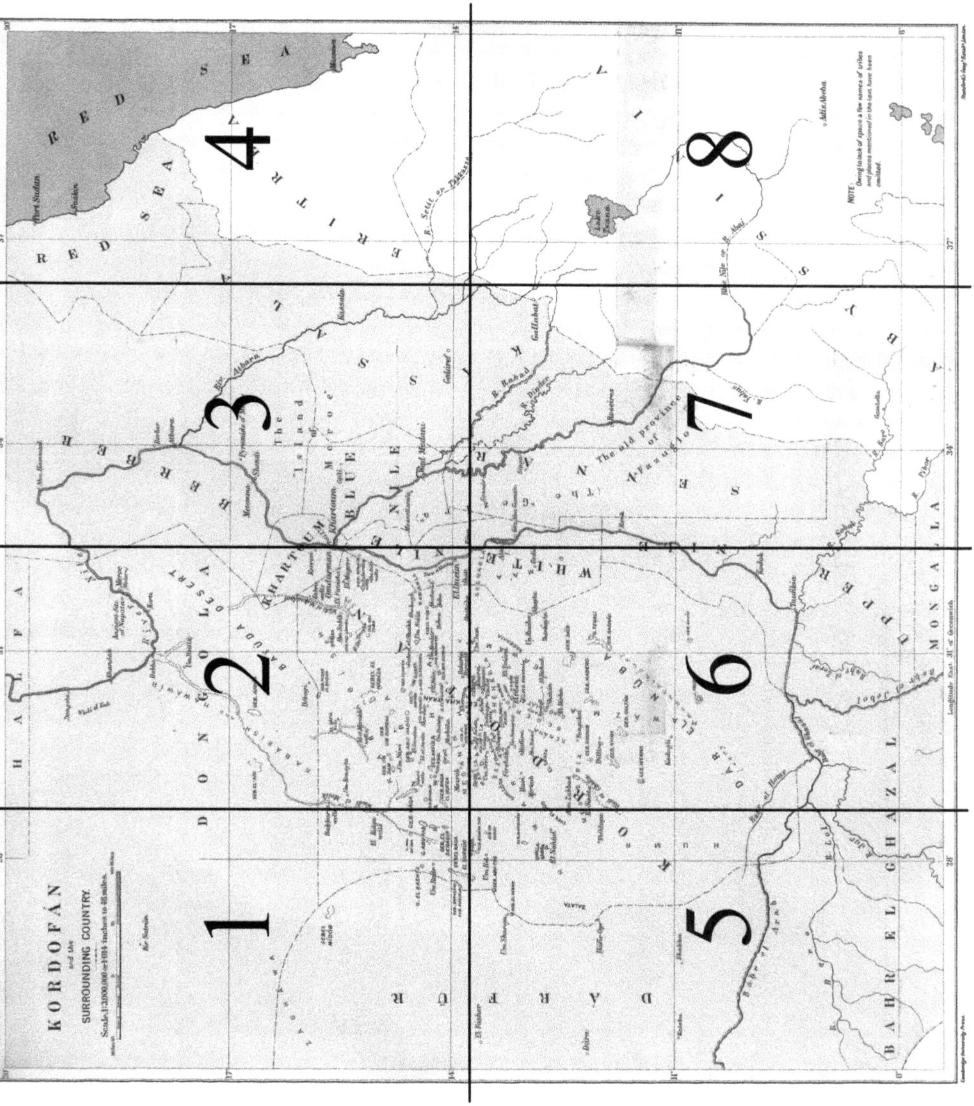

Key to following pages.

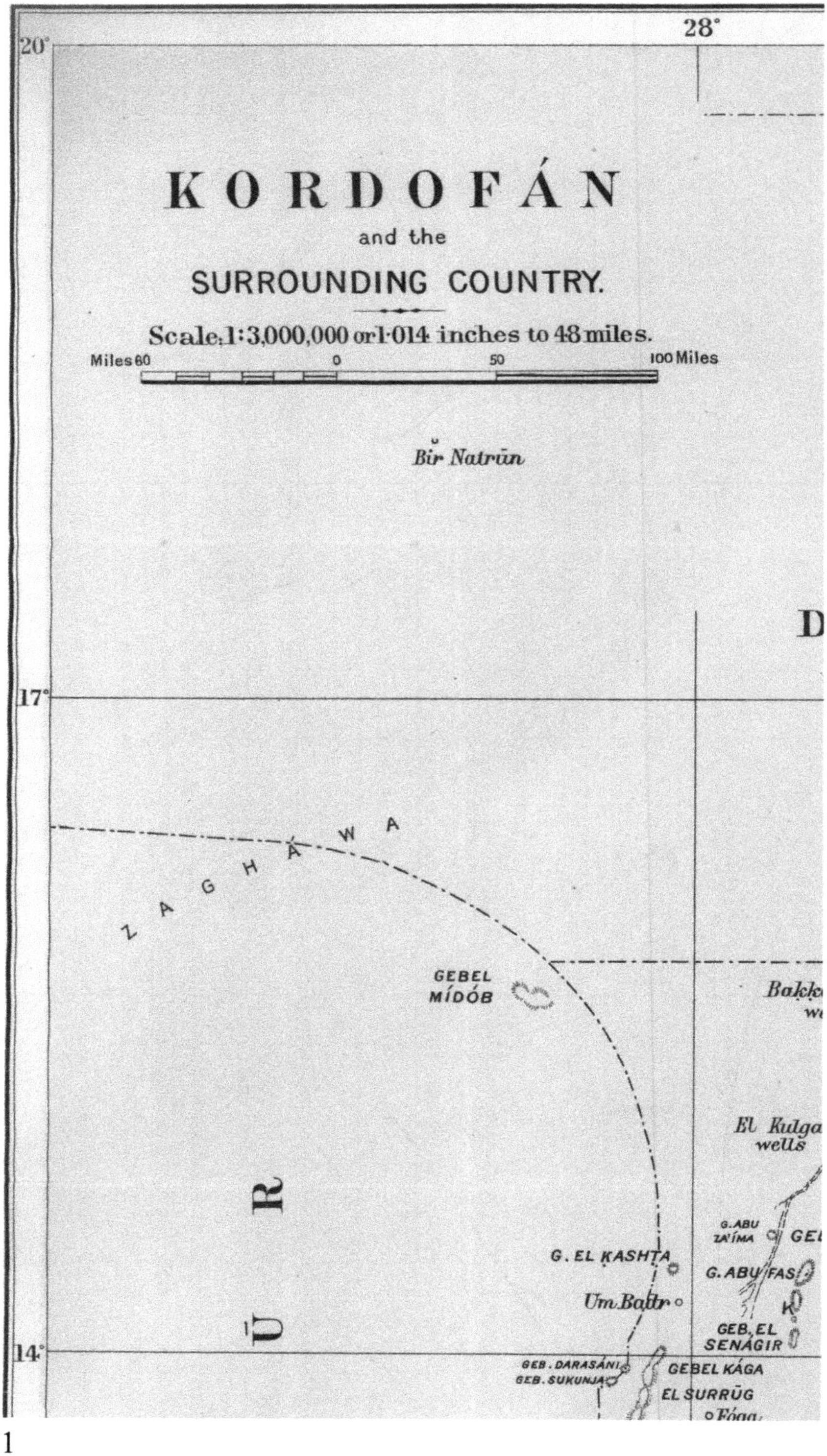
KORDOFÁN
and the
SURROUNDING COUNTRY.
Scale 1:3,000,000 or 1·014 inches to 48 miles.
Miles 60
0
50
100 Miles
20°
28°
17°
14°
Bir Natrūn
ZAGHÁWA
GEBEL MÍDÓB
G. EL KASHTA
Um Badr
GEB. DARASÁNI
GEB. SUKUNJA
GEBEL KÁGA
EL SURRŪG
Fóga
GEB. EL SENÁGIR
G. ABU FAS
G. ABU ZA'ÍMA
El Kulga wells
ŪR

1

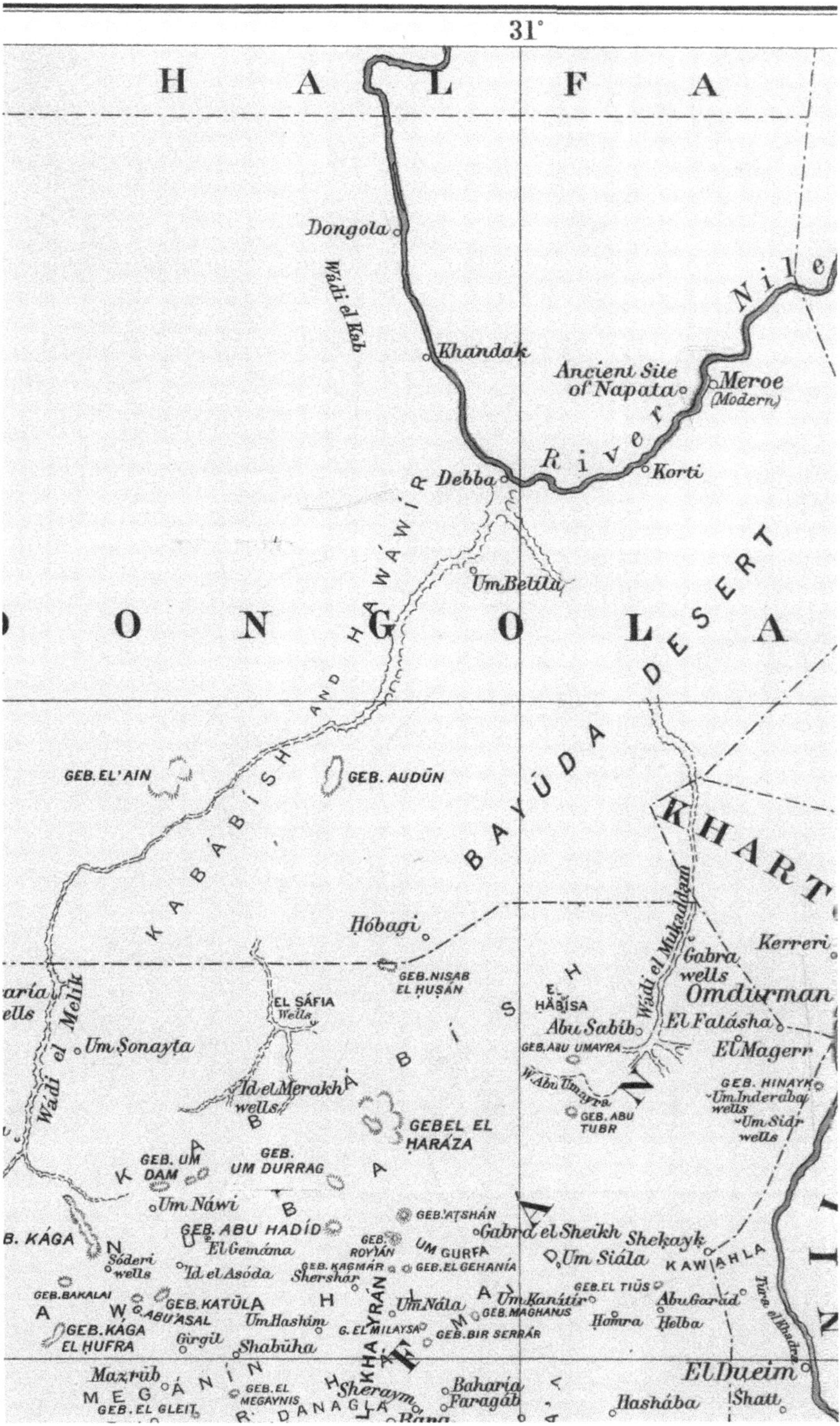
31°
H A L F A
Dongola
Wádi el Kab
Khandak
Ancient Site of Napata
Meroe (Modern)
River Nile
Korti
Debba
Um Betila
KABÁBISH AND HAWÁWÍR
D O N G O L A
BAYÚDA DESERT
GEB. EL' AIN
GEB. AUDŪN
KHART
Wádi el Mukaddam
Ḥóbagi
Kerreri
Gabra wells
Omdurman
El Fatásha
El Magerr
GEB. NISAB EL ḤUṢÁN
EL SÁFIA Wells
HÁBÍSA
Abu Sabib
GEB. ABU UMAYRA
W. Abu Umayra
Wádi el Melik
Um Ṣonayṭa
Id el Merakh wells
GEBEL EL ḤARÁZA
GEB. ABU TUBR
GEB. HINAYK
Um Inderaba wells
Um Sidr wells
GEB. UM DAM
GEB. UM DURRAG
Um Náwi
GEB. AṬSHÁN
GEB. ABU HADÍD
El Gemáma
Gabra el Sheikh
Shekayk
GEB. ROYYÁN
UM GURFA
Um Siála
KAWAHLA
Sóderi wells
Id el Asóda
GEB. KAGMÁR
GEB. EL GEHANÍA
Shershar
GEB. BAKALAI
GEB. KATŪLA
GEB. EL TIŪS
Um Náia
Um Kanátir
GEB. MAGHANUS
Abu Garád
ABU 'ASAL
Um Hashim
G. EL MILAYSA
Ḥomra
Ḥelba
GEB. KÁGA EL ḤUFRA
Girgil
Shabūha
GEB. BIR SERRÁR
Tura el Khadra
El Dueim
Mazrūb
GEB. EL MEGAYNIS
Sheraym
Baharia Faragáb
Hashába
Shatt
MEGÁNÍN
GEB. EL GLEIT
DANAGLA
KHAYRÁN

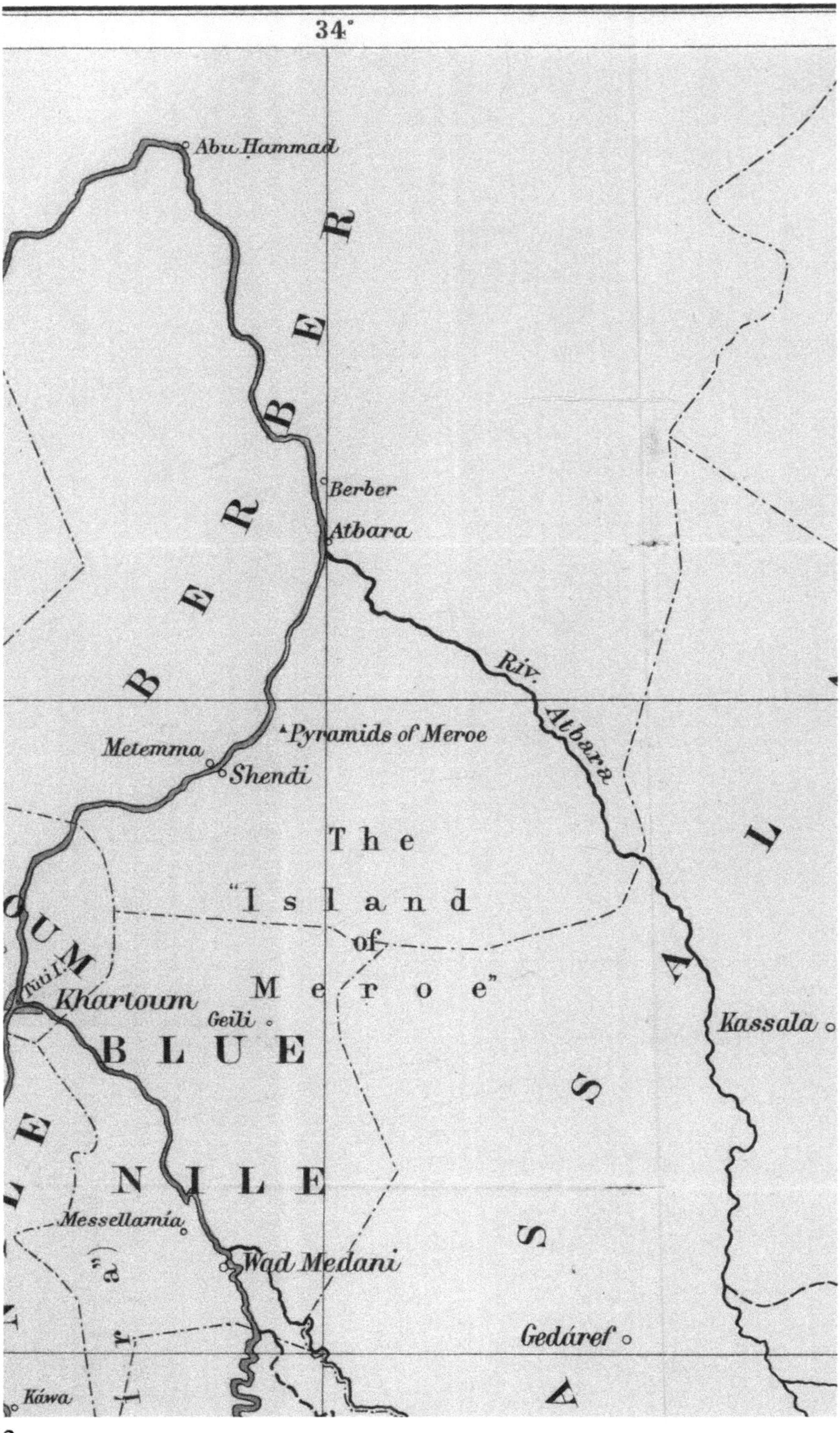
34°
Abu Hammad
BERBER
Berber
Atbara
Riv. Atbara
Pyramids of Meroe
Metemma
Shendi
The "Island of Meroe"
Khartoum
Tuti I.
Geili
BLUE NILE
Kassala
Messellamia
Wad Medani
Gedáref
Káwa

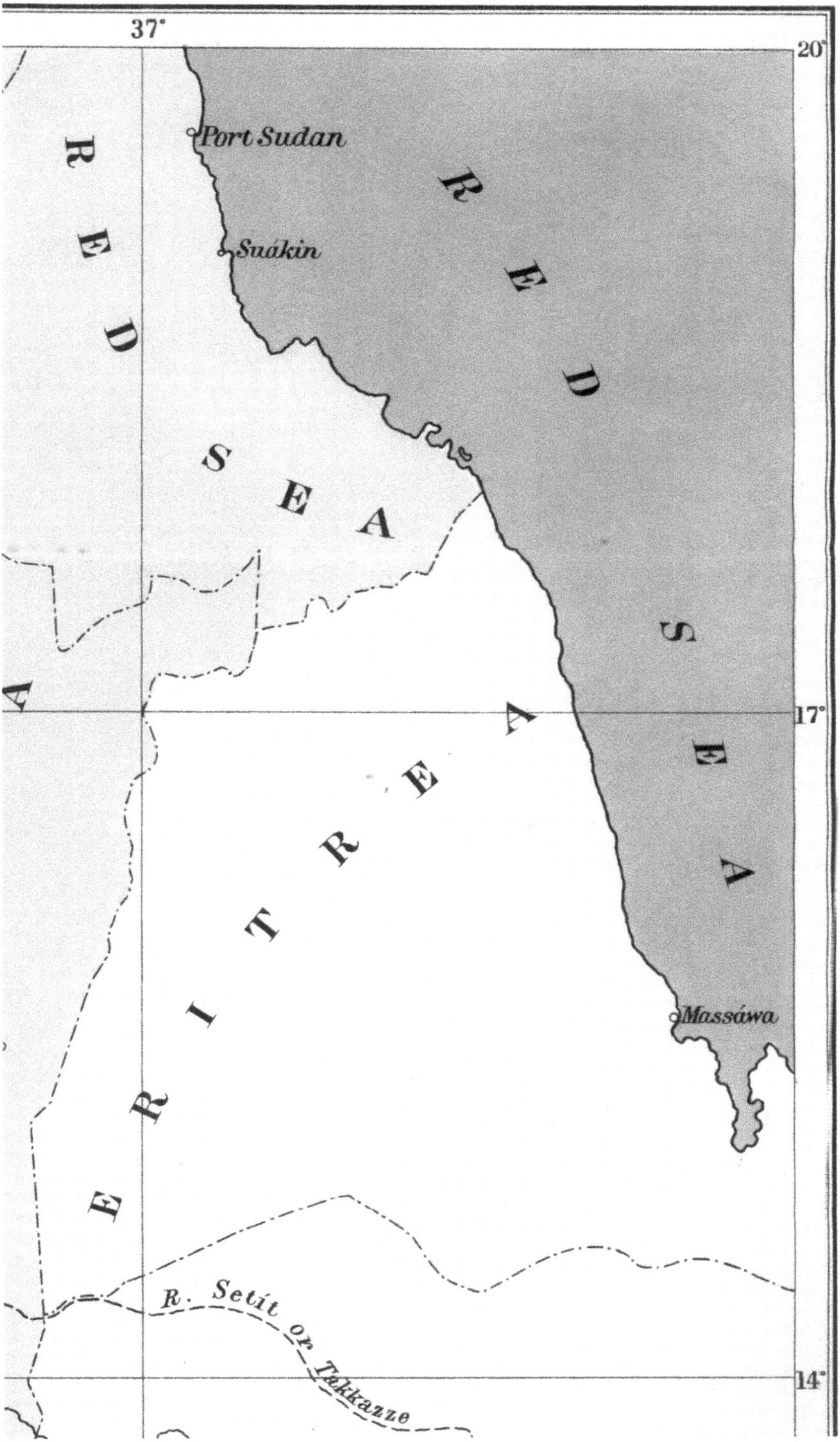
37°
20°
17°
14°
Port Sudan
Suákin
Massáwa
RED SEA
RED SEA
ERITREA
R. Setít or Takkazze

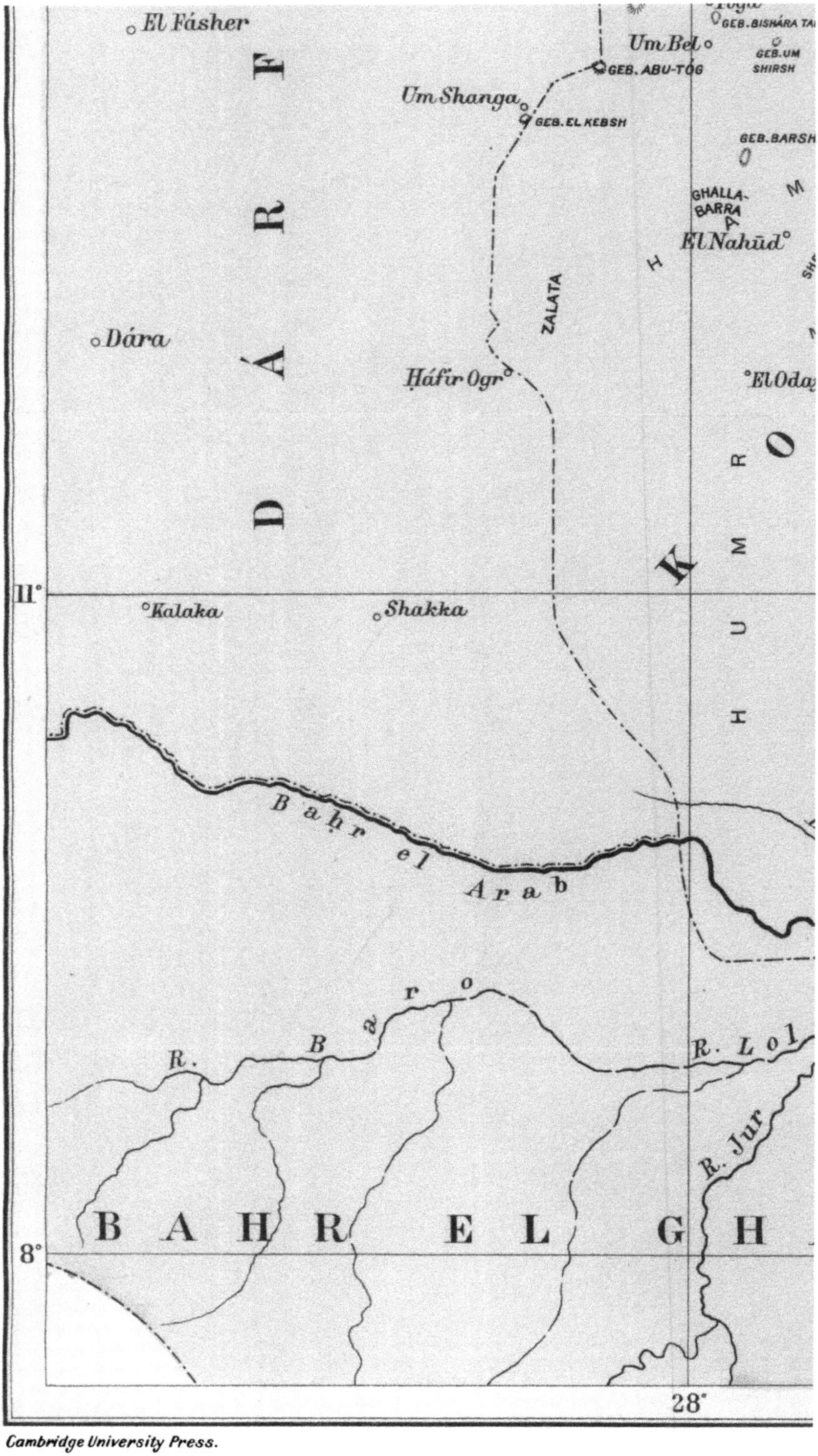

Cambridge University Press.

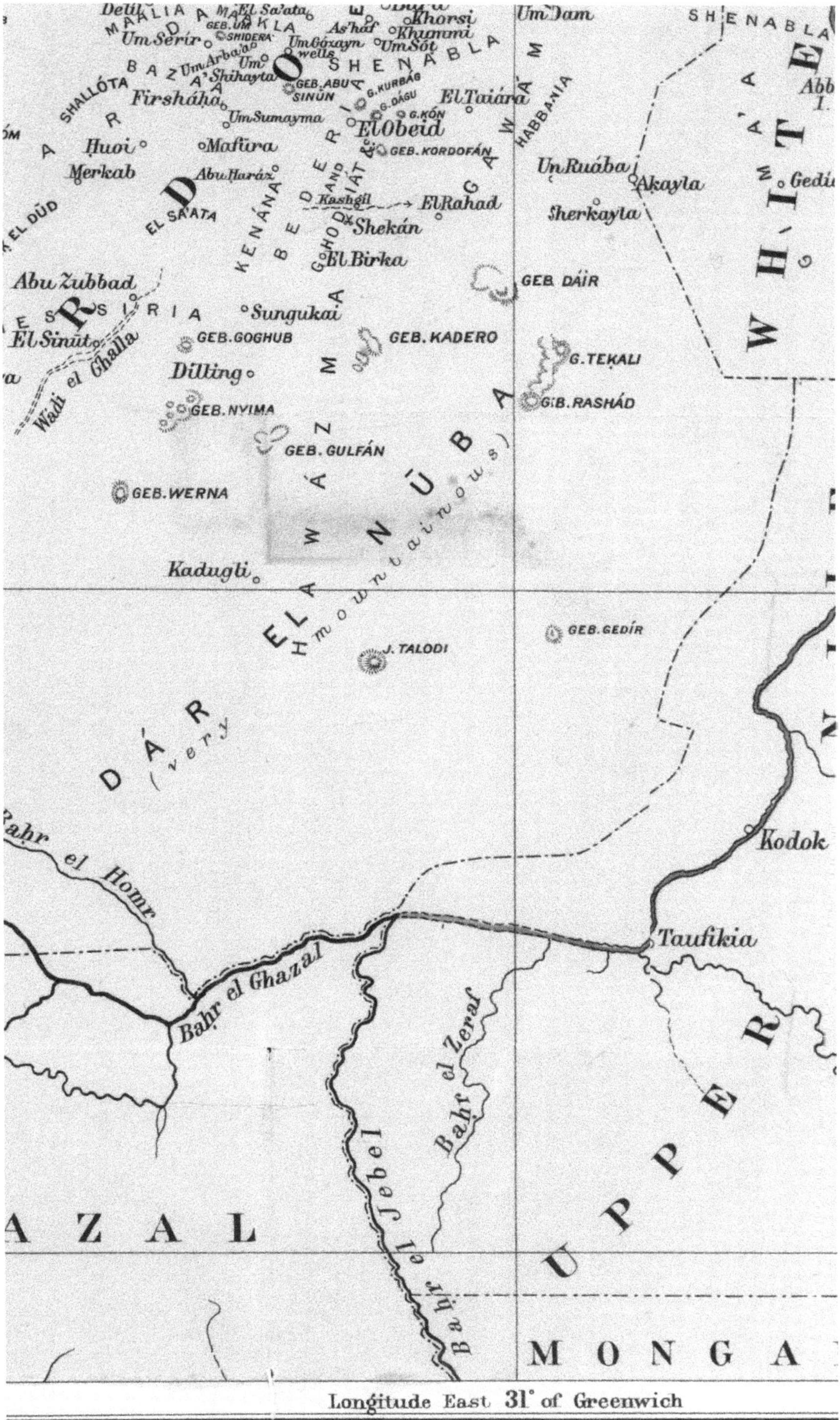

El Obeid
GEB. KORDOFÁN
El Rahad
Shekán
El Birka
Abu Zubbad
Sungukai
El Sinūt
Wadi el Ghalla
GEB. GOGHUB
GEB. KADERO
Dilling
GEB. NYIMA
GEB. GULFÁN
GEB. WERNA
Kadugli
J. TALODI
GEB. GEDÍR
GEB. DÁIR
G. TEKALI
G.B. RASHÁD
Un Ruába
Akayla
Sherkayla
El Taiára
Firsháha
Mafūra
Merkab
Abu Haráz
Huoi
Um Sumayma
Um Serír
Khorsi
Um Dam
SHENABLA
HABBANIA
WHITE
DÁR EL NŪBA
(very mountainous)
Bahr el Homr
Bahr el Ghazal
Bahr el Jebel
Bahr el Zeraf
Kodok
Taufikia
UPPER
MONGA
AZAL
Longitude East 31° of Greenwich

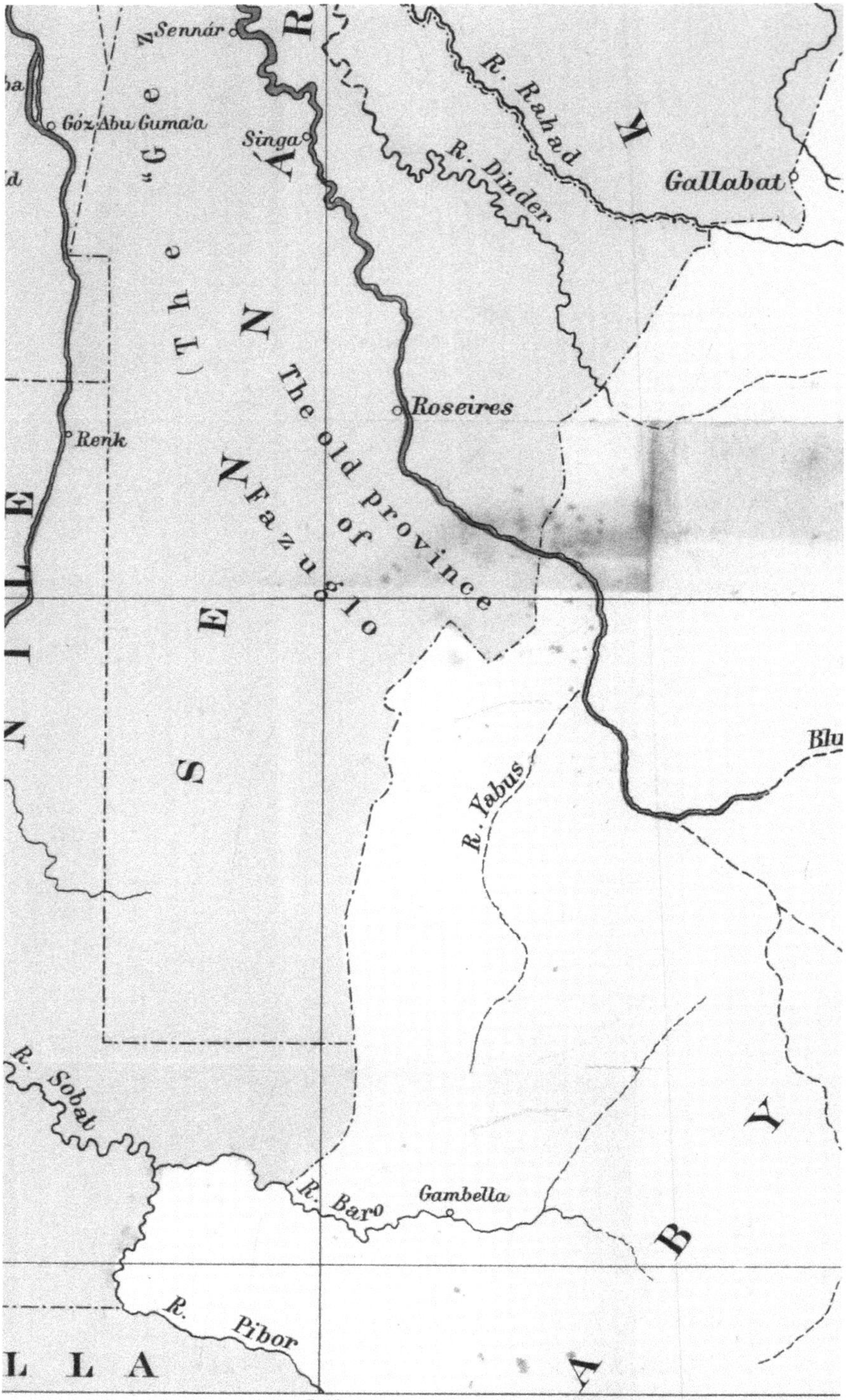
Sennár
Góz Abu Guma'a
Singa
R. Rahad
R. Dinder
Gallabat
(The "Gez
Roseires
Renk
The old province of Fazuglo
S E N N A R
N I L E
R. Yabus
Blu
R. Sobat
R. Baro
Gambella
R. Pibor
L L A
A B Y
34°

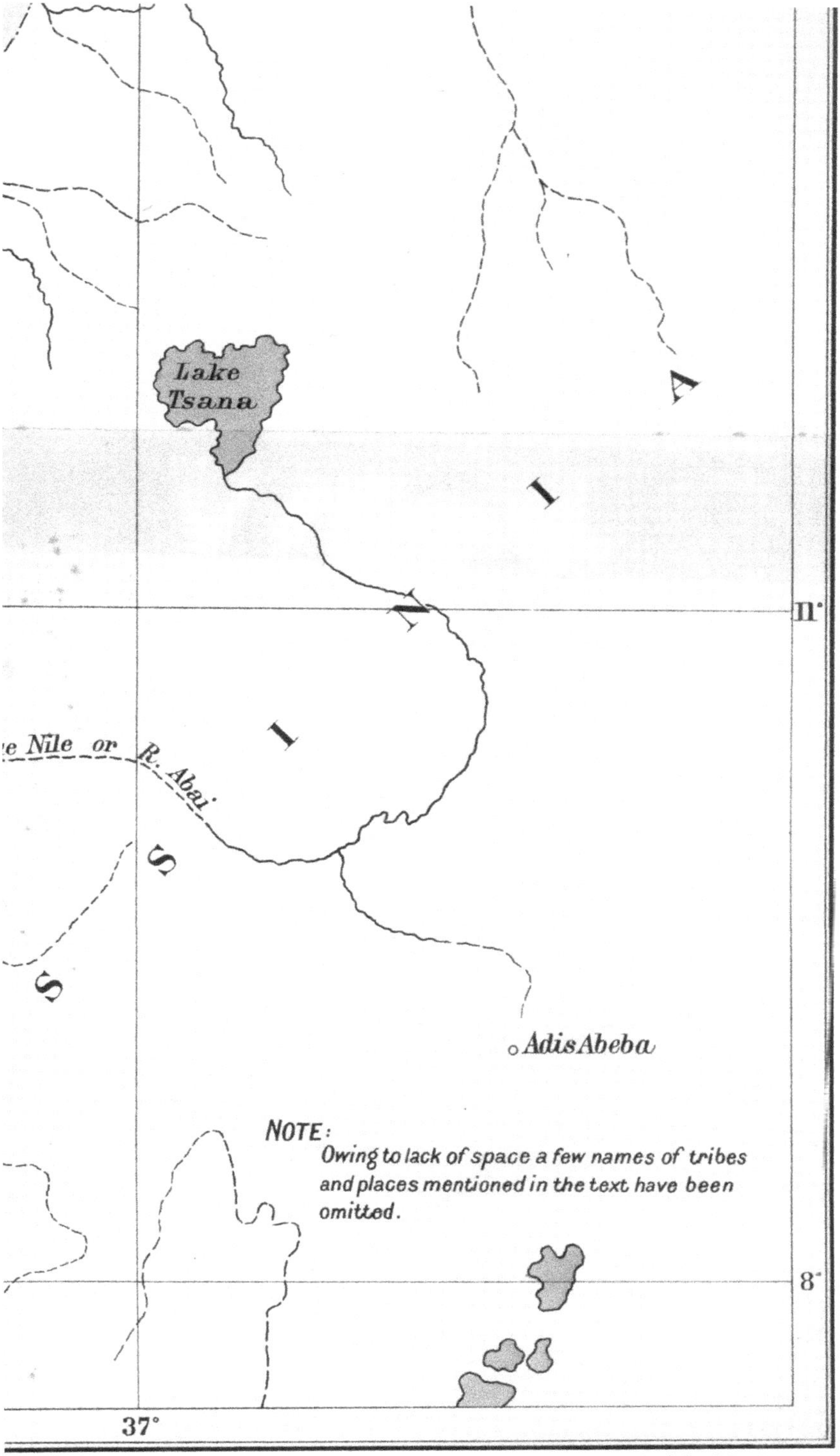
Lake Tsana
A
I
N
I
e Nile or R. Abai
S
S
Adis Abeba
NOTE:
Owing to lack of space a few names of tribes and places mentioned in the text have been omitted.
11°
8°
37°
Stanford's Geog! Estab!, London.

Milton Keynes UK
Ingram Content Group UK Ltd.
UKHW011830270923
429388UK00011B/63

9 781108 010771